Sanctions and Rewards in
A Multidisciplinary Approach

Ten experts look at the important subject of sanctions and rewards in the legal system from the perspectives of their individual disciplines. Among the issues they consider are society's selection of legal and other techniques to encourage obedience to the law, the relative effectiveness of rewards and sanctions, the usefulness of the present tort system in deterring undesirable conduct, and the question whether we are aiming our sanctions at the right persons.

This collection of essays helps us understand the dimensions of these issues by illustrating the ways in which various disciplines have dealt with them. It represents the first stage in a program on sanctions and rewards in the legal system sponsored by the Canadian Institute for Advanced Research, and is part of the institute's wider program on law in society.

MARTIN L. FRIEDLAND directs the program on sanctions and rewards of the Canadian Institute for Advanced Research. He is Professor of Law and University Professor at the University of Toronto. Among his earlier books are *Detention before Trial*, *Double Jeopardy*, *Access to the Law*, *The Trials of Israel Lipski*, and *The Case of Valentine Shortis: A True Story of Crime and Politics in Canada*.

Sanctions and Rewards in the Legal System: A Multidisciplinary Approach

edited by M.L. Friedland

March 23, 1990

To Hudson

With best wishes.

Marty

UNIVERSITY OF TORONTO PRESS

Toronto Buffalo London

© University of Toronto Press 1989
Toronto Buffalo London
Printed in Canada

ISBN 0-8020-5777-2 (cloth)
ISBN 0-8020-6688-7 (paper)

Canadian Cataloguing in Publication Data

Main entry under title:

Sanctions and rewards in the legal system

Papers presented at a symposium sponsored by the Canadian Institute for Advanced Research, May 1986.
ISBN 0-8020-5777-2 (bound) ISBN 0-8020-6688-7 (pbk.)

1. Sanctions (Law) – Congresses. 2. Reward (law) – Congresses.
I. Friedland, M.L. (Martin Lawrence), 1932–
II. Canadian Institute for Advanced Research.

K258.S35 1989   340'.1   c88-095387-x

Contents

Contributors vi

Acknowledgments vii

Introduction / 3

1 John M. Beattie, Criminal Sanctions in England since 1500 / 14

2 H. Laurence Ross, Sociology and Legal Sanctions / 36

3 Philip J. Cook, The Economics of Criminal Sanctions / 50

4 Robert L. Rabin, Deterrence and the Tort System / 79

5 Franklin E. Zimring, Methods for Measuring General Deterrence: A Plea for the Field Experiment / 99

6 Joan E. Grusec, Sanctions and Rewards: The Approach of Psychology / 109

7 Hugh J. Arnold, Sanctions and Rewards: An Organizational Perspective / 137

8 Pierre Maranda, An Anthropological View of Sanctions and Rewards / 156

9 Carolyn Tuohy, Achieving Compliance with Collective Objectives A Political Science Perspective / 179

10 Christopher D. Stone, Choice of Target and Other Law Enforcement Variables / 203

Contributors

Hugh J. Arnold is Magna International Professor of Business Strategy in the Faculty of Management at the University of Toronto.

John M. Beattie is a professor in the Department of History and Centre of Criminology at the University of Toronto.

Philip J. Cook is a professor of public policy studies and economics and the director of the Institute of Policy Science and Public Affairs at Duke University.

Joan E. Grusec is a professor in the Department of Psychology at the University of Toronto.

Pierre Maranda is a professor in the Department of Anthropology at Laval University.

Robert L. Rabin is A. Calder Mackay Professor of Law at Stanford Law School, Stanford University.

H. Laurence Ross is a professor in the Department of Sociology at the University of New Mexico at Albuquerque.

Christopher D. Stone is Roy P. Crocker Professor of Law at the Law Center, University of Southern California at Los Angeles.

Carolyn Tuohy is a professor in the Department of Political Science at the University of Toronto.

Franklin E. Zimring is a professor of law and the director of the Earl Warren Legal Institute at the School of Law, University of California at Berkeley.

Acknowledgments

The support of the Canadian Institute for Advanced Research has made this volume possible. I am grateful to Dr Fraser Mustard, the president of the institute, and to Dr Peter Munsche, its former executive director, for their continuing encouragement. I am also grateful to Timothy Endicott, a recent graduate of the University of Toronto Faculty of Law, for his valuable research assistance in helping to prepare these papers for publication; to Kathleen Johnson for her skilled copy-editing; and to my secretary, Kathy Tzimika, for expert secretarial assistance. My colleagues – in particular Robert Prichard, Kent Roach, and Michael Trebilcock – have generously given advice and guidance on all aspects of the project.

Martin L. Friedland
Faculty of Law
University of Toronto

Sanctions and Rewards in the Legal System

Introduction

One of the principal objectives of the legal system is to control and regulate human conduct. It is surprising, therefore, that relatively little research has been done by persons interested in the law on the most effective techniques for controlling and regulating conduct. Yet legislators are constantly framing laws that are based on assumptions of what does or does not work. Administrators draft regulations and policies and judges deliver judgments that are based on implicit assumptions. The research community has an obligation to help ensure that those assumptions are realistic.

This collection of papers represents the first stage in a program on sanctions and rewards in the legal system undertaken by the Canadian Institute for Advanced Research. Ten distinguished scholars examine the topic from the perspective of their own disciplines. The papers were first presented at a symposium at which other researchers who were about to embark on specific research projects on sanctions and rewards were present. The conference participants hoped to gain insights into strategies and approaches that would assist us in these further stages of the program, as well as enable us to place our work in the context of general theories of compliance. Later projects will include specific studies of compliance in the fields of income tax, traffic safety, workplace accidents, medical malpractice, environmental pollution, family violence, prostitution, and securities regulation.

In the past, as historian John Beattie shows, 'the criminal law has typically worked to control crime and social disorder by means of sanctions' rather than rewards. Capital punishment was, of course, the main deterrent for felonies. Imprisonment was not a major factor in the administration of criminal justice until the 1700s. Some of the same debates that take place today on whether certainty of penalty is more effective than severity of penalty played a role in the transition from capital punishment to imprisonment. Cesare Beccaria, for example, argued that 'the certainty of a punishment, even if it be moderate, will always make a stronger impression than the fear of another which is more terrible but combined with the hope of impunity.'[1]

The historical approach demonstrates that the sanctions that are in place today were not inevitable. The philosophy behind imprisonment, now the principal weapon against crime, has changed over the years. During the past two centuries the concepts of rehabilitation, incapacitation, vengeance, deterrence, and just deserts have had currency. Many of the philosophies seem to regain popularity on a cyclical basis.[2]

In Canada, as in many other countries, sentencing philosophy is at a crossroads. The recently released report of the Canadian Sentencing Commission stressed that 'the fundamental purpose of sentencing is to preserve the authority of and promote respect for the law through the imposition of just sanctions.'[3] According to the commission's proposed scheme, there would be less individualization of sentences in relation to the characteristics of the offender, and early release on parole would be virtually eliminated. It remains to be seen, however, whether the government will accept the commission's recommendations.

Rewards have never been widely used in the criminal law,[4] though they have been used in the administration of the law (for example, payments to informers) and the running of penitentiaries (time off for good behaviour). One major reason rewards were not used in the past was that the state had limited resources to pay for them. Today, of course, the state has enormous wealth, and some have argued that it could well afford to experiment more with this technique in areas such as traffic safety.[5]

The Law Reform Commission of Canada is surely correct in taking the position that we have relied too heavily on the criminal sanction.[6] As we move closer to a compliance-based model of enforcement there will probably be a greater emphasis on rewards because, as sociologist Albert Reiss has pointed out, 'where penalty systems primarily manipulate punishments, compliance systems principally manipulate rewards.'[7]

Sociologists have had much to contribute to an understanding of law in society. As H. Laurence Ross states in his paper for this volume, 'The fathers of modern sociology, Karl Marx, Max Weber, and Emile

Durkheim, all addressed the operation of law in their theoretical works. For Marx, law reflected the struggle between the classes, and legal sanctions functioned to guarantee the hegemony of the ruling class. Durkheim measured the basis of social cohesion by the relative predominance of either punitive or restitutive legal sanctions. Weber found in legal sanctions the ultimate guarantees of an ordered world on which modern capitalistic society rested.' Sociologists have not only theorized about the place of law in society; they have also developed techniques for empirically examining the operation of law. Many sociological studies starting in the 1960s evaluated programs based on legal sanctions. Ross himself, using the example of drunken-driving laws, has been influential in the study of what he refers to as the 'deterrence hypothesis' – that is, that the effectiveness of a threat of punishment is a function of its severity, certainty, and swiftness.[8] He concludes that 'a number of studies in widely different contexts seem to coalesce on support for the deterrent effect of measures aimed at increasing the certainty of punishment, though mainly in the short run, and on rejection of the deterrent effect of measures aimed at increasing the severity of punishment.' This is the position that Beccaria took in the eighteenth century. A further strand in the sociological literature developed by Ross is that the formal rules give us only part of the picture; we should also analyse what those who operate the justice system (for example, police officers, tax auditors, housing inspectors) do in their day-to-day practice.

A particularly fruitful approach to the study of sanctions and rewards is provided by the discipline of economics. Philip Cook takes the concept of deterrence in the criminal law very seriously. As he states in his paper, 'belief in the efficacy of the deterrence mechanism comes naturally to economists, whose theoretical perspective presupposes that observed behaviour is the consequence of well-informed, rational choice.' Cook and other economists examine the influence of the threat of criminal sanctions on the choices made by individuals regarding their participation in criminal activity. Some would object to this approach on the basis that many crimes are committed on impulse, and not by rational decision-makers. Cook's answer is that predictions about the effect of deterrence do not require that every individual act rationally. 'The prediction that crime is deterrable follows just as readily from an assumption that 10 per cent of criminals are capable of rational decision-making as from an assumption that all potential criminals have that ability.'

On the key question whether certainty of punishment is better than severity, Cook argues that the view of sociologists like Ross is supported by economic theory. Economists, says Cook, 'expect that increases in the probability of imprisonment, coupled with proportionate reductions in the prison term, will increase the deterrent value of the threat of punishment.' The same, he states, is true for fines. Laboratory experiments show that persons are not risk-averse with respect to financial losses in these cases. Thus, a stated chance of a $1,000 fine is more of a deterrent than half the stated chance of a $2,000 fine.[9]

Cook raises the important issue of the substitution of one crime for another in response to changes in enforcement patterns; for example, if shopkeepers arm themselves, thieves may switch from commercial robbery to commercial burglary (that is, without violence). This substitution can also take the form of geographical displacement; for example, exact-fare systems on buses may increase the robbery risk for convenience stores. In traffic safety, the same phenomenon is referred to as 'risk compensation.' Enhancing safety through the use of seat-belts, it is argued, causes drivers to increase the risk of an accident by driving less carefully. Some even argue what is referred to as 'risk homeostasis' – that is, that safety features are *entirely* 'used up' by the driver's adjustment to those features.[10]

The economist can also assist in the study of crime by studying the control of criminal industry. As Cook states, 'since the study of markets is the primary concern of economic science, it is natural to harness the economic paradigm to the analysis of criminal industry.' By examining, for example, the motor vehicle theft industry, he shows that apart from a concentration on prosecuting the thief, other techniques should be considered, such as more stringent regulations requiring identification numbers for auto parts, rules making it an infraction to leave a parked vehicle unlocked, and laws permitting confiscation of vehicles.

The emerging study of law and economics also has much to contribute to the effect of civil liability on conduct. Robert Rabin examines what he calls 'the uneasy case for the deterrent effect of tort liability.' Rabin states:

> In sum, there are any number of reasons to be less than sanguine about the deterrent effect of tort liability. In some instances, tort liability rules are too general to offer much guidance to potential injurers or victims. In

other instances, they are systematically unobserved. Even when tort rules are clearly communicated, they may add little to other non-legal constraints on dangerous conduct. And even if they deter, it may be that they promote too much or too little caution. Taken together, these reservations raise serious questions about the long-standing assumptions about the role of deterrence in the tort system.

It is important to study the deterrent effect of the tort system because the other justification for liability – compensation – can be accomplished better by other means, such as private or government-run accident insurance. As economist Steven Shavell states in his recent book, *Economic Analysis of Accident Law*, 'The main difference the presence of the liability system does make ... is that it creates incentives toward safety. This, then, must be said to be the chief purpose of the liability system today.'[11] Rabin argues that deterrence through the tort system may operate differently in different fields: 'There is no reason to think that doctors, drivers, and drug manufacturers respond similarly to the prospect of tort liability.'

Insurance is a particularly important factor affecting the deterrent impact of tort law.[12] If persons are insured, will they be insensitive to civil liability? Techniques that create and maintain an incentive to take care are ceilings on coverage, co-insurance, deductible amounts, and the use of experience ratings in setting premiums. We know very little about how these operate in practice. Will a no-fault insurance scheme decrease incentives to take care? Rabin states that it is 'inconceivable' that the American-style no-fault automobile insurance schemes (which still permit lawsuits for serious accidents) 'could have a negative effect on cautionary behaviour.' But is the same true in a no-fault scheme such as Quebec's, which bars lawsuits and does not provide for experience rating?[13]

Rabin suggests research on deterrence in specific areas. For example, survey research could be conducted in the drug and chemical industry to explore 'how decisions to engage in research and development or to initiate a new product line are affected by estimates of prospective tort liability.' In the manufacturing area, 'there would be great value in systematic time-series and cross-industry studies of the relationship between claims experience and investment decisions, controlling for type of product or size of firm, and like variables.' Similar studies could 'focus on the changes in medical practice that are occurring as a consequence of stringent liability rules.' In the area of traffic accidents, Rabin asks for a 'systematic study of the kinds of hazards that cause accidents and their respective susceptibility to deterrence pressure,' and would find it 'useful to analyse accident data so as to provide better information about the respective contributions of motor vehicle design, road-engineering, and driving conduct to the distressing record of highway carnage.' It should be noted that the parts of Rabin's research agenda relating to medical malpractice and traffic accidents are the subject of further studies by researchers involved with the Canadian Institute for Advanced Research.

Many of the contributors call for more empirical research into issues of deterrence. But what real-world events should the scholar seek out for study? Franklin Zimring's paper discusses the usual type of cross-sectional or time-series deterrence research, and makes a plea for what he calls 'the field experiment.' The cross-sectional or time-series approach involves '[studying] changes that occur naturally, and [attempting] to control for all the other differences that occur in nature either between areas or over time to isolate the contribution of general deterrence to differences in noted crime rates. Statistical tools ranging from simple regression to complex simultaneous equations are used to analyse the data, and significant findings are frequently reported in the literature.' One serious problem with the approach, however, is the inability to say with any degree of certainty whether differences are caused by the justice system or by non-deterrence factors.

The 'field experiment,' in contrast, 'attempts to assess the impact of changes in law enforcement or punishment policy by closely following what happens after particular policy shifts occur.' Zimring gives several examples of this approach: the Kansas City Preventive Patrol Experiment increased police patrols in certain areas of Kansas City on a random basis, and the Minneapolis wife-abuse project examined the effect of randomly changing the intervention strategy. Of course, the opportunities for such experiments are limited. The judiciary and other parts of the justice system will be reluctant to engage in 'experiments.' None the less, without controlled studies it will be difficult to make sound judgments on what techniques do or do not work.

Psychology, writes Joan Grusec, 'is a discipline that has addressed the issue of compliance at some length. Much research has been aimed at identifying the best techniques for gaining compliance from individuals and for modifying their behaviour.' The subject has been studied by social psychologists, by developmental psychologists concerned with the socialization of young children, and by behavioural psychologists interested in modifying deviant behaviour. Grusec, a developmental psychologist, criticizes behaviourist B.F. Skinner's conclusion that positive reinforcement is better than punishment. Grusec's own studies lead her to the conclusion that 'moderate levels of punishment, administered by a humane and caring agent so that the contingency between the individual's behaviour and the aversive outcome is clear, are just as effective in controlling behaviour as is the use of positive reinforcements.' What is desirable, she argues, 'is to get children to conform to the rules of society in the absence of external surveillance. Rules, values, and behaviours must be internalized; that is, they must be accepted by the individual as his or her own.' Too much coercion will defeat this objective; according to Grusec, 'children and adults who perceive that they have been coerced into conformity should be less likely to internalize moral standards (that is, to behave in accord with societal dictates in the absence of surveillance) than should those with less consciousness of having been coerced. Techniques that minimize feelings of coercion include persuasion, education, and reasoning.' Grusec would combine mild punishment with education that makes the wrongdoers aware of what they have done: 'family violence may be curtailed not only by the presence of punitive consequences, but also by the offender's sensitization to the effects of violence on spouse and children.'

Psychologists have also examined behaviour in business and other organizations. Hugh Arnold states in his paper that 'since behavioural manipulation is at the core of management, the issue whether this task is best accomplished through the use of sanctions, rewards, or some combination thereof has occupied an important place in organizational research for many years.' He concludes his paper by observing that although 'there is no doubt that punishment can and does have an impact on employee behaviour ... there is emerging consensus that the effects of punishment on performance are not as strong as the influences of reward.' The use of punishment in an organization, he points out, 'has a tendency to create resentment, anger, and hard feelings toward the punishing agent and the organization in general,' and is effective only so long as the potential and punishing agent or some monitoring device is physically present to monitor behaviour. Arnold demonstrates the effectiveness of rewards in a number of specific areas, such as absenteeism, productivity, and occupational safety. It should be observed – to use an example all the contributors are familiar with – that university faculties work almost entirely on the reward system (tenure, promotion, merit increases); sanctions are almost never applied.

Pierre Maranda, an anthropologist, reminds us that 'all societies have regulation mechanisms' – taboos, compensation mechanisms, and rewards. They vary from society to society: 'sanctions and rewards are society-specific and designed on the basis of statistical norms, and ... their function is to maintain social inertia.' This inertia 'maintains collective identity and enables the members of a society to predict the consequences of actions.' Our own legal system, he states, 'is characterized by codified and rigid sets of laws that are mostly repressive; that of other, simpler societies, by flexibility and fluid adaptation emphasizing rewards.' Maranda's ideal society would make greater use of rewards: 'When we learn to use rewards (positive incentives) rather than sanctions (fear and deterrents), we will have come a long way toward a much more dynamic and productive society.' Unfortunately, according to Maranda, it requires a greater effort to achieve compliance through rewards than through sanctions: 'The threshold of fear is relatively low, that of seduction much higher ... Fear and seduction thresholds can be measured. On the basis of studies in communication and marketing, we can state that the impact of fear on a person or group will have to be around 10 per cent of the system's inertia to be effective as a factor of change. Seduction will have to score about 40 per cent to 50 per cent on the same scale to trigger a response strong enough to override inertia.'

Compliance issues, writes Carolyn Tuohy, are also of central concern to political scientists. She examines three pure forms of compliance control from the perspective of mainstream North American liberal pluralism. The categorization helps us to sort out the myriad of techniques now used to control conduct. She sets out three basic compliance mechanisms:

> Under the *command* mechanism, B complies with A's objectives simply because A tells him to do so. B's compliance is based on a superior-subordinate relationship with A, which may be grounded in either force or consent, and which may be more or less limited in its scope (that is, in the range of matters with respect to which A can command B's compliance). Its major institutional manifestation is the apparatus of law-making, application, and adjudication – legislatures, bureaucracies, and courts.

11   Introduction

> Under the *exchange* mechanism, B's compliance with A's objectives is voluntary and is obtained at a price. A induces B to comply by offering something of value in return. The exchange mechanism's major institutional manifestations are the market and the negotiating table.
>
> Under the *persuasion* mechanism, B complies with A's objectives because A adduces arguments or principles that lead B to agree with the objectives. An institutional manifestation is less easily identified here than in the other two mechanisms (the educational system may be the best analogue).

Compliance mechanisms in practice display a mix of command, exchange, and persuasion features, and a policy decision will therefore involve changes to an existing mix. Tuohy stresses the 'symbolic' implications of such a change. For example, 'the symbolic effect of an increased emphasis on command is to highlight the social significance of compliance. The signal is, "this behaviour is socially important enough to *command*." ' She illustrates a range of research that could be conducted in the area of occupational health and safety:

> Occupational health and safety programs and disease and accident rates might be compared, for selected industries, across jurisdictions relying respectively more heavily upon command, exchange, and persuasion mechanisms: bureaucratic inspections, fines, and prosecutions; experience rating of employer premiums for workers' compensation; joint health and safety committees; and safety education programs. Are employers sensitive to experience-related increases or decreases in premiums? Does negotiation within a committee structure improve the 'intelligence' of decision-making about health standards (that is, the range of values and interests and the extent and quality of the information considered)? Does it lead to higher rates of compliance with the outcomes of decision-making? Does it encourage a mobilization of interests that either retards or accelerates change in prescribed standards of conduct? If, as is likely, the answers to these questions are contingent upon technological, economic, political, and institutional conditions, what are these conditions and what are their effects?

The beginnings of a language to categorize compliance variables is provided by lawyer Christopher Stone. He identifies four different control strategies: harm-based liability rules, penalties, standards, and rewards. Harm-based liability rules operate only when harm has been caused, and therefore minimize intrusion into private decision-making. Penalties, in contrast, are not tied to the quantum of harm that the wrongdoer has caused. Similarly, standards are not linked to the harm-causing occurrence, but operate before the harm occurs; as Stone states, they in effect 'withdraw from the enterprise the power to determine the ideal solution on its own.' Finally, he analyses rewards, pointing out that 'fears that public entry into the field would be arbitrary or, worse, subject, in the absence of recognized approaches, to improper influence' are 'easily exaggerated.' Stone raises a number of important issues, such as the question of the appropriate target of the various control strategies. Should it be the agent that actually causes the harm, or the enterprise, or both? Should the law target part of an enterprise, such as a corporate division or a plant? Should advisers such as auditors and lawyers be liable for their clients' wrongdoing? Who should monitor and enforce the rules? Stone does not provide the answers to these questions, but tries instead 'to survey some of the principal variables, the building-blocks with which we may wish to work.'

All the papers raise issues that give us insight into various approaches to compliance. They also provide an agenda for further research on sanctions and rewards. A number of themes run through many of the papers: Does deterrence actually work in the criminal and civil areas? Are rewards more effective than sanctions? Is internalization of values the best technique for gaining compliance? Will certainty of penalty have a greater deterrent effect than severity of penalty? Will enforcement displace one type of crime for another? What target or targets should enforcement be aimed at? Is it better to concentrate on 'designing out' undesirable conduct? To what extent will the answers to the above questions depend on the area of conduct being examined?

We can all profit by examining how other disciplines have looked at the question of sanctions and rewards. But there is much work still to be done.

Notes

1 C.B. Beccaria, *On Crimes and Punishments* (1764; 1963 trans. by Henry Paolucci) 58
2 See M.L. Friedland, *Sentencing Structure in Canada: Historical Perspectives*

13 Introduction

(Ottawa: Department of Justice 1988), a paper prepared for the Canadian Sentencing Commission.
3 *Sentencing Reform: A Canadian Approach* (1987) 151
4 See generally V. Aubert, *In Search of Law: Sociological Approaches to Law* (1983), and 'On Methods of Legal Influence,' in S.B. Burman and B.E. Harrell-Bond (eds), *The Imposition of Law* (1979) 9; A. Freiberg, 'Reward, Law and Power: Towards a Jurisprudence of the Carrot' (1986) 19 *Australia and New Zealand Journal of Criminology* 91.
5 See, for example, G.J.S. Wilde and P.A. Murdoch, 'Incentive Systems for Accident-Free and Violation-Free Driving in the General Population' (1982) 25 *Ergonomics* 879.
6 See *Our Criminal Law* (1976); see also *The Criminal Law in Canadian Society* (Ottawa: Department of Justice 1982).
7 'Selecting Strategies of Social Control over Organizational Life,' in K. Hawkins and J.M. Thomas, *Enforcing Regulation* (1984) 24
8 H.L. Ross, *Deterring the Drinking Driver: Legal Policy and Social Control* (rev. ed. 1984)
9 This approach appears to run counter to some influential law and economics literature in which increasing the penalty is seen as a more effective strategy. See, for example, A.M. Polinsky, *An Introduction to Law and Economics* (1983), and R.A. Posner, *Economic Analysis of Law*, 3d ed. (1986).
10 See, for example, J.G.U. Adams, *Risk and Freedom* (1985); G.J.S. Wilde, 'The Theory of Risk Homeostasis: Implications for Safety and Health' (1982) 2 *Risk Analysis* 209; and S. Peltzman, 'The Effects of Automobile Safety Regulation' (1975) 83 *Journal of Political Economy* 677.
11 S. Shavell, *Economic Analysis of Accident Law* (1987) 297
12 See M.J. Trebilcock, 'The Social Insurance-Deterrence Dilemma of Modern North American Tort Law: A Canadian Perspective on the Liability Insurance Crisis' (1987) 24 *San Diego Law Review* 929. See also Shavell, supra note 11.
13 See M. Gaudry, 'DRAG, un Modèle de la demand Routière des Accidents et de leur Gravité appliqué au Québec de 1956 à 1982,' Publication no. 359, Centre de Recherche sur les Transports, Université de Montréal (1985); see also M. Boyer and G. Dionne, 'A Description and Analysis of the Quebec Automobile Insurance Plan' (1987) 13 *Canadian Public Policy* 181.

1 Criminal Sanctions in England since 1500

JOHN M. BEATTIE*

In setting out to discuss the ways in which sanctions and rewards have been mobilized in the past in the maintenance of order, I must begin by drawing some boundaries around my subject. In the first place, as my title indicates, I will discuss mainly English evidence, though I believe similar arguments could be made for Western Europe and (in its later stages) North America, with some differences in emphasis, chronology, and speed of change. I should emphasize, too, that rather than dealing in detail with the recent past, I will be concentrating particularly on the early modern period between the sixteenth and nineteenth centuries, during which the attitudes and practices that lie behind the modern penal system took shape. And, although I will say something about the wide variety of punishments that have been available at various times to the English courts, I will deal mainly with punishments that have been deployed against offenders convicted of the gravest offences – murder, rape and other serious violence, and virtually all forms of property crime, offences long identified as felonies in English law. I will give less attention than they deserve to the interesting and important range of milder punishments that over time have been brought to bear against those convicted of lesser offences.

Finally, I must emphasize that I will be discussing mainly the nature and role of sanctions rather than rewards. Rewards have played a significant part in the history of English criminal law – to some extent in inducing compliance in individuals who might otherwise commit an offence, and especially in the administration of the law. Rewards have been paid, for example, for the prosecution and conviction of suspected offenders. Another form of reward has been immunity from prosecution offered to the accomplices of suspected felons in exchange for testifying at their trials. Less direct though none the less real rewards can be seen to have derived from the exercise of a wide range of discretionary powers that were crucial in the administration of the law before the emergence of the modern machinery of prosecution and more moderate forms of punishment in the nineteenth century – for example, the discretion of the victim of an offence to prosecute or not; the discretion of the magistrates who conducted preliminary hearings to send the case on to trial and to construct the charge against those they did commit; and particularly the immense power of the king to pardon those condemned to death or to let the law take its course. All of these discretionary powers could be manipulated to induce promises of future compliance on the part of those drawn into the legal system.[1] The place of rewards in the criminal justice system clearly deserves a more systematic and thorough treatment than I have offered here. But the criminal law has typically worked to control crime and social disorder by means of sanctions, and it is to the history of sanctions in England and particularly the origins of the modern penal system in England, and in the western world more generally, that I want to devote most of my attention.

The general theme I want to examine is the emergence of imprisonment. Prisons are not recent inventions, and imprisonment has been used as a penal device for centuries.[2] But incarceration on a large scale and as a punishment for the most serious offences came to occupy a central place in penal systems only about two hundred years ago. Until the eighteenth century the principal punishment for felonies in England was execution by public hanging. Misdemeanours and petty larceny, usually described as non-capital larceny, had long been subject to a much broader range of non-capital punishments, including some very damaging public punishments, notably whipping and the pillory, but also fines and imprisonment.[3] Over the course of the early modern period, however, that sharp distinction began to erode. Capital punishment remained at the centre of penal thinking into the nineteenth century, but the usefulness of secondary punishments that would deter by means other than terror was increasingly recognized. I hope to uncover some of the roots of the crucial shifts in penal attitudes that lie behind the making of modern penal regimes. In particular, I want to try to show why capital and corporal punishments lost their support and why imprisonment came to seem the necessary alternative. These changes in penal attitudes and practices occurred in a society undergoing far-reaching social, economic, and political changes. I will suggest that at particular times during the period the stimulus in the search for more effective punishments was a changing perception of the state of crime and social disorder, and that both the apparent and perceived threat to social order resulted from social and economic changes that polarized the society over the early modern period and gave rise to a large population of wage-dependent working poor and a relatively large middle and propertied class.

Punishment before 1500

By concentrating on the period since 1500 I do not mean to suggest that the previous period is unimportant or uninteresting. On the contrary, a number of important themes in the history of punishment emerged in the thousand years between the end of the Roman period in England and the end of the Middle Ages. Of particular significance was the transformation in attitudes and practices brought about by the Norman conquest of Anglo-Saxon England in 1066 and by the immediate successors to the Norman kings in the twelfth and thirteenth centuries.

In a sense, the Anglo-Saxon kingdoms cannot be said to have had a criminal law. The control exercised by the king was limited; certainly he had no monopoly over violence. Acts that harmed the interests of individuals were largely revenged by the individual himself and his kin. The role of the king and the state was mainly to regulate the operation of the feud, to limit and circumscribe it. To that end the laws of the Anglo-Saxon kings prescribed the amount of money (wergeld) to be paid in compensation for the killing of men of particular social status. A breach of the peace in the king's court was subject to punishment, but the 'king's peace' did not yet extend far beyond the court. There was no firmly established sense of public punishment imposed to serve public ends. The purpose of the law, and of the local courts that enforced it, was to regulate private acts of revenge and thus maintain some degree of social order.[4]

The beginnings of a system of criminal law administered across the nation had to await the emergence of an effective central government and the process of state-building: that was clearly going forward in England even before the Norman conquest in 1066, as the emergence of feudalism created hierarchical allegiances with the king at the apex and as the king's peace was gradually extended over the country. But the process of state-building went forward even more rapidly after the conquest, particularly during the reign of Henry II in the second half of the twelfth century.[5]

In the course of the next several centuries a pattern of judicial administration emerged in which royal courts and professional judges sent out from the centre imposed penalties on behalf of the king, at least for serious offences that violated the king's peace and directly threatened social order. The concept of felony crimes – generally speaking, serious offences – was clearly established by the thirteenth and fourteenth centuries, and felonies were being prosecuted and punished in the assize courts that were held in most counties by the king's judges on circuit twice a year.

The punishments these judges had at their disposal were, however, very limited. It is not surprising that in a society accustomed to the use of physical violence in the exercise of power, physical violence also dominated the penal system in the Middle Ages. The principal punishment for felonies was execution by hanging; felonies included murder, rape, arson, robbery, burglary, and grand larceny – the theft of goods worth more than a shilling.[6]

The system of criminal justice that emerged and was elaborated in the Middle Ages was limited in its ability to deal with criminal offences. For one thing, what one might call the 'community' system of justice, in which a local area dealt on its own with its crime, continued to function alongside the national system, and was to do so for many centuries to come with the blessing and support of the courts.[7] The state remained relatively weak in the Middle Ages in the face of local concentrations of private power. The level of prosecution was low – though what relation it bore to the number of events that might have given rise to a criminal charge is impossible to know – and cases were not well prepared. Perhaps for this reason, or perhaps because the only punishment available to the courts for felonies was hanging, the number of convictions was also very low. In the fourteenth and fifteenth centuries few of those charged with felonies were in the end punished. The relatively low level of hanging may have resulted from the moderating effects of community attitudes brought to bear through the jury system; there is the further explanation that in the fifteenth century a mitigating device known as benefit of clergy (discussed below) came to have wide application.[8] But more fundamental was the limited range of the criminal law and the weakness of the administrative system.

Penal Developments in the Sixteenth Century

The changes that took place after 1500 in the administrative system and the nature of punishment have done much to create the modern system of criminal justice. Changes in both areas are associated with further stages in the growth of the state and extensions of the power of the central administration, a process that can be seen at work in the sixteenth century under the Tudor monarchs. That process was further encouraged by more than a century of wars against France after 1689 for the leadership of Europe and commercial dominance abroad, and it accelerated under the impact of industrialization in the nineteenth century. The capacity of officials to catch accused offenders and the changing ways in which those convicted were punished were closely related, and both are related in turn to the growth of the state over the last five hundred years. They are also the products of changing perceptions of the nature of crime and its effect on society, and of fundamental changes in the character of society and the relative strength and influence of the social groups that felt threatened by crime.[9]

One shift in attitudes towards crime certainly began to take place in the sixteenth century, stimulated perhaps by problems deriving from a number of sharp changes in the society and economy of England, and of Western Europe generally. A strong increase in population, a steady and (for some) devastating inflation over several decades, the beginnings of a more commercialized agriculture, and a striking growth in the population of London all produced more visible poverty and large numbers of vagrants looking for work. They also produced a sharply increasing crime rate.[10] The social strains, particularly in the second half of the sixteenth century and first quarter of the seventeenth, caused a good deal of anxiety among the propertied classes, and resulted both in legislation and in more ad hoc experimentation in search of solutions to what seemed to be the most threatening dangers to the social order. The changes were as yet perhaps too piecemeal and uncoordinated to be the product of something we might call a 'policy.' But they did result in a shift of direction in some aspects of the criminal law and the way it was administered. These included important measures to strengthen the prosecution process.[11] The most significant, for my present purposes, were changes in attitudes towards punishment and in the character of the penal system.

First, there was an obvious determination on the part of the courts and Parliament to increase the deterrent capacities of the law by enlarging the use of capital punishment. This was done by manipulating the device known as benefit of clergy, which had been originally intended as a way of exempting clergymen from the jurisdiction of secular courts and reserving them to the ecclesiastical courts. Although the courts attempted to limit the privilege by restricting it to those who could read, it became widely available in practice and by 1500 was saving a large proportion of convicted offenders from the gallows. In the sixteenth century Parliament declared certain crimes (murder, rape, arson, burglary, robbery, horse theft, and pocket-picking) to be felonies 'without benefit of clergy'; in theory, no convicted offender could now escape the gallows by claiming the privilege.[12] It seems clear that Parliament wanted to enable the courts to rid the country of particular wicked individuals, and more generally to deter potential offenders by providing frequent and terrifying demonstrations of the power of the law. The determination to make the law much tougher, coupled with persistently high numbers of offences, meant that the rate of hanging went up sharply, especially toward the end of the sixteenth century and in the second and third decades of the seventeenth century.[13]

As yet, there were no established non-capital punishments for felonies: if a convicted offender was not hanged, he would be discharged by benefit of clergy with only a branded thumb. In practice, many of those convicted of felonies were either discharged in this way or pardoned by the king, and capital punishment operated essentially as a means of creating terror – and compliance – by the public execution of a few offenders chosen as examples. The punishments that were available to the courts for offenders convicted of misdemeanours – the humiliation and pain of a public scourging, public exposure on the pillory, or the infliction of some combination of fines and imprisonment – were not thought to be appropriate punishments for felonies.

It is worth trying to uncover the attitudes toward crime and punishment that lay behind a penal scheme that punished minor offenders in a variety of ways but was content to deter serious crime by hanging a few of the more notorious offenders as examples to the rest. In the first place, there was a fundamental conviction that crime was a species of immorality, that it sprang from the erosion of moral principles, and that once a man had fallen into immoral ways of even the most minor kind he was likely to go on to commit more and more serious offences. Those who failed to go to church regularly, who were lazy, who drank too much, would gradually commit worse and worse offences until their moral principles were so corroded that they would proceed to the greatest wickedness and end by murdering someone. A person in the earliest stages of this descent into moral corruption and crime could still be saved, and it was the duty of the godly magistrate to ensure that immorality was rooted out and minor offences punished. But at a certain point men became so morally corrupted that they were beyond rescue; some were so dangerous that the safety of society required that they be cut from the body politic like a diseased limb from the natural body.[14] In addition, the example provided by their public execution might frighten some of those who were themselves on the slippery slope of immorality and crime, might bring them to their moral senses and save them from the terrifying end that otherwise awaited them.

The view of crime that lay behind a penal scheme in which the courts could either free or hang convicted felons was not to be abandoned for some time. But along with the extension of capital punishment, there was another striking development in the sixteenth century, as yet without wide range or application but full of importance for the future: the creation of houses of correction, which were prisons under the direct control of county magistrates. These were places where prostitutes, recalcitrant servants, the able-bodied unemployed, and vagrants were to be rehabilitated by being whipped and made to work. They were then sent back into the world as productive citizens, reformed for their own sake and for the sake of the social order they had threatened.[15] This was one response of the state to the growth of poverty, vagrancy, and crime in the late sixteenth and early seventeenth centuries: to bring in the secular authorities to support and extend the efforts of the church to save men from the consequences of their immorality, to stop them on their way to committing felonies. As yet, it was thought that only petty offenders could be reformed; deterrence by public and violent punishments remained the central means of punishing felons. But by the second half of the seventeenth century, another significant shift in views was beginning to take place as capital punishment no longer seemed a sufficient deterrent for serious offences in and of itself. Men could not simply be terrorized into obedience; what was needed was a supplement – not yet a replacement, but a significant secondary punishment, a non-capital sanction that was more serious than branding on the thumb.

The Establishment of Secondary Punishments for Felonies: Transportation

The desire to create an effective system of non-capital punishment for serious offenders arose after 1660 for a number of reasons.[16] On the one hand, there was no support for the execution of very large numbers of offenders at once, perhaps because it was feared that too many hangings might undermine public support for the justice of the system; or perhaps because those who ran the courts were personally opposed to the massive bloodshed that would have resulted from putting the letter of the law into effect. On the other hand, there was clearly a strong feeling – at least in some parts of the country and in some sections of society (both of which I will return to) – that crime and social disorder were at such a level and posed such a threat that the courts ought to be able to punish offenders more seriously than merely branding them on the thumb and immediately discharging them back into the community. The wish to create a non-capital punishment for felons apparently was not articulated in public, or at least no evidence of it has survived. But there is no doubt that in the late seventeenth century the problem of crime produced a response that anticipated the argument of penal reformers a hundred years hence: that certainty of punishment would prove to be a more effective penal device than severity.

The desire to create a new punishment was also encouraged by the establishment of the American colonies. The possibility of sending convicts to America or the West Indies was recognized as soon as the first settlers landed, and some offenders were sent across the Atlantic in the first half of the century as a condition of royal pardon.[17] Some convicts continued to be sent across the Atlantic by a variety of subterfuges after 1660. The formal establishment of transportation as a court-ordered punishment is a complex story of false starts, colonial opposition, and English governmental weakness, but by the second half of the seventeenth century the need for such a punishment was clearly realized and widely supported. When transportation was actually authorized by statute in 1718, so many convicted felons were immediately sent to Maryland and Virginia that it is clear that the judges had wanted such a power for a long time.

Between 1660 and 1718, however, transportation failed to take root as it was first tried, and efforts were made to find alternative non-capital sanctions. A good deal of experimentation with a variety of other punishments was undertaken. Some involved increasing the pain or humiliation of established methods – branding an offender on the cheek rather than on the thumb, for example, or finding a person accused of grand larceny guilty of petty larceny in order to punish him more harshly (by whipping) than he would have been if convicted of the original charge.

The movement toward a new non-capital punishment was intensified, particularly in the 1690s, by a sense of crisis at what seemed to be a sharp increase in immorality and minor property offences in London. In fact, so strong was the sense of anxiety in the 1690s that the absence of a significant non-capital punishment led Parliament to pass several new capital statutes that removed benefit of clergy from a series of relatively minor offences, including thefts by servants and shop-lifting.

From the point of view of the history of punishment, however, the most interesting innovation at the end of the seventeenth century and the beginning of the eighteenth was not the wave of statutes that inaugurated the making of the eighteenth-century 'bloody code,' but rather the brief experimentation between 1706 and 1718 with imprisonment at hard labour in houses of correction. It is significant that much of the impetus behind the development of effective non-capital punishments, especially this effort to establish imprisonment at hard labour, came from the City of London, from members of the commercial and financial classes who felt threatened by the increase in crimes against property.

It is also significant that in the first decade of the eighteenth century men were already persuaded that those convicted of felonies not serious enough to get them hanged but serious enough to be harmful to individuals and the economy of a commercial city like London should be punished, and, moreover, punished in such a way that they could be reformed, changed by the punishment itself. This is the point, it seems to me, of the proposal to sentence them to hard labour in the houses of correction, the institutions set up to bring reformatory discipline to vagrants, prostitutes, and others who refused to be productive citizens.

All of these experiments and proposals were overtaken, however, by transportation when it was finally established by legislation in 1718.

Transportation punished offenders severely, and could be expected to act as an effective deterrent to others. It could also be imposed consistently and regularly without fear that the public would become repelled or disenchanted. The government financed it effectively and struck down American objections. It was a great success for half a century; more than half the felons convicted in English courts during the period from 1718 to 1776, when the American Revolution closed the door, were sentenced to transportation to the colonies for terms of seven or fourteen years.[18]

The Attack on Capital Punishment

In the middle of the eighteenth century it was still an unshaken belief in England, as elsewhere, that the terror of the gallows was the main defence in an unpoliced society against hordes of criminals taking to the highways or breaking into houses to threaten the lives and property of their betters.[19] None the less, the establishment of transportation as a non-capital punishment that the courts could impose directly on convicted felons was a fundamental turning-point in the history of English criminal administration. A non-capital punishment was now thought to be essential for convicted felons, and some men had clearly been persuaded that reformatory punishments might also have a role, even in dealing with other than minor offences.

The penal system that existed in the middle of the eighteenth century had thus not been formed merely by custom and long usage; it was not the product of an unresponsive, muddled, traditional 'old regime' – a view that seems to be conveyed by portrayals of the late eighteenth century as the beginning of the 'age of reform.' That label has encouraged the notion that men began to think about penal questions only when Beccaria wrote his treatise on crime and punishment in the 1760s, when Howard began to visit the English prisons, when Bentham began to think rationally about the law. It is true that another shift in penal thinking undoubtedly did take place in the late eighteenth century and the early decades of the nineteenth. Major changes were to be effected in the way the English state dealt with criminal offenders, and indeed the nature of English government and the role of government in society were also to change sharply. But without minimizing the scale and significance of those changes, it is important to emphasize that this period did not initiate the process of change. Recognizing this should discourage us from trying to tie these and other 'reforms' in a general and vague way to the Enlightenment or the industrial revolution. In addition, the earlier changes offer clues to more specific explanations of the major changes that did come in the late eighteenth and nineteenth centuries and that lie behind the modern system of punishment.

One fundamental shift that occurred in the late eighteenth century was the loss of faith in the effectiveness of violent punishments carried out in public. Public and violent punishments were meant not only to cause pain but also to shame and humiliate the offender and his family, with the intention not only of punishing him but also of deterring others. The crowds around the scaffold or along the street in which an offender would be whipped at the back of a cart were essential to the success of the demonstration of the power of the courts. The crowds helped to reinforce the moral boundaries of the society, and their participation was a crucial part of the punishment – so long as they approved the justice of the verdict and the punishment for the particular offender, which they mainly seemed to do: there are very few examples of the rescue of offenders from the rather feeble grasp of the authorities.[20]

The fundamental elements of this system of punishment – the public exposure, the physical violence – began to be questioned seriously in the eighteenth century. Partly this questioning was the result of a sense that the penal system had failed and was failing to prevent crime. I will return to that centrally important point. But that does not explain why the very bases of the old system were questioned. The answer to that is deeper and more perplexing: there was a fundamental shift of sentiment with regard to violence itself, particularly the public display of violence.[21]

By 1750, attitudes toward violence had been changing for some time. But there is no doubt that in the second half of the eighteenth century there was a sharp rise in what Elias has called the 'threshold of disgust' at behaviour that once seemed perfectly acceptable.[22] The effect of this can be seen in the way the courts dealt with defendants accused of serious violence short of murder. They began to assert the right of the community and not just the victim to extract some penalty, and began to impose large fines and terms of imprisonment for acts that in the seventeenth century and before would have been left to private negotiation.[23]

These changes in attitude did not bring to an end all violent public punishments; it was not until the 1860s that public hangings were abolished in England.[24] But they did lead to a basic reconstruction of the penal system. Between 1790 and the 1830s, whipping in public and the use of the pillory came to an end, and the number of offences punishable by hanging was sharply reduced. In all cases these changes were first effected by the courts and then confirmed by Parliament. The 1820s and 1830s saw many statutes that reconstructed virtually every aspect of the criminal law and the system of criminal administration – changes that included not only the sharp reduction of capital punishment, the abolition of other violent public punishments, and the abolition of the ancient device of benefit of clergy, but also related initiatives such as the creation of a more professional police force in London and important measures relating to prisons.[25]

Behind many of these changes there lay a real anxiety about the morality and justice of the established methods of dealing with crime. But there was also a powerful conviction that the old system was failing to solve major problems and that a better method was both necessary and at hand. In the second half of the eighteenth century the number of prosecutions increased, partly because of population growth. The English population almost doubled in the eighteenth century, and doubled again in the first half of the nineteenth. This was in itself sufficient to put pressures on all the available penal institutions and to create the appearance of an increase of crime, whatever the actual rate of offences might have been. The apprehension of growing social disorder was also a result of the massive redistribution of the population that accompanied the growth of industry and the growth of urban areas in the industrial revolution, which was well under way by 1800. But the particular trigger was the fluctuation of prosecutions for property crime. It is clear that the distinctive waves of prosecutions across the century closely correlate with the beginnings and conclusions of wars, of which there were several.[26] From 1740 to the defeat of Napoleon in 1815, England was engaged in a series of wars in Europe and overseas. Each was marked by a diminution of crimes against property as the army and navy took thousands of men from the labour force and as the economy was stimulated by the demands of the armed forces. By the same token, the coming of peace was marked by sharp increases in the number of offenders charged and a real sense of panic, especially in London, about the threat to life and property and more generally about the immorality, lack of discipline, and disobedience of the working population. At the conclusions of wars in the 1750s, the 1760s, and particularly the mid-1780s and after the battle of Waterloo

(1815), there were outcries about the state of crime, the weakness of the courts, and the need to improve the catching and prosecuting of offenders. Inevitably, the obvious failure of the punishments available to the courts to stem the tide of crime became part of the indictment. Transportation had been found wanting for this reason even before the American Revolution brought a sudden halt to the flow of convicts to the colonies in 1776. (It was to resume in 1787, with Australia as the destination, because the level of crime was so high after the war that the magistracy, especially in the more populous parts of the country, was desperate for something to do with the increasing numbers of convicted offenders.)[27] But hanging also came under attack – the scope and the uses of the gallows, and even in some quarters the very principle of capital punishment itself. The last major effort to frighten the English working population into obedience came in the 1780s. More people were hanged in 1785 than in any other year in the eighteenth century, and probably more than in any year in a century and a half. But the bloodbath did not diminish the number of thefts and other property offences committed by men unable to find work or sustain their lives by honest means. The failure to deter, coupled with the growing opposition to corporal punishment, focused the reformist ambitions of those who had been persuaded by Beccaria and others that the established means of dealing with crime could no longer be made to work.

Beccaria preached the deterrent virtues of certainty of punishment over harshness – the value of catching more criminals and making sure that all of those found guilty were punished in some way over the dependence on the violent example of the few who were hanged:

> One of the greatest curbs upon crime is not the cruelty of punishments, but their infallibility, and consequently, the vigilance of magistrates, and that severity of an inexorable judge which, to be a useful virtue, must be accompanied by a mild legislation. The certainty of a punishment, even if it be moderate, will always make a stronger impression than the fear of another which is more terrible but combined with the hope of impunity; even the least evils, when they are certain, always terrify men's minds.[28]

Much of this message had been accepted in practice in England since the seventeenth century; that seems to me to have been what the establishment of transportation signified. But the reformers also made an argument –

now an insistent, demanding, and ultimately convincing argument – for a particular kind of punishment that had also been tried in England earlier, but that had been given up when transportation became available: imprisonment at hard labour.

In the 1760s and thereafter, the belief that confinement in the right circumstances would provide an answer to crime took root in England and elsewhere as a central conviction of penal thinking. It was not a new idea, as I have tried to demonstrate. But it emerged in the late eighteenth and early nineteenth centuries with new force and new point, partly because of the evident failure of the established system.[29]

The strength of the imprisonment idea was reinforced by other elements in the changing society. The industrial work force was growing rapidly in towns and industrial villages by the end of the eighteenth century, and the size and relative importance of the middle classes in society were also increasing – professionals (doctors, lawyers, bankers), traders, shopkeepers, manufacturers, and industrialists. Such men sought rather different kinds of protection from society and government than did the landed gentry. They owned movable, not landed, property; they lived in proximity to the poor, not behind the high walls of country houses; they valued orderliness and regularity, especially in those who worked for them; they wanted a work force and a society that was orderly, reliable, and disciplined. Many felt a religious obligation to create a society in which they and others would be encouraged to live a moral life and so come at last to salvation. They also thought that government should be responsive to the needs of the property-owning classes in society, and that government should be actively engaged in creating conditions in which morality and prosperity would flourish. I think that such men had also been responsible for the push toward more effective punishments in the seventeenth century. London had had an experience of crime in the seventeenth and eighteenth centuries very different from that of the rest of the country – more offences, more violence, and much more wildly fluctuating levels of prosecutions over the short term.[30] It was from London that the strongest impetus for non-capital punishments was to come. London's social and political institutions were dominated by the commercial and professional middle classes, and such men were even more numerous, more widespread, and more active by the end of the eighteenth century.

The means by which opinion could be mobilized were strengthened and greatly expanded during the eighteenth century by the creation and widespread establishment of a newspaper press that by 1800 served the entire country.[31] The focusing of such public opinion might not in itself have convinced a Parliament dominated by the landed gentry and aristocracy of the need for massive legal and penal reform if that class of men had not themselves become persuaded of the threat of crime and disorder. But the moving force behind reform, both in debate and in the press, was provided by the lawyers and middle-class reformers, many of whom were moved by religious convictions and by what seemed to be the growing immorality and irreligion of the poor.

The Establishment of Imprisonment

The rejection of violent public punishments was thus accompanied by a conviction that what was required was a sanction that would have the positive effect of correcting the immorality that had led the offender into trouble in the first place. I do not think that there was a fundamentally new view of crime in the late eighteenth and early nineteenth centuries. Reformers and non-reformers alike continued to think of crime as a moral choice made by an individual. But there were so many offenders by the end of the eighteenth century that it was difficult to think of crime as the product of a few wayward individuals who could be frightened into obedience by the public suffering of a small number of men on the gallows. Crime seemed more and more to be the product of a whole class of people – a criminal or dangerous class, people who were so steeped in immorality as to be beyond the influence or control of religious duty or social obligation.[32]

By the fourth decade of the nineteenth century, the conviction was widespread that crime could be diminished only if the source of the problem was treated – that is, the immorality, the laziness, and the irreligion of the criminal class. Capital punishment might still be appropriate for murderers and a few other offenders. Transportation to Australia could take off others. But Australia could never absorb the number of convicts that had been sent to America. Hanging and transportation could not now touch the heart of the problem. If men committed crimes because they were immoral, lazy, or irreligious, the only effective punishment was one that would transform them and give them the right attitudes. That required institutions in which they could be isolated from the evil influences that had caused their downfall. That was the essence of the reform campaign led by John Howard in the 1770s and carried on thereafter by a small group of reform-minded men. They sought to create prisons in which offenders would be rehabilitated, made to feel remorse for their offences, and armed with moral principles and work habits that would enable them to support themselves honestly in the future. It was essential, in this view, that the discipline of the prisons be such that inmates would be made to feel penitent, an aim reflected in the name given to the new institutions in the legislation that first authorized them in 1779. 'And whereas,' the preamble of the Penitentiary Act runs, 'if many offenders, convicted of crimes for which transportation hath been usually inflicted, were ordered to solitary imprisonment, accompanied by well-regulated labour, and religious instruction, it might be the means, under providence, not only of deterring others from the commission of like crimes, but also of reforming the individuals, and inuring them to habits of industry.'[33] In the penitentiaries, deterrence by a public assault on the bodies of a few convicts was abandoned in favour of rehabilitation by an assault on the hearts and minds of many.

The history of the establishment of prisons and of the attempts to create an environment and a discipline in which the reformation of offenders could be achieved is complex and tangled, and I can do little more here than sketch in some of the main points.[34] It is certainly the case that in terms of numbers, imprisonment became for the first time in the 1770s the main punishment imposed on convicted felons in England. It was a fundamental view that prisons should be forbidding institutions and sufficiently frightening to act as a deterrent to crime. No reformer would have denied that intention. But it was also believed that prisons should be a reformatory experience. How the dozens of local jails actually worked is another matter. Conditions probably improved at least marginally in most of them; the buildings probably were better built and more sanitary than their counterparts in the past. But the extent to which the new penitentiary ideology was imposed in practice was highly variable, both from one institution to another and over time;[35] none the less, one can distinguish a number of broad characteristics of the new custodial sentences.

In the Penitentiary Act of 1779, Parliament accepted the principle that the national treasury should support the creation of penal institutions. The first phase of the effort to establish those institutions lasted into the middle of the nineteenth century, when the impulse to make reformative discipline work ran out of steam. Even at the height of reformatory enthusiasm, the day-to-day conditions in English prisons rarely came close to matching the intentions of the reformers. But in several institutions a very strict discipline was imposed. Broadly speaking, there was from the beginning a difference of opinion between those who thought that the reformation of prisoners would be best accomplished by work discipline, and those who thought that religious training was the only real route to a full rehabilitation of the sinner who had been led to commit criminal offences. These views gave rise to different forms of prison discipline and very different kinds of institutions.

Tension between the proponents of the two schools of thought was frequently apparent.[36] By the 1820s the apparent failure of the earliest schemes and the continuing conflict over the best way to organize prisons was a matter of profound importance, for by then the numbers of offenders had increased sharply and the abolition of capital punishment for all but a handful of relatively rare crimes made the effective disposition of the imprisonment issue a matter of urgency. It was in these circumstances and for these reasons that the experience of American penitentiaries became so important and so valuable. Two U.S. prison systems were built in the 1820s that exhibited in pure form the two opposing routes to convict rehabilitation: these were the prisons in Philadelphia and New York.[37] In Philadelphia, Quaker influence lay behind the creation of a prison in which the prisoners were to be entirely isolated. The Philadelphia plan was to keep prisoners in solitary confinement so that they might, in time and with reflection, come to a realization of their sin, and by spiritual training overcome it on their release. In New York, at Auburn State Prison and Sing Sing, the conviction that prisoners should be isolated from the other inmates and the contagion they represented was united with the belief that prisoners had committed offences in the first place because they lacked good work habits. If they were to be rehabilitated, they had to be inured to 'habits of industry,' as the Penitentiary Act had put it. At Auburn, therefore, the prisoners were to work during the day, though in silence and in as much isolation as possible. At night they were locked up in single-occupancy cells.

These American prisons were inspected by many English and European visitors, and by Canadians; Kingston Penitentiary, which was opened in 1835, was modelled on Auburn. The 'separate' system – cellular and with total isolation – became the model for Pentonville, the major English experiment in penitentiary discipline, which opened in 1842. The 'silent,' or Auburn, system of associated labour was instituted in a number of other English prisons. The results in both cases were horrendous. Isolation brought hundreds of men quietly to insanity, and the silent system of associated labour could be imposed only by means of unrelenting brutality.[38] The hideous results no doubt explain why the effort to root out the causes of crime by 'grinding men good' had begun to wane by the 1850s, even before that goal was explicitly rejected by the Carnarvon committee of 1863 and in the provisions of the Prison Act of 1865. With the winding down of both transportation and the hulks (prison ships) at mid-century, imprisonment came to be the principal punishment for all classes of serious offenders. At the same time, imprisonment came to be seen mainly as a deterrent, and the emphasis in prison administration shifted toward the practice of exacting as severe a punishment as possible without damaging the health of the prisoner. Separation and hard labour were no longer valued as agents of rehabilitation, but more as punitive measures designed to deter released convicts from returning to crime.[39]

The ideal of reformation began to fade after mid-century, in part because it had been such a conspicuous failure, as shown by the rates of recidivism. But it was also the case that in the 1860s and after, the rates of property crime and violence also began to wane in England and elsewhere. There was a greater sense of well-being and prosperity in the second half of the century, and while no one was prepared to say that a problem no longer existed, the sense that society was in danger of being undermined by a tide of crime and immorality was clearly diminishing.[40]

The history of punishment over the previous five hundred years had seen a number of aims and intentions developing in layers, as it were – one coming to overlay the others without entirely displacing what had been there before but none the less causing a shift in policy and practice. Deterrence by terror was supplemented by the deterrent and punitive effects of transportation in the seventeenth century and by reform and rehabilitation in the eighteenth and nineteenth. The new penal ideas were complex responses to what seemed to be a changing criminal problem and, more broadly, a changing problem of the governance of the poor. Reformation did not replace deterrence as a penal strategy, even in the new prisons of the nineteenth century, whose proponents saw in their disciplinary regimes the key to social order and the elimination of crime. But reformation did not disappear entirely, even when those extravagant hopes were dashed. Rehabilitation resurfaced in a different guise at the end of the nineteenth century, and remains now a recurring hope occasionally reinvented by reformers. What to do about imprisonment continues to trouble governments and policy-makers; but a discussion of how imprisonment has been adapted in the last hundred years, how it has been modified and reinforced by early-release incentives, parole and community orders, and by prisoners' rights, and how other and alternative sanctions have been elaborated would require another paper, or several.

Notes

* Professor, Department of History and Centre of Criminology, University of Toronto. I wish to thank Alan Darnell for research assistance, and to express my gratitude for financial support to the Social Sciences and Humanities Research Council of Canada and to the Ministry of the Solicitor-General of Canada through its contributions grant to the Centre of Criminology, University of Toronto.

1 On discretion and the criminal law, see D. Hay, 'Property, Authority and the Criminal Law,' in D. Hay, P. Linebaugh, and E.P. Thompson (eds), *Albion's Fatal Tree: Crime and Society in Eighteenth-Century England* (1975) 40–9; P. King, 'Decision-Makers and Decision Making in the English Criminal Law, 1750–1800,' (1984) 27 *Historical Journal* 25, at 27. On the role of rewards in criminal law administration, see L. Radzinowicz, *A History of the English Criminal Law and Its Administration from 1750*, vol. 2 (1957) 33–167; J.W. Langbein, 'Shaping the Eighteenth-Century Criminal Trial: A View from the Ryder Sources,' (1983) 50 *University of Chicago Law Review* 1 at 106–10; J.M. Beattie, *Crime and the Courts in England, 1660–1800* (1986) 50–5.

2 On the origins of imprisonment in the Middle Ages, see C. Harding, B. Hines, R. Ireland, and P. Rawlings, *Imprisonment in England and Wales: A Concise History* (1985) chapters 1–2; R.B. Pugh, *Imprisonment in Medieval England* (1968); and two studies by Margery Basset: 'The Fleet Prison in the Middle Ages' (1943–4) 5 *University of Toronto Law Journal* 383, and 'Newgate Prison in the Middle Ages' (1943) 18 *Speculum* 233.

3 Beattie, supra note 1, 456–68

4 F. Pollock and F.W. Maitland, *The History of English Law before the Time of Edward I*, vol. 1 (1895) chapter 2

5 N.D. Hurnard, *The King's Pardon for Homicide before A.D. 1307* (1969) 8–9; F. Pollock, 'The King's Peace in the Middle Ages' (1900) 13 *Harvard Law Review* 177; H.G. Richardson and G.O. Sayles, *The Governance of Mediaeval England from the Conquest to Magna Carta* (1963) chapters 9–10; D.N.P.

Stenton, *English Justice between the Norman Conquest and the Great Charter, 1066–1215* (1965)

6 J. Bellamy, *Crime and Public Order in England in the Later Middle Ages* (1983) chapter 6; B. Hanawalt, *Crime and Conflict in English Communities, 1300–1348* (1979) 44

7 B. Lenman and G. Parker, 'The State, the Community and the Criminal Law in Early Modern Europe,' in V.A.C. Gatrell, B. Lenman, and G. Parker (eds), *Crime and the Law: The Social History of Crime in Western Europe since 1500* (1980) 18–23

8 On the rates of conviction in the fourteenth century, see Hanawalt, supra note 6, 56–62, 268. On the mitigation exercised by juries, see T.A. Green, *Verdict According to Conscience: Perspectives on the English Criminal Trial Jury, 1200–1800* (1985) chapters 2–3. On the origins of benefit of clergy, see L.C. Gabel, *Benefit of Clergy in England in the Later Middle Ages* (1929).

9 The relationship between the growth of the state and changes in criminal law and punishment has been explored by Pieter Spierenburg in *Spectacle of Suffering: Executions and the Evolution of Repression from a Preindustrial Metropolis to the European Experience* (1984). See also Lenman and Parker, supra note 7, 11–48.

10 A.L. Beier, *Masterless Men: The Vagrancy Problem in England, 1560–1640* (1985); A.L. Beier and R. Finlay (eds), *London 1500–1700: The Making of the Metropolis* (1986); P. Clark and P. Slack (eds), *Crisis and Order in English Towns, 1500–1700* (1972); R. Finlay, *Population and Metropolis: The Demography of London, 1580–1650* (1981); D.M. Palliser, *The Age of Elizabeth: England under the Later Tudors, 1547–1603* (1983) chapters 2–5; P. Slack, 'Vagrants and Vagrancy in England, 1598–1664' (1974) 27 *Economic History Review* 360

11 J.H. Langbein, *Prosecuting Crime in the Renaissance: England, Germany, France* (1974) 5–125

12 J.F. Stephen, *A History of the Criminal Law of England*, vol. 1 (1883) 463–6; J.H. Baker (ed.), *The Reports of Sir John Spelman*, vol. 2 (1978) 327–34; J.S. Cockburn, *Calendar of Assize Records, Home Circuit Indictments, Elizabeth I and James I, Introduction* (1985) 117–21; benefit of clergy was finally abolished by the Criminal Law Act of 1827.

13 Cockburn, supra note 12, 125; J.A. Sharpe, *Crime in Seventeenth-Century England: A County Study* (1983) chapters 9 and 11; Sharpe, *Crime in Early Modern England, 1550–1750* (1984) chapter 3; P. Jenkins, 'From Gallows to Prison: The Execution Rate in Early Modern England' (1986) 7 *Criminal Justice History* 51

14 R. McGowen, 'The Body and Punishment in Eighteenth-Century England' (forthcoming)

15 J. Innes, 'Prisons for the Poor: English Bridewells, 1555–1800,' in F. Snyder and D. Hay (eds), *Law, Labour and Crime in a Historical Perspective* (1989)
16 For the evidence upon which the discussion of the period 1660–1718 in the next several paragraphs is based, see Beattie, supra note 1, chapter 9.
17 Cockburn, supra note 12, 126–9
18 A.R. Ekirch, 'Bound for America: A Profile of British Convicts Transported to the Colonies, 1718–1775' (1985) 42 *William and Mary Quarterly* 184; Ekirch, *Bound for America: The Transportation of British Colonists to the Colonies, 1718–1775* (1987); A.E. Smith, *Colonists in Bondage: White Servitude and Convict Labour in America, 1607–1776* (1974) 89–135
19 D. Hay, 'Property, Authority and the Criminal Law,' and P. Linebaugh, 'The Tyburn Riot against the Surgeons,' in Hay, Linebaugh, and Thompson, supra, note 1, chapters 1 and 2
20 Spierenburg, supra note 9, chapters 2–4
21 Ibid., chapter 6; R. McGowen, 'A Powerful Sympathy: Terror, the Prison and Humanitarian Reform in Early Nineteenth-Century Britain' (1986) 25 *Journal of British Studies* 312
22 N. Elias, *The Civilizing Process* (1939; 1978 trans. by Edmund Jephcott)
23 Beattie, supra note 1, 89–91, 136–7, 608–10
24 On the campaign against public hangings in the nineteenth century, see D. Cooper, *The Lesson of the Scaffold: The Public Execution Controversy in Victorian England* (1974).
25 L. Radzinowicz, *A History of the English Criminal Law and Its Administration from 1750*, vols. 1–3 (1948–56); Philips, '"A New Engine of Power and Authority": The Institutionalization of Law Enforcement in England, 1780–1830,' in Gatrell, Lenman, and Parker, supra note 7, chapter 6.
26 D. Hay, 'War, Dearth and Theft in the Eighteenth Century: The Record of the English Courts,' (1982) 95 *Past and Present* 117; Beattie, supra note 1, chapter 5
27 On the re-establishment of transportation in 1787, see A.G.L. Shaw, *Convicts and the Colonies* (1966) chapter 2; Beattie, supra note 1, 592–601.
28 C.B. Beccaria, *On Crimes and Punishments* (1764; 1963 trans. by Henry Paolucci) 58
29 On the renewed interest in imprisonment at the end of the eighteenth century, see C. Harding, B. Hines, R. Ireland, and P. Rawlings, supra note 2, chapter 5; U.R.Q. Henriques, 'The Rise and Decline of the Separate System of Prison Discipline' (1972) 54 *Past and Present* 61, at 61–70; M. Ignatieff, *A Just Measure of Pain: The Penitentiary in the Industrial Revolution, 1750–1850* (1978) chapter 3; S. McConville, *A History of English Prison Administration, 1750–1877*, vol. 1 (1981); R. Evans *The Fabrication of Virtue: English Prison Architecture, 1750–1840* (1982) chapter 2.

30 Beattie, supra note 1, 215-35
31 J. Black, *The English Press in the Eighteenth Century* (1987); G.A. Cranfield, *The Development of the Provincial Newspaper, 1700–1760* (1962); M. Harris, *London Newspapers in the Age of Walpole: A Study in the Origins of the Modern English Press* (1986)
32 For the notion of a 'criminal class,' see J.J. Tobias, *Crime and Industrial Society in the Nineteenth Century* (1967) chapter 4.
33 19 Geo. III, c. 74, s. 5 (1779)
34 For more detailed studies, see Evans, supra note 29, chapters 3-8; Harding, Hines, Ireland, and Rawlings, supra note 2, chapter 6; Henriques, supra note 29, 70–89; Ignatieff, supra note 29, chapters 4-6; McConville, supra note 29; L. Radzinowicz and R. Hood, *A History of the English Criminal Law and Its Administration from 1750*, vol. 5 (1986).
35 For an excellent evaluation of the results of various programs of prison reform in one county, see M.E. DeLacy, *Prison Reform in Lancashire, 1700–1850: A Study in Local Administration* (1986) chapters 4-7; DeLacy, 'Grinding Men Good? Lancashire's Prisons at Mid-Century' in V. Bailey (ed), *Policing and Punishment in Nineteenth-Century Britain* (1981) chapter 8.
36 On this theme, see Henriques, supra note 29, 70-8; Harding, Hines, Ireland, and Rawlings, supra note 2, 143–54.
37 D. Rothman, *The Discovery of the Asylum: Social Order and Disorder in the New Republic* (1971) chapter 4
38 Ignatieff, supra note 29, chapter 4; S. Webb and B. Webb, *English Prisons under Local Government* (1922). On the brutality of the Kingston Penitentiary in the two decades after it was founded on the Auburn model, see J.M. Beattie, *Attitudes towards Crime and Punishment in Upper Canada, 1830–1850* (1977) 15-35.
39 On imprisonment in the last half of the nineteenth century, see Harding, Hines, Ireland, and Rawlings, supra note 2, 154–61, 187–235; Radzinowicz and Hood, supra note 34.
40 V.A.C. Gatrell, 'The Decline of Theft and Violence in Victorian and Edwardian England,' in Gatrell, Lenman and Parker, supra note 9, chapter 9.

2 Sociology and Legal Sanctions

H. LAURENCE ROSS*

The interest of sociologists in legal sanctions, though present from the birth of the discipline in the late nineteenth century, has flowered in the second half of the twentieth century. Two distinct approaches to the study of legal sanctions can be discerned in the contemporary law-and-social-science movement. The first, labelled the criminological approach, takes the obedience and disobedience of legal rules as the central issue. It focuses on the deterrence proposition, which states that obedience is increased by the provision of severe, sure, and swift sanctions for disobedience. The second, labelled for convenience the sociology of law, inquires into the process by which sanctions are applied. It centres on the operation of discretion among legal officials, and leads to the proposition that legal rules, when applied in practice, are simplified, liberalized, and rendered arbitrary in comparison with the formal statement of the law. This paper reviews these lines of inquiry and summarizes the research they have yielded.

Background

One might describe sociology as the study of the interaction between behaviour and rules; laws can be seen as the most formal and central of social rules. The fathers of modern sociology, Karl Marx, Max Weber, and Emile Durkheim, all addressed the operation of law in their theoretical works. For Marx, law reflected the struggle between the classes, and legal sanctions functioned to guarantee the hegemony of the ruling class.[1] Durkheim measured the basis of social cohesion by the relative predominance of either punitive or restitutive legal sanctions.[2] Weber found in legal sanctions the ultimate guarantees of an ordered world on which modern capitalistic society rested.[3]

Despite the classical concern of sociologists with law, an empirical research tradition was slow to be established, largely because, as sociology developed in early twentieth-century America, the phenomena of informal social control appeared to be more dramatic and interesting. Legal effects were regarded as banal and could be assumed, whereas the impacts of family, peer, and neighbourhood institutions, especially in the immigrant urban ghettoes, were unanticipated and therefore more exciting.

During this period of relative indifference to law among sociologists, the stewardship of interest in the capacities and limitations of legal sanctions passed to academic lawyers in the intellectual traditions of sociological jurisprudence, exemplified by Roscoe Pound,[4] and legal realism, exemplified by Karl Llewellyn.[5] Sociological jurisprudence attacked the classical conception of law as self-contained, logical, and independent of social influences. It introduced the idea of 'law in action' as opposed to what might be called 'law in concept.' Law was seen both as a social institution and as a body of doctrine. Legal realism continued this tradition of scepticism, but relied more self-consciously on the social sciences. Realists engaged in empirical research as well as in theoretical speculation, and some of the studies of these law-trained scholars exceeded in scale many of the subsequent accomplishments of social scientists. One investigation of comparative procedure utilized a data base of 70,000 cases.

Sociological interest in law revived strongly in the 1960s, partly owing to an infusion of public funds into research evaluating a variety of law-based programs designed to address social problems in the United States. The Great Society showed signs of also being the Experimental Society,[6] although critics pointed out the difficulties in maintaining objectivity in publicly funded evaluations of publicly funded programs. None the less, a number of major evaluations were undertaken of programs based on legal sanctions. These included programs offering incentives as well as traditional punitive ones, and the studies added greatly to our understanding of the use of law as a tool of reform. The law-and-social-science enterprise in general and sociological studies of law in particular were also fostered by support from private foundations, especially the Russell Sage Foundation, which financed the Law and Society Association and its journal, the *Law and Society Review*. The same foundation supported interdisciplinary programs at several universities, and provided incentives for training and retraining legal scholars and social scientists in the companion disciplines. Academic enterprises in North America also were affected by a rise in student interest in legal careers and in undergraduate courses related to law. The ensuing growth of legally oriented sociology was paralleled by developments in disciplines such as anthropology, psychology, political science, and history. In all the social sciences, investigations into and understanding of law have increased greatly over the past quarter-century. Both the efficacy and the limitations of legal sanctions as tools for ordering behaviour are better understood than previously, and gaps in the knowledge base are better identified. We now know better what we do and do not know.

Criminology

One of the two centres of the current sociological interest in law is criminology, which can be defined as the science of explaining the violation of legal imperatives. Historically, criminologists tended to consider the law as a given, a passive definer of phenomena to be explained on the basis of biological, psychological, or social structural variables. Beginning with the seminal work of Paul Tappan,[7] however, criminologists in recent years have posited an active role for the legal process in the creation of criminality. Conformity to law is not automatic; some laws attract more compliance than others. The reasons are to be found in the nature of the rules and the manner in which they are applied as much as in the characteristics of the individuals and organizations to which they are addressed.[8] Violation of some criminal laws is so widespread as to be characterized as 'folk crime'[9] – for example, the rate of failure to comply with laws requiring the use of seat-belts in automobiles ranges from 5 per cent in England to 79 per cent in Japan; the typical rate is somewhere between 60 and 70 per cent.[10] Resistance, like that of U.S. school boards to desegregation orders of the Supreme Court,[11] and of police departments to landmark civil rights cases,[12] is common, predictable, and comprehensible.

Although criminological research has not been characterized by immersion in general theory, during the past two decades attempts have been made to explore and refine the deterrence proposition in sociological (non-market) contexts. In economics, this proposition is known as the law of demand, which states that as the price of a commodity increases, consumption will decline. Its confirmation in the marketplace is general, if not universal. Understood in the form of a prediction that stiffer legal penalties will reduce crime, however, its validity is highly questionable.

The traditional statement of the deterrence hypothesis, which originated in eighteenth-century utilitarian thought, is that the effectiveness of a threat of punishment is a function of its severity, certainty, and swiftness. Critics have noted that the hypothesis is fundamentally psychological, and that these variables must be understood as perceived rather than objective.[13] Those attempts to investigate the deterrence hypothesis that employ such measures as actual risk of apprehension necessarily assume a correlation that is generally plausible but possibly incorrect. The threat of punishment must be communicated, and it must be credible if a deterrent effect is to be expected. Moreover, the impact of the threat may be enhanced or diminished by such factors as whether the receiver is relatively present-oriented or future-oriented, optimistic or pessimistic, and risk-seeking or risk-averse, and whether the behaviour at which the threat is aimed is of great or little importance, instrumental or expressive, etc.[14]

Most current research concerns objective threats and assumes the linkage with perception described above; a number of studies in widely different contexts seem to coalesce on support for the deterrent effect of measures aimed at increasing the certainty of punishment, though mainly in the short run, and on rejection of the deterrent effect of measures aimed at increasing the severity of punishment. Criminal acts as diverse as subway robberies, muggings on the streets, and drunken driving seem to be reduced in number by publicized campaigns of police enforcement. A recent example, showing some impressive accomplishments over the medium as well as the short term, is the practice of random breath-testing in New South Wales, Australia, where a million such tests are conducted annually in a total population of about six million drivers.[15] In contrast, studies examining the results of raising penalties from conventional levels to draconian ones in such matters as drug-dealing[16] and drunken driving[17] find little evidence of deterrent effect. Such studies commonly report that the severe punishments are greatly moderated in practice through the discretion of criminal justice officials.[18]

There has been very little research on the third of the deterrence variables, swiftness of punishment, perhaps in part because of the scarcity of policies that increase swiftness without also significantly affecting certainty and severity. One current policy that may permit this is administrative driving-licence revocation for drunken driving. This kind of law permits police immediately to take away the licence of a driver who fails a breath test. Some preliminary studies in the United States are yielding encouraging findings.[19]

Unfortunately, the validity of much of the deterrence knowledge base is currently in question.[20] Many studies are cross-sectional, and rely on associations that lack a time component to help distinguish cause from effect. For example, if fewer jail sentences are associated with higher crime rates, is this fact evidence favouring deterrence? Or are large numbers of criminals swamping available detention facilities?

Those deterrence studies employing econometric techniques face the technical problem of specification errors in the mathematical modelling necessitated by the techniques. Furthermore, most deterrence studies, like criminological research in general, are necessarily founded on reported data of limited completeness and representativeness, and are conducted using conventional groups and venial crimes, with very limited ranges of the three principal variables. This is especially the case for certainty of punishment, which is nearly always negligible.

The attention of the research community has been directed mainly at criminal law penalties; civil law penalties and tax consequences of behaviour have been overlooked, despite their obvious importance in specific offences.[21] The interactions between deterrence variables and other social factors such as peer-group norms are also generally overlooked.[22]

These facts militate against easy generalization from the research literature to the broad theoretical proposition of deterrence. It is important to note that an important strain of scholarship in the Scandinavian countries[23] views the effects of legal threats to be operative over a much longer period, through such mechanisms as moral education and habit formation. Scholars of this persuasion find that the time scale of virtually all reported research is too limited for these mechanisms to have their predicted effect.[24]

The Sociology of Law

Criminological studies, especially those founded on deterrence theory, help to define the abstract potential of legal sanctions. The application of those sanctions would be less controversial if all law were self-enforcing – if rules jumped off the pages of the statute-books and furnished realistic and enforceable guides for behaviour. The body of scholarship which I term here 'the sociology of law' attempts to show how and why the circumstances of application of legal rules modify the formal statements in the statute-books and redefine the rights and obligations of members of society.

There are two key perceptions in the sociology of law as it applies to the capabilities and limitations of legal rules in regulating behaviour. First, the formal rules are often ideal, expressing hopes rather than expectations; second the rules are often an onerous overburden on the system charged with applying them. The sociology of law views this system much more broadly than does traditional legal scholarship. The system encompasses not only the paraphernalia of lawyers and courts, but also, and far more commonly, numerous paralegal bureaucracies. The vast bulk of law application in contemporary societies is performed by agencies such as police departments, insurance companies, and administrative agencies charged with regulating the quality of food, water, housing, and the environment, the payment and collection of taxes, and the provision of educational and welfare services. If we are to understand the nature of rights and duties under law, attention must be paid to the circumstances and persons involved in the day-to-day application of the law.

The officials charged with applying and enforcing the law attempt a virtually impossible task. The mere heft of a modern motor vehicle statute or a housing code, not to mention an income tax act, will assure the observer that strict enforcement is an unreasonable expectation; add to this the fact that complexity and multiplicity of origins are likely to produce contradictions and inconsistencies in a statute's provisions. Because it is not in the spirit of modern legislation to declare priorities among the conflicting demands of various statutes, the resolution of these problems – defining what is important and what will be overlooked, and which demand takes precedence in the event of conflict – is shifted from legislators to administrative agencies. Furthermore, it is rare that the higher, and supposedly most responsible, levels of officialdom dare to remedy a legislative default by taking into their own hands the formal interpretation, organization, and necessary partial nullification of the codes. The task therefore ends up in the hands and at the discretion of the frontline officials, Lipsky's 'street-level bureaucrats.'[25] I am speaking here of the police officer, the insurance adjuster, the tax auditor, the meat or milk or air pollution or housing inspector, the customs official, and similar workers. These persons exercise wide discretion in the matter of whether and how the formal rules will be applied in the population to which they are directed. Many of these workers ply their trades with relative freedom from supervision. Their work is accomplished in the field, far from the physical presence of the supervisor, or in conferences or over the telephone where it cannot be directly observed. Indeed, the guarantee of front-line discretion lies in the fact that the supervisor generally has no access to the 'real world,' but develops his or her procedures according to a picture that has been painted and provided by the worker whose decisions have to be evaluated. The worker, knowing the criteria that will be applied, can to an important degree create a 'file' that supports what he or she has decided to do.

A considerable case-study literature now illuminates the practice of law application. The overzealous police officer knows that physical brutality will be most readily tolerated if it is directed at an accused who has assaulted an officer, and appropriate assault charges against the accused and corroborating narrative details are routine in such cases.[26] The insurance adjuster anxious to quiet a pesky claimant may photograph a fictional (usually nearby) accident scene that better justifies paying a claim than the place originally identified.[27]

A major theme in occupational sociology, equally or more applicable in the sociology of law, is that workers act to minimize role strains. The behaviour of front-line workers can be understood by heeding the pressures they experience as they go about their rounds. Classical descriptions involve the patrol officer faced with the 'symbolic assailant'[28] or the supervisory quota,[29] and more recent studies of workers in non-criminal law areas also point to strong pressures both from those they serve (claimants, clients, complainants) and from those who command them.

These generalizations have long received support in sociological studies of the police. A major study of three police departments undertaken by the American Bar Foundation more than two decades ago found informal agendas to be highly influential in determining whether the patrol officers used the arrest power where it was warranted.[30] (Alternatives to arrest included warnings, harassment, or disregard of behaviour that clearly violated one or more criminal laws.) Arrests were not made when in the opinion of the patrol officer the laws in question were ideal, or not meant to be applied literally; when the offences were judged trivial; when they were committed by and against minority-group members in ways deemed typical of the subculture; when the victim was predicted to be uncooperative, or was himself in part to blame for the offence; and when arrest would involve treatment deemed inappropriate, such as excessively harsh sentences. The category of weak evidence for prosecution, the only formally legitimate one, appears almost as an afterthought. In contrast, behaviour that ordinarily would have escaped punishment led to arrest when it was seen as likely to recur, and thus to strain police resources, or when it was seen to indicate disrespect for the police; when arrest was seen as necessary to maintain an image of full enforcement; when arrest could be used to punish different conduct that was difficult to prove; and to aid in the investigation of irrelevant matters, such as detaining a witness to a different crime.

By exercising selectively the power of arrest, the police are effectively changing the criminal law. Activities that meet with tolerance have been decriminalized in a real sense, and in other situations the police enlarge the boundaries of criminality. This finding is a major contribution of the sociology of law to the understanding of legal sanctions.

That things are seldom what they seem, or are supposed to be, though perhaps a discovery in itself, does not exhaust the sociological insights in this area. The possibility arises of specifying the general sources of role strain among law-applying personnel and, even more significantly, of predicting the consequences of official discretion for the nature and quality of the legal system as it is experienced on a day-to-day basis. This point can be illustrated by comparing the outcomes of official action in settling tort law claims for automobile bodily injuries[31] and enforcing the housing code in response to complaints.[32]

Insurance adjusters are faced with a historic and complex set of doctrinal principles. The law of negligence is intellectual, precise, and subtle. the estimation of personal injury damages is as demanding and perplexing as any task of appraisal. The job of applying tort law rules in varied fact situations might suggest endless study and investigation for all but the most routine incidents. However, the front-line employees of insurance companies are required to investigate, evaluate, and negotiate dozens of personal injury claims every month. Time and other resources are limited for all but the most serious injuries. Yet the task is accomplished within the resource constraints in a way that satisfies supervisors, claimants, and attorneys in all but a tiny fraction of claims, as is evidenced by high settlement rates and a general avoidance of litigation.

The key to the satisfactory functioning of the system lies in the acceptability of bureaucratic handling of what at first seems like intractable material. Bureaucracies function best when a task can be converted into routine classification of fundamentally simple cases. The uniqueness of human experience has to be in large part disregarded or defined as irrelevant. For example, a postal clerk takes only the weight and size of a parcel into consideration when calculating the cost of postage, and this fact does not burden anyone's conscience. In contrast, when similar criteria are used to classify candidates for admission to college, we are uneasy. In insurance claims, issues of liability and damage are bureaucratically resolved by substituting the provisions of the relatively simple traffic code for the complex and subtle law of negligence. The rules of traffic law offer quick and easy guidelines for driver behaviour, and they have come to be accepted by all parties to insurance claims as sufficient substitutes for negligence law in routine cases. They reduce the cost of determining the validity of claims to a level bearable by the system. Similarly, the task of evaluating intangible damages, such as pain and suffering, can be accomplished by applying simple multipliers to easily ascertained objective indexes – for example, medical bills.

Thus, one of the characteristics of the law in action in routine automobile personal injury claims is simplification – the reduction of complex mandates to simple ones easily manageable by the available organizational machinery.

A second major characteristic of the law in action is liberalism. The job of the adjuster is to pay claims, and payment is usually the means whereby the files can be closed and the workers can go on to other cases. Although one might characterize the insurance company's stance as adversarial to the claimant, this does not prevent payment being made in nine out of ten cases in which claims are presented, even when the company is armed with the defence of the claimant's contributory negligence. The files of a major insurance company have been found to contain several cases in which payment was made on a liability claim when the claimant rear-ended another car – cases in which common sense and the simplified law of negligence would suggest that no payment be made. The amounts paid in these cases can be described as token; they enabled the adjusters to close the cases, and the payments were justified by them on the grounds that it was cheaper to make the payment than to continue to refuse when the (misguided) claimant seemed determined to press the case.

The third characteristic of the law in action is arbitrariness. Given what seem to be highly similar liability and injury situations, some kinds of claimants are paid much more than others. The successful claimants can best be described as sophisticated – educated, middle-class individuals. Perhaps the most sophisticated claims of all are those presented by attorneys. Represented claims obtain considerably higher payments than similar claims put forward directly by claimants.

In short, observation of the law in action in the case of automobile injury tort claims finds that situational pressures on the personnel responsible for resolving claims produce outcomes that are based on simpler rules, that are more liberal, and that arbitrarily reward formally irrelevant factors. These outcomes are to be contrasted with expectations that are based on principle or 'black-letter law.'

Similar patterns appear in the very different context of applying the housing code in an industrial city. An observation of the behaviour of housing inspectors reveals, first, a simplification of the complex code through informal 'prioritization.' Some provisions are considered important, and compliance is demanded; others are ignored. These are not the same throughout the city: most work orders in middle-class areas are for exterior violations related to sightliness (for example, peeling paint), whereas in areas inhabited by poor tenants the bread and butter of the inspectorate is the absence of heat and hot water.

Liberalism in housing inspection also takes the form of underenforcement of the code. The ideal nature of the code is evident in that it promises a middle-class home to everyone, but provides no resources (other than what can be extracted from landlords) to build or maintain these homes. Inasmuch as many homeowners are themselves poor, and even wealthy ones are generally unable to fulfil the housing code's implied promise to large numbers of limited-income tenants, the task of the inspector may be regarded as non-enforcement of much of the code. One of the principal ways in which non-enforcement can be legitimated is to pretend that the code violation is in the process of being remedied, and to allow additional time for compliance. If the case seems hopeless, as when the landlord is known to be without resources (the proverbial widow on Social Security), the inspector may search for a new daub of paint as evidence that an extension is warranted. Unlike the insurance claimant, the property owner will make no waves if the disposition is postponed indefinitely, barring any countervailing pressures from either supervisors or complainants.

Not surprisingly, code inspection outcomes are influenced by formally irrelevant matters, and consequently the law in action appears arbitrary. A case in point is the characterization of landlords as 'good apples' or 'bad apples.' The good ones are expected to comply with the code if and when the resources can be made available. The bad ones are seen as deliberate evaders, and are treated with much less patience and forbearance than other property owners.

In these two disparate cases and elsewhere[33] the law in action appears simpler, more liberal, and arbitrary in comparison with the formal statements of the applicable law. A realistic understanding of legal sanctions must encompass these distortions, for they determine how, when, and where the sanctions are experienced by the relevant target group. Likewise, intelligent and effective policy that relies on legal sanctions to accomplish deterrence or inducement will take the effects of law application into account. The policy-maker will ask about the circumstances in which the sanctions are applied, including the organizational and personal characteristics of law application, and will design incentives and inducements to ensure that the law in action conforms closely to his intentions.

Conclusion

The findings of researchers in the sociology of law may help to explain some of the disappointing outcomes of criminological studies based on deterrence expectations. In particular, it seems possible to explain the counter-theoretical findings concerning the effects of severe punishments. Many common criminal acts appear vastly to exceed the numbers of fulfilled threats of punishment. For example, the ratio of drunken-driving incidents to arrests – not convictions – can be estimated at close to a thousand to one. Moreover, the sanction is applied arbitrarily in the sense that police patrols are concentrated in place and time, and suspicion is likely to land on some kinds of drivers and vehicles more than others. Young men, for instance, are arrested more often than their numbers warrant.[34] Thus, the average driver who is tempted to drink is faced with extremely small objective probabilities of apprehension. We know from the psychological literature that although moderately low probabilities of loss tend to be overestimated, extremely low probabilities are treated as negligible – as though they were zero.[35]

If we regard the deterrence proposition as at least roughly multiplicative, then a very severe penalty with a probability of near zero cannot be expected to yield greater deterrent results than a mild penalty. Indeed, the expected deterrent value of both is close to zero, and a negative result for the police does not constitute a fair test of the deterrence proposition. From the policy viewpoint, this example points to the necessity for effective legal sanctions to be applied with reasonable probabilities. Although patrol services bear up-front costs, it is not possible to avoid these and obtain the same effects merely by increasing penalties for those offenders who are caught. Harsh punishments imposed haphazardly upon a small and arbitrary sample of a large population may strike us as both unfair and unavailing. The legal system provides no exceptions to the truism that the things we want are not free.

Notes

* Professor, Department of Sociology, University of New Mexico at Albuquerque
1 M. Cain and A. Hunt, *Marx and Engels on Law* (1979)
2 E. Durkheim, *The Division of Labor in Society* (1964)
3 M. Weber, *On Law in Economy and Society* (1966)
4 R. Pound, 'The Scope and Purpose of Sociological Jurisprudence (Part II)' (1912) 25 *Harvard Law Review* 140
5 K. Llewellyn, *Jurisprudence: Realism in Theory and Practice* (1962)
6 D.T. Campbell, 'Reforms as Experiments' (1969) 24 *American Psychologist* 402, advocates the use of public policy as a sociological research tool and the use of sociological theory as a public policy tool.
7 P.W. Tappan, *Crime, Justice, and Correction* (1960)
8 A.L. Stinchcombe, 'Institutions of Privacy in the Determination of Police Administrative Practice' (1963) 69 *American Journal of Sociology* 150
9 H.L. Ross, 'Traffic Law Violation: A Folk Crime' (1961) 8 *Social Problems* 231
10 A.C. Grimm, 'Restraint Use Laws by Country as of August, 1984' (1984) 15 *UMTRI Research Review* 1
11 J.H. Wilkinson III, *From Brown to Bakke: The Supreme Court and School Integration 1954–1979* (1979)
12 See the discussion of *Mapp v. Ohio* (1961) 367 U.S. 643, in D.L. Horowitz, *The Courts and Social Policy* (1977) 220–57.
13 J. Gibbs, *Crime, Punishment and Deterrence* (1975) 105–44

14 F. Zimring and G. Hawkins, *Deterrence: The Legal Threat in Crime Control* (1973) 98–118
15 R.J. Homel, *Policing the Drinking Driver* (Australian Federal Office of Road Safety, 1986)
16 Association of the Bar of the City of New York, *The Nation's Toughest Drug Law: Evaluating the New York Experience* (1977)
17 H.L. Ross, *Deterring the Drinking Driver: Legal Policy and Social Control* (1982)
18 National Institute of Justice, *Mandatory Confinement for Drunk Driving: Impacts on the Criminal Justice System* (1983)
19 See, for example, National Highway Traffic Safety Administration, *State and Community Program Area Report* (1985).
20 See A. Blumstein, J. Cohen, and D. Nagin (eds), *Deterrence and Incapacitation: Estimating the Effects of Criminal Sanctions on Crime Rates* (1978) 4–7.
21 E.H. Sutherland, *White Collar Crime* (1949)
22 H. Grasmick and D. Green, 'Legal Punishment, Social Disapproval, and Internalization as Inhibitors of Illegal Behavior' (1980) 71 *Journal of Criminal Law and Criminology* 325
23 See, for example, J. Andenaes, *Punishment and Deterrence* (1974), especially chapter 4, 'The Moral or Educative Influence of Criminal Law' (110–28).
24 J. Snortum, 'Another Look at the "Scandinavian Myth"' (1983) 6 *Law and Policy* 5
25 M. Lipsky, *Street-Level Bureaucracy: Dilemmas of the Individual in Public Services* (1980)
26 See P. Chevigny, *Police Power: Police Abuses in New York City* (1969) 140–6, for a discussion of police use of 'cover charges' to conceal cases of brutality.
27 H.L. Ross, *Settled out of Court: A Sociological Study of Insurance Claims Adjustment* (1970)
28 J. Skolnick, *Justice without Trial* (1966). Skolnick defines 'symbolic assailants' as 'persons who use gesture, language, and attire that the policeman has come to recognize as a prelude to violence' (at 45).
29 J. Gardiner, *Traffic and the Police: Variations in Law-Enforcement Policy* (1969)
30 W.R. LaFave, *Arrest: The Decision to Take a Suspect into Custody* (1965)
31 See Ross, supra note 27.
32 P. Ould, 'The Enforcement of Law: A Study of the Housing Code in Action in Buffalo, New York' (PH D dissertation, State University of New York at Buffalo 1985)
33 See, for example, K. Hawkins, 'Bargain and Bluff: Compliance Strategy in the Enforcement of Regulation' (1983) 5 *Law and Policy Quarterly* 35 on water pollution inspectors; E. Bardach and R.A. Kagan, *Going by the Book: The*

Problem of Regulatory Unreasonableness (1982) on other kinds of inspectors; and the extensive literature on the police (for example, Skolnick, supra note 28, and Chevigny, supra note 26).

34 R.J. Homel, 'Young Men in the Arms of the Law: An Australian Perspective on Policing and Punishing the Drinking Driver' (1983) 15 *Accident Analysis and Prevention* 449

35 For example, D. Kahneman and A. Tversky, 'Choices, Values and Frames,' in N.J. Smelser and D.R. Gerstein (eds), *Behavioral and Social Science: Fifty Years of Discovery* (1986)

3 The Economics of Criminal Sanctions

PHILIP J. COOK*

This is an essay on the economists' theoretical perspective of how rewards and sanctions influence criminal activity. Although I include an occasional reference to the empirical evidence, Franklin Zimring's essay (elsewhere in this volume) precludes the necessity of a more complete account. In any event, as an economist I run true to form in placing precedence on developing the theory: as the joke has it, an economist is someone who, told that something is true in practice, wonders whether it is true in theory.

Economics is unique among the social sciences in having a well-developed paradigm for guiding theoretical inquiry on any topic that an economist chooses to investigate. This paradigm is well illustrated in the modern literature on the economics of crime, beginning with the seminal articles by Becker[1] and Ehrlich.[2] In essence, the paradigm has five parts:
1. Identify the relevant decision-makers and the objectives that motivate their behaviour, usually by assuming self-interest and rationality.
2. Given these objectives, and a characterization of the available options, develop the implications for how behavioural choices will respond to changes in opportunity.
3. Specify the conditions of interaction or exchange among the decision-makers.
4. Derive a characterization of the aggregate consequences of this interaction, with special attention to the characteristics of 'equilibrium'.
5. Analyse the effects on this equilibrium of changes in contextual variables.

Of course, economists traditionally have applied this approach to the analysis of prices and quantities in the context of a market system of exchange, and efforts to expand the domain of economic inquiry to include topics such as criminal behaviour have met with resistance from other social scientists. The bulk of this essay is devoted to an account of the 'economic' characterization of the behaviour of the potential (or actual) criminal, together with a discussion of the common objections to this characterization.

This account covers only the first two of the five parts that constitute the economic paradigm. The entire paradigm is briefly illustrated in a subsequent section of the essay, with an analysis of the crime of motor vehicle theft. The conclusion discusses research priorities.

The Crime Decision: Theoretical Perspectives on the Deterrence Process

The role of theory in the study of criminal deterrence, as in other scientific inquiries, is to generate interesting, testable hypotheses and provide a framework for interpreting empirical observations. A 'good' theory explains known facts in a parsimonious way and generates accurate predictions. There are two main issues to be considered in a complete theory of criminal deterrence: first, the influence of the threat of criminal sanctions on the choices made by individuals regarding their participation in criminal activity; second, the effectiveness of various criminal justice system activities in producing threats. The discussion here is limited to the first issue.

The Rational Potential Criminal

An increase in the probability or severity of punishment for a particular type of crime will reduce the rate at which that crime is committed, other things being equal. This assertion is not an assumption, but is derived from a theoretical argument developed primarily by economists in recent years.[3] Observed crime rates are viewed as the aggregate result of choices made by rational individuals. Potential criminals weigh the possible consequences of their actions, both positive and negative, and take advantage of a criminal opportunity only if it is in their self-interest to do so. Jeremy Bentham expressed the point this way: 'The profit of the crime is the force which urges a man to delinquency: the pain of the punishment is the force employed to restrain him from it. If the first of these forces be the greater the crime will be committed: if the second, the crime will not be committed.'[4]

A satisfactory characterization of the 'rational potential criminal' must elaborate on Bentham's proposition to take into account the subjectivity of 'profit' and 'pain,' as well as individual differences in objective circumstances. Individuals respond differently to equivalent criminal opportunities, for reasons that include the following:

1 Individuals differ in their willingness to accept risks. The consequences of committing a crime (arrest and conviction) are always less than certain, and for some common crimes the probabilities are small indeed. The consequences of conviction are also uncertain, owing to the wide discretionary power of judges in sentencing. Potential criminals will differ in their assessment of the probability of 'losing' the gamble offered by a particular criminal opportunity, and they will also differ in the degree to which they are risk-averse.

2 Individuals differ with respect to 'honesty preference' – the strength of their preference for behaving in a law-abiding manner. How much net 'profit' is required to persuade an individual to overcome his ethical concern for staying within the law? Furthermore, for crimes that are *mala in se*, the individual's ethical concern may extend to the criminal act itself.

3 Individuals differ with respect to their evaluation of the 'profit' to be gained from a crime. These differences are largest for crimes for which the payoff is not money (which almost everyone values) but is 'in kind'; consider, for example, crimes of violence, vandalism, draft evasion, and double-parking.

4 Individuals differ in their objective circumstances – their income, the value they place on their time, their skill in committing crimes successfully and evading capture, and their reputation in the community. An arrest for shop-lifting, followed by a dismissal of charges, may be of little consequence for an unemployed teenager, but may ruin the life of a college professor. An individual's circumstances also influence the nature of criminal opportunities available to him; few of us are in a position to embezzle money, fix prices, or commit treason.

Thus, the 'profit' and 'pain' associated with equivalent criminal opportunities will be evaluated differently by different individuals. Some may find criminality very worthwhile, others will be close to indifferent, and a third group will view it as highly unattractive. The key point is that a change in either the probability or the average severity of punishment will cause some people to change their minds about whether the opportunity is, on balance, attractive, and thereby change their behaviour. A small change will affect only those who were previously close to indifference (the perceived 'profit' and 'pain' are about equal); changing the behaviour of others will require a larger change in the probability or severity of punishment.

Most discussions of the deterrence mechanism distinguish between general and special deterrence. 'Special deterrence' refers to the deterrent effect of punishment on those who have been punished. This concept is somewhat vague.[5] It is possible that those who have suffered a criminal sanction once are more likely to be deterred by the threat of punishment thereafter, but there is no evidence to support this notion.

The threat of punishment may play a greater role than simply acting as a debit in the potential criminal's cost-benefit analysis of a crime opportunity. It may also have a socializing and moralizing effect.[6] Punishment in the form of incarceration reduces crime by incapacitating inmates.[7] Correctional treatments may also reduce crime by rehabilitating some convicts, although existing programs appear to be largely ineffective.[8]

Objections to the Theory

The economists' theory of criminal deterrence has been useful in developing the implications of a long-neglected notion in the criminology literature – that criminals can be viewed as rational decision-makers intent on furthering their personal welfare in an environment that provides crime opportunities coupled with sanction threats. However, some critics find this assumption of rationality in the decision to commit a crime highly implausible and inconsistent with descriptive evidence of criminal behaviour. Herbert Jacob succinctly states the two major objections to that assumption:

> (a) It implies that people who contemplate committing a crime have a realistic perception of the probabilities of being sanctioned and of the severity of the sanction ... The little evidence we have on perceptions of legal sanctions by the general public indicates that these perceptions are incorrect and variable ... (b) It implies that people who commit crimes

act after rational calculation rather than on impulse. We have much reason to believe that many crimes are committed on impulse, either under the influence of alcohol or simply as the result of opportunity and need intersecting.[9]

Jacob's arguments are persuasive, and have led many criminologists to conclude that common appropriative crimes and much violent crime are not very responsive to the threat of punishment. But this conclusion does not follow from his argument. The existence of a strong deterrent effect does not require that potential criminals be fully informed or fully rational in their crime decisions. A theoretical model that postulates full rationality on the part of criminals is clearly 'unrealistic,' but may none the less generate valid predictions because it contains essential elements of truth. The assumptions of a rational choice/full information model can be relaxed without undermining the prediction that an increase in the threat of punishment will reduce crime. I will deal with Jacob's objections in reverse order, since the second point is more fundamental.

Limits on Rational Calculation

It may be true, as Jacob suggests, that many criminals do not consider the consequences of their acts, other than those consequences that are obvious, certain, and immediate. This impulsiveness is often thought to be particularly characteristic of youths and of people who are intoxicated, in a state of high emotional arousal, deviant, or emotionally disturbed. These groups constitute a large percentage of the perpetrators of some types of crime. Are these crimes deterrable? Two affirmative arguments are worth mentioning.

Deterrence theory is concerned with making predictions about aggregate behaviour. The accuracy of such predictions does not require that every individual act predictably. The prediction that crime is deterrable follows just as readily from an assumption that 10 per cent of criminals are capable of rational decision-making as from an assumption that all potential criminals have that ability; assuming, that is, that the remaining 90 per cent do not respond to a change in the threat level in a systematically perverse fashion.

The deterrence mechanism does not require that each crime opportunity be evaluated separately or fully. Herbert Simon[10] and his followers[11] have developed the notion of 'limited rationality' as a descriptively more accurate alternative to the 'full rationality' notion propounded by economic theorists.[12] Limited rationality models of decision-making incorporate observed limitations on people's capacity to acquire and process information. In particular, it is thought that people tend to economize on this scarce capacity by adopting rules of thumb, or 'standing decisions,' which eliminate the need to completely analyse every new decision. A person whose judgment is impaired by emotion or inebriation may still be guided by his personal standing decisions, which in turn may reflect his concern with the threat of punishment. Most of us have long ago adopted standing decisions to refrain from robbery and assault, no matter what the circumstances. An increase in the threat of punishment may have the effect of persuading more people to adopt such decisions, thus inhibiting them from acting on impulse when next an attractive crime opportunity arises.[13]

This defence of the rational choice model is not entirely satisfactory. The remaining concern is that those potential criminals who are sufficiently thoughtful and aware to respond to changes in the threat of punishment will, in some circumstances, violate the norms of rational decision-making in some systematic and predictable fashion. If so, it would be possible to gain improved predictive power from a theory that took these systematic deviations from rationality into account. For example, extensive experimentation by psychologists using human subjects demonstrates that people tend to make certain predictable errors in decision-making tasks involving choices between lotteries.[14] An example is the tendency of experimental subjects to ignore low-probability events entirely – a tendency that is confirmed by the failure of most residents of flood plains to buy heavily subsidized flood insurance policies.[15] In circumstances where people do take low-probability events into account (for example, shark attack), there is a tendency to place an inappropriately large weight on the low-probability outcomes. Most of this experimental work has not employed criminal choice problems, although the analogy should be clear. An exception is Carroll's report of experimental findings involving crime choice with convicted criminals as subjects. Carroll's perspective is worth quoting: 'The proposed approach thus offers a new model of how the person decides about crime opportunities. He or she is not viewed as the "economic person" making exhaustive and complex calculations leading to an optimal choice. Rather, it is the "psychological person," who makes a few simple and concrete examinations of his or her opportunities and makes guesses that can be far short of optimal.'[16] The challenge to deterrence theorists is to find predictable ways in which the 'psychological person' deviates from the 'economic person.'

Threat Communication

Jacob's first objection to the rational choice model of criminal behaviour concerns the reliability of the threat communication process.[17] Rational choice models provide a framework for analysing the effect of the individual's perception of the threat of legal sanction on his participation in illegal activities. This relationship is of theoretical interest, but is not directly relevant to policy: what policy-makers need is information on the effect of actual (rather than perceived) criminal justice system activities on crime rates. If perceptions were sufficiently accurate, there would be no need to distinguish between, say, the actual probability of arrest for a particular criminal act and the probability as perceived by various potential criminals. If the link between the actual and the perceived probability is weak, then one can question the claim that increased enforcement efforts will deter crime. A third possibility is that public perceptions are not accurate, but do tend to be systematically related to criminal justice system activities. This possibility serves as the basis for a response to Jacob's first criticism of rational choice models of criminal behaviour.

What are the important channels by which information on the certainty and severity of punishment is communicated to potential criminals? Three channels are discussed below: the media, the visible presence of enforcers, and personal experience and observation. Although these channels do not provide potential criminals with accurate information, the information they do provide is systematically related to the truth. That systematic relationship is sufficient to generate predicted deterrent effects.

The threats generated by criminal justice system activities are 'advertised' in the media, primarily through reporting of legislative actions, newsworthy crimes and criminal court cases, and new programs and policies. Occasionally, officials will launch an effort to publicize a particular law enforcement effort, such as a crackdown on speeding. A dramatic example of the possibilities for a media 'advertising' campaign is the intensive publicity given the British Road Safety Act of 1967; most of the British public was aware of the provisions of this act by the time it was implemented.[18] But such success is surely rare.

Verbal messages concerning specific provisions of the law, the likelihood of being caught, or both are communicated through a variety of other means: bumper-stickers remind us of the 55 mph speed limit in the United States; road signs inform us that there are penalties for littering, that the local traffic enforcement unit is equipped with radar, and that residential areas are protected by neighbourhood watch organizations; official documents announce the legal penalties for supplying false information; and stores and residences post signs warning that shop-lifters will be prosecuted and that goods or belongings have been marked for later identification. The use of such official verbal communications is like other forms of advertising. The effectiveness of the messages might well be enhanced by a systematic application of the techniques by which the media are used to inform and persuade, but Madison Avenue has not yet entered the crime control business to any great extent.

The proximity of police emits a potent signal that the probability of arrest for a crime committed in the immediate vicinity is high. A police cruiser eliminates driving infractions in its immediate area, an effect that is extended by citizens' band radio communication between motorists. Private guards in stores, airports, and other public locations produce an analogous signal for would-be robbers, hijackers, and shop-lifters.

The resources devoted to routine patrol activity by police would presumably be hard to justify unless the visible police presence had an effect beyond the immediate vicinity. If the police are seen frequently in an area, potential criminals may be persuaded that there is a high likelihood of arrest in that area owing to a short response time and the chance that the police will happen on the scene while the crime is in progress. Although the relation between police visibility and public perceptions of their effectiveness has not been examined directly, there are a number of studies of the deterrence effect of the density of police patrol.[19]

Active criminals accumulate personal experience during the course of their criminal career; that experience surely has a powerful effect on perceptions of the effectiveness of the criminal justice system among the group that is of greatest importance in the crime picture. If active criminals find that they are rarely arrested, unlikely to be convicted if arrested, and unlikely to be sentenced to prison terms if convicted, then they may acquire a justified sense of invulnerability. The effect of arrest and subsequent proceedings on the criminal's perception of the system's effectiveness is the key issue in the study of special deterrence – the deterrent effect of the punishment threat on an individual who has been convicted.

An arrest can push the criminal's overall perception of the risk of punishment up or down, depending on whether the consequences of arrest are more or less unpleasant than he expected. Probation and parole dispositions are interesting in this context when viewed as an effort to persuade the convict that he will be closely watched and is very likely to be imprisoned if rearrested.

Victims, witnesses, and jurors also acquire personal experience with the effectiveness of the system, and that experience may influence their perception of whether 'crime pays.' Furthermore, an active criminal's friends and associates may be somewhat aware of his criminal activities and their legal consequences. Thus, on the one hand, each arrest, court proceeding, and sentence may have a large influence on the perceptions of a relatively few people. On the other hand, the public at large is not likely to know about or be influenced by any one criminal trial, unless it is highly newsworthy.

This communication mechanism suggests that the deterrence process may often operate in a strikingly different fashion from that which is typically assumed in the rational choice models of criminal behaviour. Those models implicitly assume that each potential criminal in some fashion monitors the overall probability of apprehension and punishment for each crime type. By this assumption, each arrest and criminal disposition has some marginal (infinitesimal) effect on the perceptions of all potential criminals. This assumption seems highly unrealistic, given that even criminologists working with volumes of statistics have difficulty in measuring changes in these probabilities accurately (although the first two communication channels discussed above may provide potential criminals with some vague sense of the overall performance of the system). The alternative possibility, suggested here, can be stated as follows: *Each arrest and disposition has a relatively large effect on the perceptions of a small number of potential criminals (including the accused), and goes essentially unnoticed by all others.* I have developed a model incorporating this assumption that simulates the criminal behaviour of a population of robbers.[20] The main features of this model can be summarized as follows:

1 At any time, a robber's perception of arrest and punishment is influenced by his own recent experience and that of a few 'friends.' Perceptions differ widely among robbers, because each observes only a small fraction of the actions taken by the system.

2 Even if the true effectiveness of the system remains constant, there is considerable turnover among active robbers: robbers are deterred and undeterred according to their own experiences and those of their friends.
3 An increase in the true effectiveness of the system results in a corresponding increase in the mean of robbers' perceptions of effectiveness, and an increase in the number of robbers who are deterred. These changes do not occur because the robbers observe that the system has become more effective, but because the likelihood that a robber will observe one or more friends apprehended is increased when the overall effectiveness of the system increases.

This model is abstract, and can be criticized for its simple mechanistic assumptions concerning the complex phenomena of perception, communication, and criminal behaviour. It does serve to demonstrate, however, that the deterrence process does not require that criminals' perceptions of the risk of punishment be accurate or that they be derived from observations of the overall performance of the criminal justice system. It may also serve the useful purpose of provoking further research into the communication processes that link official activity to individual perceptions of the threat of punishment.

The three communication channels discussed above do not exhaust the possibilities. In some instances, direct word-of-mouth communication among criminals with similar interests may be important; rumours concerning police and judicial activities circulate and at times have considerable potency. It is also possible that potential criminals make judgments on the basis of direct observation of the extent of criminal activity in the area: if 'everyone' is doing it, it must pay. One familiar example is our judgment of how 'safe' it is to exceed the speed limit; if the traffic is averaging 70 mph with a 55 mph limit, it seems safe to assume that the probability of being ticketed for driving 70 mph is very low.

In general, it is reasonable to assume that the relative importance of each of the several channels of information on the effectiveness of the criminal justice system differs with the type of crime, the degree to which the potential criminal associates with criminally active people, and other factors. The link between official activities and the public's perception of them constitutes half of the deterrence story. A better understanding of this link could be exploited to the advantage of crime control efforts. Two examples are worth noting. First, the initial publicity given to the British Road Safety Act apparently succeeded in giving Britons a greatly exaggerated impression of the true likelihood of their being caught and punished for drunken driving. While this impression evidently was corrected after several years of experience, many lives were saved in the interim. Second, an intensive police presence in the New York subway system during high-crime periods initially caused a deterrent effect, not only during those periods but also during the rest of the day (when police manning levels were not changed). It has been suggested that this 'phantom effect' could have been sustained by random changes in police assignments.[21]

Jacob's observations that potential criminals are poorly informed, and that in some cases they act impulsively, are valid but not sufficient to negate the predictions of deterrence theory. These predictions do not depend on every criminal's being fully informed and rational. A limited rationality on the part of some fraction of potential criminals, combined with an information transmission mechanism that is systematic if not completely accurate, is sufficient to generate deterrent effects. Indeed, there is a great deal of evidence that criminals, like other people, respond to objective changes in their opportunities as if they were rational. It would be unfortunate to reject the claims of deterrence theory on the a priori grounds of implausibility. Nevertheless, careful descriptive studies and laboratory experiments investigating the way in which individuals acquire information and evaluate opportunities may yield insights into criminal decision-making that will help refine the predictions of rational choice models, and may even suggest means of increasing the effectiveness of the system in deterring crime.

The preceding discussion developed a basic perspective on the deterrence process, focusing on information-processing and decision-making by the potential criminal. Three specific issues are examined below from this perspective: the determinants of the extent to which an individual participates in criminal activity; the relative importance of the probability and severity of punishment in deterring crime; and the influence of sanction threats for one type of crime on the relative attractiveness of other types of crime.

Degree of Involvement in Crime

So far we have discussed the deterrence phenomenon as if criminal activity were an all-or-nothing decision. Yet criminals differ widely in their degree of involvement in crime. The number of robberies committed in a year is the product of the number of active robbers and the average number of robberies committed by each. The deterrence process may influence both factors: the rate at which active robbers commit crimes, and the decision to enter the robbery 'business' at all.

The basic question with respect to intensity of criminal activity is this: what limits are there on the participation in illicit activity of a potential criminal who decides that it is worthwhile to commit his first offence? I suspect that a large proportion of the population is opportunistic with respect to property crimes. Without making a special effort many people occasionally encounter an extraordinarily good opportunity to steal, and take advantage of it. Examples include taking towels from a hotel, walking out of a shop without paying because the checkout lines are momentarily left unattended, and so forth. We can imagine each person having a standard rule of thumb by which he judges whether such opportunities are worthwhile; the more stringent one's standard (in terms of legal risks and payoff), the less frequently will one encounter suitable opportunities in the normal course of daily activities. An increase in the effectiveness of the criminal justice system or in the severity of punishment will reduce the number of suitable opportunities for those who are opportunists, with a corresponding reduction in their individual theft rates.

A more active involvement in theft is characteristic of people we ordinarily think of as 'robbers,' 'burglars,' and 'shop-lifters.' Instead of a series of yes-or-no decisions on opportunities supplied by the individual's environment, more active thieves are concerned with searching out and developing opportunities, and make explicit decisions about the intensity of their illicit activity. Two limiting factors for such people are the opportunity cost of time, and the effects of increased income on the willingness to take risks.

The latter effect seems relevant to understanding employee theft and embezzlement, income tax evasion, and other economic crimes for which time is not an important input.[22] Given that the magnitude of the offence is positively correlated to the risk of detection and punishment (and perhaps also to the severity of punishment), the miscreant can be viewed as choosing a risk-payoff combination from a continuum of possibilities. An increase in the effectiveness of the system for detecting and punishing criminals in these cases will make this type of crime less attractive and persuade some to drop out completely. For those who remain active, it is not obvious whether the augmented risk of punishment will cause an increase or decrease in the rate of offending. A perverse result of increased effectiveness may occur, for example, if the increase in effectiveness is concentrated at the low end of the theft spectrum; those who do not drop out may move up the continuum after the difference in risk for large and small thefts is reduced.

For crimes that require substantial time to execute, such as fencing, running numbers, and prostitution, the opportunity cost of time may be an important limiting factor in the extent of the offender's involvement. The legitimate wage rate influences both the entry decision and the decision with respect to degree of involvement.[23] Once again there is a theoretical possibility that an increased probability of apprehension will increase criminal activity levels for those who do not drop out. For example, if police start to arrest prostitutes more frequently, some prostitutes may increase their workload in order to maintain their standard of living while meeting the additional costs of bail, legal fees, and fines. This result is analogous to the theoretical possibility of a backward-bending labour supply curve; there is nothing intrinsically irrational about people choosing to work harder in response to a reduction in the net rate of return for their efforts.

While these models of participation in illicit economic activities admit of a theoretical possibility that an increase in the likelihood of detection will increase the overall crime rate, the actual importance of that possibility is uncertain. It seems more plausible that if more effective measures are taken against a particular type of criminal activity, the dominant effect will be to cause criminals to act with greater caution or to switch into other illicit or licit activities.

Certainty versus Severity of Punishment

One of the intriguing issues in the deterrence literature is whether crime rates are more responsive to changes in the likelihood or the severity of punishment. The importance of this issue is suggested by two relevant policy dilemmas. First, sentencing authorities must allocate scarce prison capacity among convicts; one consideration is whether prison sentences should be relatively common but short, or relatively uncommon but long. Second, prosecutors have to decide whether to use their scarce resources to produce a high conviction rate with relatively low-quality convictions (through generous offers in plea-bargaining), or to concentrate their resources on gaining high-quality convictions of a relatively few defendants while dismissing the remaining cases. The first alternative in each case is compatible with the commonly held view that the likelihood of punishment has a greater deterrent impact on crime rates than does the severity of punishment.

A precise illustrative statement of this hypothesis can be expressed as follows: *A 10 per cent increase in the average severity of punishment for a crime will have a smaller deterrent effect than a 10 per cent increase in the likelihood of punishment.* For example, if the only form of punishment for convicted robbers is imprisonment, an increase in average sentence from 3 years to 3.3 years will have less deterrent effect than an increase in likelihood of imprisonment from 0.050 to 0.055.

The usual assumptions made in the economic analysis of decision-making under uncertainty support this claim when the punishment is imprisonment, but support the opposite conclusion when the punishment is a fine. The argument behind these conclusions can be illustrated by the following two 'lotteries' involving prison sentences. In the first lottery, there is a 10 per cent chance of receiving a one-year prison sentence; the second lottery offers a 5 per cent chance of a two-year prison sentence. These two lotteries have the same expected value (one-tenth of a year in prison), but most people would not view them as equally threatening; if two years in prison is not viewed as being twice as bad as one year, then the second lottery would be preferred, and the first lottery would have a greater deterrent value. In general, we expect that increases in the probability of imprisonment, coupled with proportionate reductions in the prison term, will increase the deterrent value of the threat of punishment.

The second example involves punishment in the form of a fine. Suppose now that the prison terms in the two lotteries specified above are replaced with fines of $1,000 and $2,000 respectively. Once again the two lotteries have the same expected value ($100). If people are risk-averse, a common assumption in economic theory, they will prefer the first lottery: a $2,000 loss is subjectively more than twice as bad as a $1,000 loss to a risk-averse person. However, Tversky and Kahneman report that in laboratory experiments most subjects are not risk-averse with respect to financial losses, and would actually choose the smaller probability of a proportionately larger fine.[24] Once again, then, the first lottery should have greater deterrent value, and the conventional wisdom (among criminologists, but not necessarily economists) regarding certainty and severity of punishment is reaffirmed. Although this sort of theoretical analysis and laboratory experimentation seems rather remote from criminal behaviour, it is interesting to observe that this type of evidence does support the conventional wisdom.

The claim that certain punishment is a more effective deterrent than severe punishment is often buttressed by an assertion that crime rates are unresponsive to variations in severity. If that is true, the sentencing authorities could reduce average sentences a great deal without any noticeable effect on the crime rate. The most compelling issue, and the one given the greatest scholarly attention, is whether capital punishment is a greater deterrent to murder than a long prison term. At the other end of the spectrum are questions concerning the potential loss of deterrent effect resulting from the increased use of diversion programs, suspended sentences, and fines in place of incarceration.

It is commonly acknowledged that the threat of a severe penalty will cause defendants to put more effort and resources into their defence. Indeed, one of the social costs of capital punishment, mandatory sentencing provisions, and related efforts to increase the severity of punishment is that these cases take up an increased portion of court resources through appeals and other efforts to resist or overturn conviction. It seems implausible that the severity of punishment should be highly salient to the criminal after arrest but not before.

While we would expect a rational criminal to respond in some degree to increases in the severity of punishment, it is certainly plausible that the marginal deterrent effect of increasing prison sentences declines rapidly as the length of the sentence increases, because of the tendency of people to discount the future. A simple mathematical model may be helpful in illustrating this point.[25] Suppose that an individual assigns one unit of 'disutility' to a year in prison, and has a time discount rate of 15 per cent per annum. It would then be true, in present value terms, that a two-year prison term has about 87 per cent more disutility than a one-year term. Under these assumptions, however, a twenty-year term has only 25 per cent more disutility than a ten-year term. It is plausible, then, that increasing the severity of punishment when punishment is mild may have a greater deterrent effect (even proportionately speaking) than increased severity when punishment is already severe.

Substitutes and Complements

Establishing rational sentencing policies and setting appropriate priorities in prosecutions and police investigations are complicated by the possibility that variations in the threat of punishment for one type of crime may affect the incidence of other types of crime. First, because of limited police, court, and corrections resources, giving one type of crime a higher priority necessarily entails lowering the priority of one or more other types of crime. Second, in deciding whether to commit one type of crime, criminals will be influenced by the legal threat not only to that crime type but also to related types of crime. This latter mechanism must be given consideration in any complete characterization of the deterrence process. An analogy from the economic theory of consumer demand provides insight and useful terminology for discussing this mechanism. Suppose the price of gasoline increases by 50 per cent because of a change in policy by the OPEC cartel. The primary effect of the price increase would be to reduce the quantity of gasoline purchased. Secondary effects include an increase in the demand for public transportation, fuel-efficient autos, and central-city housing, and a decrease in demand for luxury autos and suburban housing. Commodities that become more desirable when the price of gasoline increases are known as 'substitutes' for gasoline; those that become less desirable are 'complements.' Although the analogy is by no means perfect, I will use these terms to discuss the secondary effects of a change in the threat level to a particular type of crime.

Various types of property crime are presumably substitutes for each other. Recidivism data demonstrate that there is a great deal of crime-switching among active criminals; for example, 22 per cent of the men arrested for burglary in the District of Columbia in 1973 were subsequently arrested for robbery within three years (compared with 33 per cent who were rearrested for burglary).[26] The Rand study of self-reported crime by a sample of forty-nine incarcerated robbers found that they admitted having collectively committed 1,492 auto thefts, 2,331 burglaries, 855 robberies, and 1,018 other serious thefts during their criminal careers.[27] Given this sort of versatility, one would expect that an increase in the relative effectiveness of law enforcement against robbery would result in an increase in other types of theft crimes. Variations in other sorts of crime-specific deterrents can be predicted to have the same effect:

if shopkeepers arm themselves, then thieves may switch from commercial robbery to commercial burglary; an increased use of burglar alarms would have the opposite effect.

A second dimension of the substitution phenomenon is geographic displacement. A large increase in the number of police assigned to one precinct in a city may result in some increase in crime in neighbouring precincts. A homeowner who posts an Operation Identification sticker (which indicates that his goods have been marked for easy identification) increases the burglary risk to his stickerless neighbour. Intensive police manning of the subway system may cause an increase in taxicab and bus robberies. Exact-fare systems on buses may increase the robbery risk to convenience stores. I know of no studies of crime displacement across state lines or between distant metropolitan areas, but it is likely that some buyers of illicit merchandise (drugs, machine-guns, stolen goods) travel some distance in order to take advantage of more lax law enforcement in another jurisdiction. Organized crime operations can be expected to locate their activities so as to minimize legal risks to the extent that other considerations permit; an example in this context would be the criminal's decision where to land illicit drug shipments smuggled in from South America or Mexico.

A very important aspect of the substitution phenomenon frequently arises in the design of criminal sentencing policy. It is thought that the structure of criminal sentences must include a strong marginal deterrent to the use of threat or violence to reduce the likelihood of violent resistance to arrest. If the typical sentence for robbery without violence is a long term of imprisonment, robbers may be more inclined to kill their victims and other witnesses on the ground that they have nothing to lose. Defendants who are faced with the likelihood of conviction and severe punishment will be more tempted than others to jump bail and intimidate witnesses, knowing that even if they are caught there is little more that the system can do to them; this is the reasoning behind denying defendants the right to bail in capital cases.

Zimring and Hawkins discuss this aspect of sentencing policy in terms of the 'fortress' and the 'stepladder.'[28] The 'fortress' approach is to erect a high and more or less uniform 'barrier' around the domain of criminal activity. The 'stepladder' approach adjusts the punishment to the seriousness of the crime in the hope that if the potential criminal does decide to act, the penal code will provide an adequate incentive to limit the seriousness of his crimes. If the preceding discussion of the deterrent effect of changes in the length of prison term is correct, the bottom rungs of the stepladder must be kept low in order to allow room for effective differences in sentencing between robbery, robbery with victim injury, and robbery murder; the usual sentence for robbery should not be more than a year or two in prison. This type of policy must be evaluated in the context of priority-setting by police and prosecutors: if sentences are relatively uniform, then a greater burden is placed on officials to create a stepladder effect through gradations in the likelihood of arrest and conviction.

Complementarity arguments have been extremely important in motivating criminal justice policy with respect to heroin and hand-guns. A key argument for vigorous law enforcement efforts to interdict the flow of heroin and other illicit drugs is that an increase in the 'effective price'[29] of such drugs resulting from law enforcement efforts will reduce the incidence of property crimes. Similarly, the crimes of illegal acquisition, possession, and carrying of hand-guns are thought to be complementary to robbery and murder. Both these claims of complementarity are highly controversial, of course, and even if there is such a relation it must be demonstrated that these indirect techniques for reducing property crimes or murder are the most effective use of resources in the fight against crime.

Concluding Thoughts on the Deterrence Process

Belief in the efficacy of the deterrence mechanism comes naturally to economists, whose theoretical perspective presupposes that observed behaviour is the consequence of well-informed, rational choice. Perhaps the most important contribution economists have made to the study of criminal behaviour is resurrecting the deterrence mechanism from the dustbins of jurisprudence and instituting it as a topic worthy of serious consideration by social scientists. Once considered carefully, the claims made for the deterrence mechanism seem quite plausible and robust against arguments that criminals as a group are insensitive to the legal consequences of their actions.

The 'Market' for Criminal Activity: Placing the Deterrence Mechanism in a Broader Context

The deterrence mechanism characterizes the influence of sanction threats on crime-related decisions. But knowledge of this link is not a sufficient basis for guiding legal intervention in some criminal contexts. Much criminal activity is not simply the result of individual decisions; it involves a number of actors with differentiated roles engaging in a variety of transactions that mimic legitimate business in many respects. Market-oriented complexes of criminal activity support most forms of vice and theft. Since the study of markets is the primary concern of economic science, it is natural to harness the economic paradigm to the analysis of criminal industry. One purpose of this effort is to develop a strategy to guide the use of legal sanctions – criminal, civil, and regulatory – against the complex of activities that support a particular crime type. The discussion that follows is limited to the single example of motor vehicle theft. The example is used to illustrate the economic perspective, but lacks the formality, precision, and empirical work that would characterize a complete econometric analysis.

The Motor Vehicle Theft Industry

Approximately one million vehicles are reported stolen each year in the United States, of which about 60 per cent are recovered. (These figures do not include thefts of motor vehicle accessories or theft of contents from motor vehicles.) The average value of a stolen vehicle in 1984 was about $4,000.[30]

The National Automobile Theft Bureau estimates that 15 per cent of all auto thefts reported are fraudulent. Usually the owner's objective in making the report is to collect on his insurance. The owner may arrange to have his car taken before reporting the theft; and in such cases the car will become part of the illicit commerce in stolen vehicles. An owner 'give-up' of this sort is profitable if the insured value of the car exceeds its resale value, as is often the case when the vehicle needs expensive repairs. The remaining reported thefts are either joy-riding cases or thefts for the purpose of sale. The fact that the police recover over one-half of the vehicles reported stolen suggests that the bulk of reported thefts are for joy-riding purposes. My interest here, however, is in the last category

– theft for the purpose of sale. This is the kind of theft associated with the 'industry' of auto theft. Stolen cars are resold in one of several ways. They may be repainted and retitled (perhaps using the documents from a salvage vehicle of the same model and year), and then sold on the legitimate used vehicle market; they may be shipped abroad and then sold, with or without some effort to camouflage them first; or they may be cut up by a 'chop-shop' operator, and the parts sold to body-shops and the like.

In sum, this black market for stolen autos includes three types of transactions: *removal* from the owner, *alteration* to conceal the vehicle's true identity, and *sale* to a more or less knowledgeable purchaser. The important actors in this market are the owners, the thieves, the middlemen (including the chop-shop operators), and the ultimate buyers. An enforcement strategy that is limited to sanctioning thieves will be less effective than a comprehensive strategy based on an understanding of the structure of this black market.

Market Structures and Enforcement Options

The profitability of the business of dealing in 'hot' autos will depend on the costs of removal and alteration and on the price for used vehicles and parts.[31] (The going price for a legitimate used car sets a ceiling for its hot counterpart.) During periods of strong demand for used cars, prices for both licit and illicit units will rise, thereby drawing more operators into the black market.[32] We can presume that the costs of obtaining vehicles for sale in the black market (for example, by purchase from a thief) will depend on the perceived risk of arrest and punishment for theft, and on the extent to which owners protect their vehicles by alarms, locks, and careful parking arrangements. The cost of alteration may be increased by special enforcement efforts against illicit dealers, and by more stringent regulation of car-part identification numbers and transaction records. Any measures that increase the cost of doing business in the black market should reduce profitability and therefore, ultimately, the volume of theft. These ideas are developed more fully below.

Owners

We can think of vehicle theft as a sort of extraction industry, with the stock of vehicles in circulation as the ore. The quality of this ore and the costs of removal will depend on decisions made by owners: what types of vehicles to purchase and how much care and expense to undertake in protecting them against theft. If the owner equips his auto with an alarm and parks it only in protected parking areas, it is riskier and more difficult to steal it than if the owner is lax in his security precautions. The owner's theft protection decisions will be influenced by, among other things, the perceived risk of theft; the financial loss to him if his vehicle is stolen (which will depend on his insurance coverage); and the cost and convenience of protected parking and anti-theft devices. This list suggests several means of encouraging owners to better protect their vehicles. Insurance regulators could require a relatively high deductible provision for theft insurance, and could offer a reduction in premiums for vehicles equipped with effective anti-theft devices. Cities could regulate parking so as to discourage the parking of vehicles in places vulnerable to theft. More intrusive measures are also imaginable: in some European countries, leaving a parked vehicle unlocked is an infraction punishable by a fine. And of course it is possible simply to require that new vehicles be equipped with anti-theft devices, as has been done with the steering-wheel lock in the United States.

Any of these regulations could increase the cost of 'removal' to the auto theft industry. As in any other competitive business, an increase in the cost of raw materials will tend to cause a reduction in the purchase and use of those materials by firms in the business.

Thieves

Vehicle thieves may free-lance, or may work for chop-shop operators or illicit dealers. In either event, they are likely to possess information that is of potential use to police investigators in identifying the middlemen. The police are faced with choosing whether to target enforcement efforts on thieves or on those who process and alter stolen vehicles. The latter group tends to employ more capital equipment and be more skilled than the thieves, and may represent a relatively scarce resource; shutting down one active chopping operation is more disruptive to the industry than jailing a number of thieves, who are more readily replaceable. Police investigators may be well advised to plea-bargain with arrested thieves for the purpose of gaining intelligence useful in making a case against the middlemen. Undercover operations can also be targeted to the illicit dealers and chop-shop operators rather than the thieves.

Middlemen

The middleman's primary task is to obtain stolen vehicles and alter them so that they (or their parts) can be passed off as legitimate in the used-car market. There are a variety of regulatory methods for increasing the costs and risks of alteration. U.S. federal regulations require that identification numbers be stamped in a number of places on each newly manufactured car or truck, and that records be kept on transactions involving each vehicle throughout its history, from first sale to final disposal. The export of stolen vehicles is apparently less carefully regulated, and is difficult to interdict once the vehicle is sealed in a container.

The illicit dealer bears the costs of obtaining suitable stolen vehicles, altering them, and arranging sales. Presumably, the price he receives is no higher than the price of equivalent parts from licit vehicles and may be much less if he is not able to do a convincing job of representing the stolen vehicles as licit after they are altered. Middlemen are also threatened with the possibility of legal sanctions. In protecting themselves against this threat, middlemen have to exercise care in choosing the people they deal with, something that law enforcement authorities can encourage by undercover work. Investigators posing as thieves trying to unload hot cars or as shady body-shop operators looking for a good deal on parts can increase the risk of doing business and discourage black-market operators from dealing with strangers. The objective is to disrupt the smooth functioning of the black market, and ultimately to reduce the volume of business.

In addition to standard criminal penalties, law enforcement authorities may be well advised to consider the possibility of asset confiscation in punishing illicit dealers. The threat of confiscation may be particularly effective in deterring legitimate businessmen from accepting some illicit business on the side.

Interactions

In analysing the effects of law enforcement directed at the thieves and illicit dealers operating in this black market, it should be noted that 'success' (measured by reduced vehicle theft rates) may be undermined to some extent by the feedback to owners. If owners perceive a reduction in the likelihood of theft, and respond by reducing their level of care in theft prevention, then theft rates may be stimulated by the increased availability of vehicles.[33] In other words, the deterrent effect of the increased threat of legal sanctions for theft will be undermined by the greater ease of stealing a vehicle.

Further Thoughts on the Economic Perspective

The preceding discussion illustrated the economist's perspective as applied to the analysis of crime. The discussion presumed that the behaviour of the actors in the automobile black market was sensitive to normal economic incentives. On the basis of this presumption, a multifaceted strategy was suggested for reducing vehicle theft by reducing the payoff to participation in the black market.

Completely absent from the discussion was any reference to normative economics. Normative economics is primarily concerned with the implications of economic efficiency for evaluating alternative ways of stimulating, organizing, and guiding economic activity. The economists' contributions to legal studies have been equally concerned with positive and normative issues: indeed, the seminal work by Gary Becker is primarily normative.[34] The economist's normative perspective is well illustrated by Robert Rabin's contribution to this collection.

Notes on a Research Agenda

Research relevant to understanding and managing the criminal deterrence process includes a wide range of topics and methods. The four topics discussed below strike me as deserving of greater attention by criminologists. These topics are easily accommodated within the economist's framework, but are by no means limited to economists. Several more uniquely 'economic' topics are suggested at the end of this section.

Comparative Studies of Risky Decision-making

Laboratory experiments in decision-making under conditions of uncertainty can provide information on how decisions are influenced by the threat of adverse consequences of varying probability and severity. Extrapolating from the artificial laboratory setting to the real world is difficult, of course, but some questions are hard to investigate in a natural setting. One such question is the extent to which such factors as age, emotional arousal, and inebriation are related to 'deterrability.' Are people more willing to risk adverse consequences when drunk than when sober? A more important issue is whether the willingness to risk adverse consequences is less responsive to changes in the threat level when the subject is drunk.

Threat Communication

The extent to which the threat of punishment deters crime depends to some extent on how the threat is 'marketed.' Several lines of research might prove useful in this regard:
- an analysis of research findings on commercial advertising, dissemination of information on new products, etc., as a source of hypotheses concerning threat communication;
- interviews with active and potential criminals to determine what sorts of information they regularly acquire on the effectiveness of law enforcement activities;
- studies of the criminal's response to specific environmental cues related to the likelihood of arrest and punishment, including visible police patrol, signs posted to warn would-be violators ('shop-lifters will be prosecuted'), and so forth.

Complements and Substitutes

The incidence of one type of crime will be influenced by the effectiveness of law enforcement efforts against closely related types of crime. A crackdown on fencing may reduce the rates of armed assault and robbery; an increase in the severity of sentencing for selling heroin may increase the rates at which defendants jump bail and attempt to intimidate witnesses before trial. Research on such interconnections among crime types should aid in targeting law enforcement resources.

Other Preventive Effects of Punishment

Deterrence effects have almost been ignored in discussions of the other preventive effects of punishment. This sort of compartmentalized thinking is dangerous for policy prescription and costly to the scientific development of criminology. If the threat level influences the rate at which active criminals commit crimes, as well as the number of criminals who are active, then the measurement of incapacitation effects cannot ignore the deterrence phenomenon.[35] Similarly, the outcome measure almost always used in studies of correctional rehabilitation – some sort of recidivism rate – will be influenced through deterrence by the threat environment facing the released convict. A related concern is the possibility that a correctional program will have a large enough effect on the severity of punishment to undermine the deterrent effect of punishment; a finding of reduced recidivism is insufficient to demonstrate that the rehabilitation program reduced crime.

Together, these four topics would substantially expand the range of deterrence research, and they by no means exhaust the list of interesting possibilities. But to an important extent productive research projects cannot be identified deductively; there should be a large element of opportunism in the choice of projects. The richest source of raw material for deterrence research has always been dramatic changes in criminal justice policy in state and local jurisdictions, and this will continue to be the case. The keys to exploiting this raw material are early involvement and special data collection efforts.[36]

Economists have made important contributions to the study of deterrence during the last two decades, but have no monopoly on the subject. Indeed, the interesting topics, such as the four suggested above, are more in the realm of psychology than economics. For the future, the unique contributions of economists to criminology are likely to take the form of the analysis of the effects of sanctions in the context of market systems. The economic paradigm starts with a characterization of individual behaviour, but only as a building-block in constructing an account of the aggregate structure of economic activity. The brief account presented above of the auto theft industry is one illustration, albeit sketchy. Peter Reuter has pioneered the economic analysis of illicit markets and organized crime,[37] and others will no doubt follow him. A second line of inquiry focuses on crime within the context of licit structures, led by economists such as Michael Block on price-fixing and Susan Rose-Ackerman on corruption.[38] Understanding how individuals respond to the threat of punishment is just the beginning.

Notes

* Professor of public policy studies and economics and director of the Institute of Policy Science and Public Affairs, Duke University, Durham, North Carolina. Portions of this essay were first published in 'Research in Criminal Deterrence: Laying the Groundwork for the Second Decade,' in N. Morris and M. Tonry (eds), *Crime and Justice: An Annual Review of Research*, vol. 2 (1980).
1 G.S. Becker, 'Crime and Punishment: An Economic Approach' (1968) 76 *Journal of Political Economy* 169
2 I. Ehrlich, 'Participation in Illegal Activities: A Theoretical and Empirical Investigation' (1973) 81 *Journal of Political Economy* 521
3 See J.M. Heineke, 'Economic Models of Criminal Behavior: An Overview,' In J.M. Heineke (ed.), *Economic Models of Criminal Behavior* (1978) 1, for a review. Gary Becker gave the first statement of this theory in modern times (supra note 1); his work was extended by Ehrlich (supra note 2), and in M.K. Block and R.C. Lind, 'An Economic Analysis of Crimes Punishable by Imprisonment' (1975) 4 *Journal of Legal Studies* 479.
4 Quoted in F.E. Zimring and G.J. Hawkins, *Deterrence: The Legal Threat in Crime Control* (1973) 75
5 See N. Walker, 'The Efficacy and Morality of Deterrents' (1979) *Criminal Law Review* 129, at 131.
6 P.J. Cook, 'Punishment and Crime: A Critique of Current Findings Concerning the Preventive Effects of Punishment' (1977) 41 *Law and Contemporary Problems* 164
7 See J. Cohen, 'The Incapacitating Effect of Imprisonment: A Critical Review of the Literature,' in A. Blumstein, J. Cohen, and D. Nagin, *Deterrence and Incapacitation: Estimating the Effects of Criminal Sanctions on Crime Rates* (1978), and Blumstein et al., *Criminal Careers and 'Career Criminals,'* vol. 1 (1986).
8 For a survey of rehabilitation programs, see D. Lipton, R. Martinson, and J. Wilks, *The Effectiveness of Correctional Treatment* (1975), and L.B. Sechrest, S.O. White, and E.D. Brown (eds), *The Rehabilitation of Criminal Offenders: Problems and Prospects* (1979).
9 H. Jacob, 'Rationality and Criminality' (1978) 59 *Social Science Quarterly* 584, at 584
10 In *Models of Man* (1957)
11 See J.W. Payne, 'Information Processing Theory: Some Concepts and Methods Applied to Decision Research,' in T.S. Wallsten (ed.), *Cognitive Processes in Choice and Decision Behavior* (1980) 95.
12 See J.S. Carroll, 'A Psychological Approach to Deterrence: The Evaluation of Crime Opportunities' (1978) 36 *Journal of Personality and Social Psychology*

1512, for a discussion of this issue in the context of the crime decision. See also E. Johnson and J. Payne, 'The Decision to Commit a Crime: An Information-Processing Analysis,' in D.B. Cornish and R.V. Clark (eds), *The Reasoning Criminal: Rational Choice Perspective on Offending* (1986) 170.

13 John Conklin's interviews with convicted robbers in Boston, reported in *Robbery and the Criminal Justice System* (1972), yield some anecdotal evidence on impulse control. A few offenders stated that they could not trust themselves with loaded firearms; they feared that in a confrontation with a resisting victim they might 'lose their heads' and shoot (at 111). This attitude was not reported to be caused by the threat of punishment, but it shows that the offender is able to manage his impulsive actions in some circumstances.

14 Two interpretive summaries of this literature are provided by D. Kahneman and A. Tversky, 'Prospect Theory: An Analysis of Decision under Risk' (1979) 47 *Econometrica* 263, and A. Tversky and D. Kahneman, 'Judgment under Uncertainty: Heuristics and Biases' (1974) 185 *Science* 1124. Some crimes, such as robbery, are usually committed by two or more perpetrators working together. The crime decision in this case must involve some sort of group process. Social psychologists have studied group decision-making in the face of risky choices, and have documented a fascinating effect known as 'risky shift'; the reference is to the tendency of a group discussion to shift the preferences of members of the group toward more risky choices than they would have selected before the discussion. This effect is observed only if the individuals who make up the group are already inclined to a relatively risky choice before the discussion. See D.G. Myers and H. Lamm, 'The Group Polarization Phenomenon' (1976) 83 *Psychological Bulletin* 602, for a review of this and other 'group polarization' effects.

15 H. Kunreuther and P. Slovic, 'Economics, Psychology, and Protective Behavior' (1978) 68(2) *American Economic Review* 64, at 66

16 Carroll, supra note 12, 1513

17 See Jacob, supra note 9, 584.

18 See H.L. Ross, 'Law, Science, and Accidents: The British Road Safety Act of 1967' (1973) 2 *Journal of Legal Studies* 1. The British Road Safety Act creates a precise standard by which to judge whether a driver is legally under the influence of alcohol (his blood alcohol content must be in excess of 0.08 per cent), and it establishes a mandatory one-year suspension of driving privileges for drivers who are convicted of violating this standard.

19 These studies are reviewed in P.J. Cook, 'Research in Criminal Deterrence: Laying the Groundwork for the Second Decade,' in N. Morris and M.H. Tonry (eds), *Crime and Justice: An Annual Review of Research*, vol. 2 (1980) 211.

20 P.J. Cook, *A Unified Treatment of Deterrence, Incapacitation, and Rehabilita-*

tion: A Simulation Study (Durham, NC: Duke University Institute of Policy Sciences and Public Affairs 1979)
21 J.M. Chaiken, M.W. Lawless, and R.A. Stevenson, 'The Impact of Police Activity on Subway Crime' (1974) 3 *Urban Analysis* 173
22 See M.G. Allingham and A. Sandmo, 'Income Tax Evasion: A Theoretical Analysis' (1972) 1 *Journal of Public Economics* 323, for a formal model of this sort.
23 Ehrlich (supra note 2) develops a model of this sort, which is criticized by Heineke (supra note 3). See also M.K. Block and J.M. Heineke, 'A Labor Theoretic Analysis of the Criminal Choice' (1975) 65(3) *American Economic Review* 314.
24 Supra note 14
25 The model postulates that the individual's subjective evaluation of the prison terms is equal to the sum of the disutilities discounted to the present. If the disutility of one year in prison is denoted by d, and the discounted present value of n years in prison is denoted by D_n, then

$$D_n = \sum_{i=1}^{n} d\left(\frac{1}{1.15}\right)^{t-1}$$

The value chosen for d does not influence the value of the ratios reported in the text, and was set equal to 1.
26 P.J. Cook and D. Nagin, *Does the Weapon Matter?* (1979)
27 J. Petersilia, P.W. Greenwood, and M. Lavin, *Criminal Careers of Habitual Felons* (1978)
28 Zimring and Hawkins, supra note 4
29 A term coined by Mark Moore in 'Policies to Achieve Discrimination on the Effective Price of Heroin' (1973) 63(2) *American Economic Review* 270
30 National Automobile Theft Bureau, *1985 Annual Report* (1986)
31 W. Vandaele, 'An Econometric Model of Auto Theft in the United States,' in Heineke, supra note 3, 303
32 P.J. Cook and G.A. Zarkin, 'Crime and the Business Cycle' (1985) 14 *Journal of Legal Studies* 115
33 Cook, supra note 6; P.J. Cook, 'The Supply and Demand for Criminal Opportunities,' in M. Tonry and N. Morris (eds), *Crime and Justice: An Annual Review of Research*, vol. 7 (1986)
34 Becker, supra note 1
35 P.J. Cook, 'Criminal Incapacitation Effects Considered in an Adaptive Choice Framework,' in Cornish and Clarke, supra note 12, 202
36 See F.E. Zimring, 'Policy Experiments in General Deterrence: 1970–1975,' in Blumstein, Cohen, and Nagin, supra note 7; also Zimring, 'Methods for

Measuring General Deterrence: A Plea for the Field Experiment,' elsewhere in this volume.
37 In P. Reuter, *Disorganized Crime: The Economics of the Visible Hand* (1983)
38 M. Block, F. Nold, and J. Sidak, 'The Deterrent Effect of Antitrust Enforcement' (1981) 89 *Journal of Political Economy* 429; S. Rose-Ackerman, *Corruption: A Study in Political Economy* (1978)

4 Deterrence and the Tort System

ROBERT L. RABIN*

From the advent of the industrial revolution, the Anglo-American courts self-consciously worked at designing a system of negligence law that governed tort liability for unintended harm. In his classic study of the common law published in 1881, Oliver Wendell Holmes sought to articulate the moral basis for this system and located it in the notion of foreseeability; an individual should be in a position to act with reference to a set of principles that indicated as clearly as possible the norms of permissible conduct.[1] To put it another way, tort law constituted a system of sanctions against unreasonably dangerous conduct.

Almost a century later, another legal scholar, Guido Calabresi, surveyed the tort system from the distinctively contemporary vantage-point of the lawyer-economist.[2] The establishment of no-fault compensation schemes, the rise of enterprise liability, and the influence of strict liability for defective products had, in tandem, dramatically tarnished the image of the negligence system. But Calabresi stressed the enduring power of the deterrence rationale as a foundation for tort liability. His conception of general deterrence anticipated a market economy in which the prospect of tort liability, recognized as a cost of operations, forced those engaged in injury-generating activity to choose a level of production that promoted allocative efficiency.[3] Once again, tort as a system of sanctions offered a compelling rationale for civil liability.

As these capsule summaries indicate, tort theory draws upon a set of assumptions about real-world behaviour. On the surface, at least, most injury-causing activity appears to correspond to the preconceptions of the theorists: the core ideas of fault and defect provide relatively clear signals as to the circumstances in which one will be responsible for harm. The driver who gives a moment's thought to the question realizes that speeding or tail-gating is virtually certain to result in liability for injuries caused. Similarly, the manufacturer of a malfunctioning widget or an exploding soda-bottle recognizes in advance that the company is likely to be held responsible for the defective product. Routine injury situations of this kind no doubt account for the overwhelming majority of two-party cases of accidental harm.

Yet I would guess that most serious students of the tort system have grave reservations about acknowledging the effectiveness of tort as a system of sanctions these days.[4] The challenge, then, is to account for the growing disillusionment with the deterrent capacity of tort law and to assess whether the criticism is warranted.[5]

In my view, there are a number of problems associated with the signalling function of tort liability – 'noise' in the transmission, reception, and precision of the signal, as well as doubts about whether tort adds anything to coexisting mechanisms for controlling risky conduct. I will discuss these problems in the next section of this paper. In addition, a comprehensive treatment of tort sanctions requires a more detailed look at how deterrence operates in specific fields of tort liability. There is no reason to think that doctors, drivers, and drug manufacturers respond similarly to the prospect of tort liability. Consequently, I will later examine some discrete categories of harm-producing activity – toxic substances, products liability, medical malpractice, municipal liability, and motor vehicle accidents – as a way of rounding out the discussion. My intention is twofold: to explore briefly the problematic case for the deterrent effect of tort law and to suggest areas in which research might relieve some of our doubts about the efficacy of the system.

The Deterrence Rationale: Some General Reservations

Signals Transmitted and Received

Oliver Wendell Holmes, the ardent proponent of the negligence principle, recognized that foreseeability – the linchpin for maximizing individual autonomy – might be seriously compromised if the concept of reasonable conduct was left to the unguided discretion of juries. Who would be able to predict in advance what a jury might find 'reasonable' in a given set of circumstances? As a consequence, he argued that judges should take a strong hand in articulating fixed rules of conduct to govern garden-variety accidental injuries of a repetitive kind.[6] A half-century later, in 1927, sitting on the U.S. Supreme Court as Mr Justice Holmes, he was able to put his long-held views into practice in the well-known *Goodman* case, in which his opinion for the court announced that a failure to stop, look, and if necessary survey the scene on foot at a railroad grade-crossing was contributory negligence as a matter of law.[7]

Alas, this was not to be a case where patience brought its own rewards. In the short space of seven years, *Goodman* was disapproved in an equally famous opinion by Mr Justice Cardozo, an opinion that graphically illustrated the difficulties in specifying rules of reasonable conduct even for a fact-pattern as common as driver behaviour at a railroad grade-crossing.[8] A simple proposition emerges from this famous exchange: to the extent that human conduct, particularly in everyday affairs, is, as Cardozo insisted, almost infinitely variable, the deterrent effect of tort law is seriously diminished. The featureless generalization that unreasonable conduct is proscribed can hardly be expected to have a meaningful ex ante impact on our personal activity.

Of course, the more routinized, self-conscious character of business affairs is another matter altogether. The product manufacturer counts costs carefully, and frequently turns out a relatively standardized item. Here, however, a different reservation about foreseeability and care must be entered. In these days of strict liability for product defects, it may well be necessary to distinguish between so-called manufacturing defects on the one hand, and design or warning failures on the other.[9] While the exploding soda-bottle may predictably occur one time in a million units (a prototypical instance of a manufacturing defect), the inadequate drug warning is intrinsic to every unit of the product, as is a design defect, and may, as a consequence, lead to mass or multiple tort liability. For present purposes, the key point is that design and warning cases are often decided under a featureless liability standard akin to the negligence approach, which has dubious deterrent value.[10] Holmes's complaint resurfaces: if the principles of tort liability have no predictive power, a deterrence rationale for the system is in serious trouble.

The deterrence potential of the system turns not just on whether a signal is clearly transmitted by the tort rules, but also on whether it is received by the relevant parties. In daily life, we tend to be notably unaware of the rules of civil liability. The consequences of tort rules sanctioning excessive drinking, failure to use safety devices, or indifference to warnings (via defences of assumed risk or contributory negligence) are largely lost on individuals as they go about their everyday affairs. To a lesser but still substantial extent, tort rules fail to engage the personal conduct (as distinguished, again, from business conduct) of individuals as they move from the role of potential victim to potential injurer – from pedestrian to driver, from visitor to homeowner, and from consumer to vendor of a risky product. As a consequence of either indifference or ignorance, the law of tort is simply remote from our daily conduct.

Constraints Apart from Tort

The deterrent function of tort is further undermined by its irrelevance in many situations. To begin with, there is an array of criminal and regulatory sanctions that establish guideposts for behaviour. To take a notable example, consider the mandatory warning of the dangers associated with smoking. A recent U.S. Court of Appeals decision took the regulatory standard, which requires a warning of health risks to appear on the package, to be a sufficiently comprehensive sanction to pre-empt tort liability altogether.[11] Less dramatically, criminal and regulatory sanctions apply to the intoxicated driver; auto safety standards are addressed to the motor vehicle manufacturer; new drug regulations must be adhered to by the pharmaceutical producer.[12] The question in each case is whether tort liability provides an additional measure of safety through its deterrent effect.

As a general proposition, I would argue that tort does play an affirmative role here. By and large, health and safety regulations emerge from a process embedded in political considerations and coloured by budgetary constraints; consequently, the regulations are often expressions of minimum standards. In practice, courts have largely reflected this thinking and have treated administrative regulations as a baseline rather than a standard of civil liability.[13]

None the less, there are situations in which tort liability adds little if anything to extralegal, informal sanctions. In some cases these non-legal constraints operate in the realm of personal behaviour: an individual may exercise caution both out of fear of self-injury and because of genuine moral compunctions about injuring others.[14] Although these constraints affect the entire range of everyday behaviour of most individuals in risky pursuits, it may be that a high proportion of accidents is caused by a small 'deviant population' that is largely immune to the constraints.

In other cases, extralegal constraints operate in business or professional conduct. It seems unlikely that airlines, for example, are significantly motivated to achieve higher levels of care by the prospect of tort suits when they contemplate the impact that mass disasters occurring in quick succession would have on their business. For them, bad publicity is sanction enough. Architects, lawyers, doctors, and others who are affected by reputational considerations that operate, to some extent at least, independently of tort liability are similarly motivated to exercise a high degree of care, whatever the standard of civil liability. At the same time, however, in some of these situations the prospect of publicity may turn on the existence of tort liability, since professional malpractice does not automatically attract the same degree of public attention as an airplane crash.

Perhaps most prominent on the list of extralegal factors affecting the deterrent impact of tort is the institution of insurance. Rather than making tort liability superfluous, however, as do the constraints in the situations discussed above, insurance perversely creates the prospect of making legal liability irrelevant. To the extent that the insurer shields injury-producing behaviour from financial responsibility, there is the prospect of 'moral hazard' – that the insured will be indifferent whether he acts cautiously or carelessly.[15]

The impact of insurance turns on the interplay between coverage and personal exposure on the one hand, and between coverage and the internal dynamics of the insurance industry on the other. In the first instance, insurance will not necessarily diminish the impact of tort liability as long as coverage under the policy involves co-insurance, a deductible amount, or a low ceiling on liability.[16] In each of these cases, since the insured remains residually liable, tort rules retain their deterrent effect in varying degree. In the second instance, the internal dynamics of the insurance business dictate the extent to which experience-rating is utilized.[17] Again, the deterrent effect of tort is not necessarily undercut by insurance coverage; if premium levels are linked to the likelihood of tort liability, the inducement to avoid accidents may be virtually as strong for an insured as for an uninsured party.

These general observations about insurance strongly suggest a caveat. One cannot really assess the impact of insurance on the deterrent role of tort rules without some context; in other words, it is essential to look at insurance in the setting of a particular field of harm-producing activity. But the same observation can be made about the other non-legal constraints on risky activity – publicity, regulatory sanctions, moral compunctions, and the like. Each plays out somewhat differently, depending on the context of harm – a subject I will pursue more concretely after addressing a final general consideration, the precision of the deterrent signal.

Overdeterrence and Underdeterrence

Deterrence theory is premised on a liability system that provides quantifiable signals about the costs of accidents.[18] Judge Learned Hand captured this notion in his much-discussed negligence formulation when he defined unreasonable conduct as the failure to act when the burden of adequate protection is less than the likelihood of harm multiplied by its magnitude.[19] The fundamental premise is that harm to another should entail liability only if the marginal costs of an added $1 in safety measures would have yielded more than $1 in accident prevention. Although such precise foresight – or, for that matter, judicial hindsight – may seem illusory, it represents an aspirational social welfare goal: achieving an optimal investment in safety.[20] It follows, of course, that mandating a $2 expenditure on safety to avoid $1 in injury costs represents an overinvestment in safety, and, conversely, that tolerating a 50-cent investment in safety by the generator of $1 in injuries – that is, failing to assign the cost of injuries to such a party – constitutes an underinvestment in cautionary behaviour.

The question is whether tort liability functions as a welfare-sensitive regulatory mechanism rather than simply as a deterrent that operates in a largely erratic fashion. Consider the criticism that was frequently levelled at the principal tort replacement scheme, workers' compensation, in the decades after the Second World War. In many states, workers' compensation benefits appeared to be woefully inadequate because of a sustained political unwillingness to recognize the impact of inflation.[21] To the extent that this criticism was accurate, it seems virtually certain that industrial investment in safety was suboptimal, since there was no built-in incentive adequate to avoid accident costs. Consider, however, the consequences if workers' compensation had been 'reformed' by adopting a regulatory scheme of industry surcharges for occupational accidents – a scheme in which the surcharge was set at a rate far exceeding the average loss actually suffered by workers. Obviously, a social welfare critic would argue that the scheme would put an unacceptable damper on business activity.

But what of the tort system? The precision of the signal emanating from the tort system is a direct function of the clarity of the right-hand side – the injury-cost side – of the Learned Hand formula. If either the likelihood of harm or its potential magnitude eludes rational assessment, the deterrent function of tort law is seriously compromised. Indeed, the same is true under a strict liability system wherein the costs of injury are privately measured against the need to invest in safety, without reference to an ex post determination of reasonableness by the judiciary.[22] Here too an informed judgment about the appropriate level of care is dependent on a clear view of the likely injury costs associated with various ways of conducting an activity.

Much of the recent perception of crisis in the tort system has been a by-product of the contention that predictive judgments about cost can no longer be made with any degree of confidence.[23] In its broadest manifestation, this critique is an indictment of non-economic damage awards in tort cases generally. There is a growing perception that awards for pain and suffering, as well as punitive damages, have been increasing at a rate that indicates a breakdown in the system.[24] To mention one specific context, in the modern mass tort case the claim of tort crisis centres on the vagaries of establishing causation.[25] In essence, the claim that causation is highly indeterminate in these cases can be taken to mean that affected parties have no way of determining in advance the dimensions of their potential liability. Deterrence is the crux of the matter. When the risks associated with low-probability, high-magnitude drugs or chemicals come to fruition, they may impose a cost burden that is beyond the capacity of even the largest industrial concerns. The mere prospect of such 'crushing liability,' critics assert, is bound to have aberrant effects on corporate decision-making.[26]

In sum, there are any number of reasons to be less than sanguine about the deterrent effect of tort liability. In some instances, tort liability rules are too general to offer much guidance to potential injurers or victims. In other instances, they are systematically unobserved. Even when tort rules are clearly communicated, they may add little to other non-legal constraints on dangerous conduct. And even if they deter, it may be that they promote too much or too little caution. Taken together, these reservations raise serious questions about the long-standing assumptions about the role of deterrence in the tort system. Still, they do not constitute a comprehensive treatment of the subject. It is necessary to go further, by examining how the considerations I have been discussing come into play in specific areas of tort activity.

The Deterrence Rationale: Area Studies

Commercial Activities: Toxic Substances

In a recent book on the asbestos cases, Paul Brodeur argues persuasively that tort litigation played a central role in revealing information about industry efforts to ignore and conceal the accumulating evidence of health risks associated with asbestos.[27] Moreover, Brodeur suggests, the asbestos litigation demonstrated that tort law is a double-edged sword: not only have the cases exposed the callous indifference of the industry, but they serve as a warning to other producers of potentially toxic products that ignoring serious health risks in the course of their profit-seeking activities will lead to devastating financial consequences.

There are a number of reservations that might be entered to Brodeur's thesis; one might cite the contemporaneous data indicating that two-thirds of the payout in asbestos tort litigation went to lawyers rather than to victims.[28] For present purposes, however, the key question is whether the deterrent effect noted by Brodeur – and one need look no further than the bankruptcy petition of the Johns-Manville Corporation, an otherwise going concern, to find convincing evidence of a deterrent effect – has in fact been a salutary development.[29] The answer is by no means clear.

There are two particularly salient characteristics in cases involving toxic substances such as asbestos, Agent Orange, DES, and the like: the long latency period between exposure and crystallization of harm, and the great uncertainty about the underlying contribution of the toxic product to overall risk.[30] Taken together, these factors seriously undermine the deterrent potential of tort law. When there is major uncertainty about the probability and extent of harm associated with a product, the projections that guide production and design decisions are often based on little more than guesswork. Correlatively, the guesswork is based on attempts to predict judicial decisions a generation later, when courts will be required to isolate a particular firm's contribution to an environment of background risk.

These projections must take account of likely damage assessments – far in the future – of pain and suffering, punitive damages, and harm to unborn generations. Risk-managers must also engage in a parallel tracking of future economic growth in order to discount accurately the future payouts to present value. They engage in this process of crystal-gazing cognizant of the fact that their errors of judgment will probably be revealed long after the present management team has turned over the reins of decision-making responsibility to others.

In this milieu, the tort system seems to operate in a totally wilful fashion as a constraint on risk-related decision-making. Indeed, it is virtually impossible to say whether the tort system is likely to grossly over-deter or under-deter the risk-related decision-making of an enterprise in any given case.

These doubts suggest a fertile field for study. It would be extremely useful to have something more than conjecture to rely upon in assessing how corporate management in the drug and chemical industries is influenced by the prospect of tort liability in the case of toxic substances. A survey research study might be designed to explore how decisions to engage in research and development or to initiate a new product line are affected by estimates of prospective tort liability and predictions of co-ordinate regulatory standard-setting.[31] If tort law is, as I have suggested, an exceedingly blunt instrument, does it in fact over-deter or under-deter the production of socially beneficial drugs and chemicals that have certain undesirable side-effects?

Commercial Activities: Products Liability

Putting aside the special problems of toxic substances, products liability is arguably the prime example of a field of activity in which tort law might be expected to have a strong deterrent effect. The mass manufacturer of soda-bottles, automobiles, or power lathes experiences systematic feedback from the tort system, including the settlement process, on the injury toll generated by its product. In most cases this experience, along with a general sense of the production design alternatives and costs faced by others in the industry, should provide the kind of information that makes risk-benefit analysis (if not taken too literally) feasible. These are the prerequisites for tort liability's fulfilling a bookkeeping function of sorts; that is, generating the kind of data on the cost of accidents that create incentives to optimal investment in safety.

There are some unarticulated assumptions in this argument, however. If the manufacturer operates on a small scale or introduces a novel product, it may be that there is simply no historical basis for estimating costs in any meaningful way. Often, the uncertainty is exacerbated by the fact that feedback from the tort system is slow in coming; it may be four or five years after a new product line is introduced before the courts and the settlement process begin to generate data on the risks associated with its use.[32] In these circumstances, whether the manufacturer carries liability insurance or self-insures, tort liability serves as a blunt instrument in affecting risky production techniques. Eads and Reuter suggest that although manufacturers are indeed sensitive to the prospect of products liability, they aren't quite sure what to make of it; they only know that it looms as an ominous cloud on the production horizon.[33] The smaller the producer, the greater the imprecision in estimating the consequences of potential tort liability.

Moreover, a distinction must be made between manufacturing defects and design or warning inadequacies. For manufacturing defects, the standard of liability is generally clear: 'defect' means that the harm-producing unit has manifested dangerous characteristics beyond those typically found in the product. By contrast, in a design-defect case the question is whether the basic structure of the product is flawed; in warning cases the issue is whether a safety initiative has been omitted which indicts the entire product line.

There is much debate in these cases about whether risk-benefit analysis is the appropriate substantive standard of liability, or whether strict liability implies a more stringent approach.[34] From a deterrence perspective, however, the key point is the great uncertainty generated by the courts' inability to fashion tort rules that establish a tolerable degree of predictability about the allocation of loss. As in mass tort cases, the prospect of a court's finding a design or warning failure signals potential liability, but the signal often lacks the clarity to serve as an effective deterrent.

The need for further study in this area is apparent. There would be great value in systematic time-series and cross-industry studies of the relationship between claims experience and investment decisions, controlling for type of product or size of firm, and like variables. To enhance the value of any such study, the dynamics of insurance coverage – experience-rating practices, safety monitoring, and so forth – warrant careful attention.

Professional Activities: Medical Malpractice

Insurance plays a particularly important mediating role in the area of physicians' tort liability. Virtually all doctors carry liability insurance, and, from all the evidence, it appears that they are particularly sensitive to the implications of the steadily rising numbers of malpractice claims and the corresponding growth in the average size of awards.[35] On the surface, insurance practices in the medical malpractice field might be thought to create a shield from the direct impact of tort liability. Malpractice policies generally do not contain deductibles or co-insurance provisions, and there is virtually no experience-rating of individual doctors.[36] As a consequence, 'moral hazard,' or indifference to personal liability, might at first blush appear to be of concern.

But there are substantial reasons, admittedly hard to document, that suggest otherwise. While there is no practice of individual experience-rating, there is a sharply defined experience-rating by type of practice. As a consequence, there is extreme variation in insurance costs among areas of specialization. Testimonial evidence within the high-litigation areas suggests that a good deal of defensive medicine is practised, and even that there is a growing tendency on the part of physicians to abandon high-exposure areas of practice.[37] In addition, close observers of the malpractice field report that doctors greatly fear the prospect of becoming involved in litigation and the possible damage to their professional reputations.[38]

Thus, even if malpractice insurance provides a shield against the direct consequences of litigation, it may well be the case that tort law has a strong deterrent effect on medical practice. Once again, however, there is substantial reason to question the precision of this effect. Defensive medicine may have salutary benefits, but it may simply raise the costs of medical treatment through added procedures that are essentially a buffer against litigation exposure and nothing more. Similarly, category-wide experience-rating may establish a correspondence between premium costs and high-risk areas of practice, but the lack of individual experience-rating is comparable, perhaps, to the exceedingly blunt deterrent effect of tort liability on small-scale product manufacturers. Worse yet, it is possible that the high-premium specializations correlate with areas of practice in which patients have unreasonably high expectations, rather than areas in which the incidence of actual negligence is substantial.

Speculation about deterrence ought to be better informed by further research on the deterrent effect of malpractice liability. There is a modest beginning in the study and informed speculation regarding therapists' responses to a California case in which therapists were found to be liable in some situations to the victims of patients with dangerous propensities.[39] But much more needs to be done.[40] It should be possible to target high-incidence areas of specialization for cross-sectional or time-series studies that focus on the changes in medical practice that are occurring as a consequence of stringent liability rules.[41]

Municipal Liability

The singular characteristic of the municipal liability field is the lack of a competitive constraint similar to that which operates on the physician or the product manufacturer. In considering private entrepreneurial liability, it is implicit that marginal injury costs exceeding marginal costs of prevention will ordinarily lead to greater investments in safety as a means of generating more revenue and higher profits. These assumptions are inapplicable to the municipal liability situation. While there may be a host of political reasons for keeping costs down, municipalities are not subject to the normal constraints of the market. Within wide limits, people are not likely to make permanent residence decisions on the basis of the impact of accident costs on local tax rates and municipal services. Municipalities may be sensitive to rising accident costs, particularly when they are brought home by skyrocketing liability insurance premiums, but it does not follow that any disciplining mechanism comparable to market pressure exists.

Moreover, the mediating impact of liability insurance is hard to assess. On the one hand, municipal liability policies, unlike medical malpractice policies, typically contain large deductibles and co-insurance provisions, thus promoting the direct impact of tort judgments. On the other hand, there appears to be no meaningful effort to arrive at experience-ratings of individual communities; again, this omission lessens the deterrent impact of tort rules.[42] Of course, if insurance-premium increases appear to be random, or intolerably burdensome, communities will self-insure, and will expose themselves directly to the effects of the tort system. In such cases the question arises, once more, whether the self-insuring municipality is insensitive to tort rules in any event because of the absence of market constraints.

In the current atmosphere of tort crisis, these cross-cutting considerations regarding municipal liability have been further complicated by the problem of joint and several liability. Municipalities have sometimes been held fully responsible for awards in cases where their share of responsibility is minimal when compared with that of an insolvent co-defendant.[43] Clearly, this situation has major implications for the deterrent effect of tort law. If municipalities are bearing, on a more or less random basis, the full costs of minimal flaws in road design or facility maintenance – situations in which a relatively improbable risk is brought to fruition by the serious misconduct of an insolvent third party – an element of unpredictability created by the tort rules will seriously undermine the system's deterrent function.

Municipal liability is an area ripe for research. Because of the distinctive non-market constraints on municipalities, there is a threshold question of the underlying sensitivity of these entities to tort judgments. Assuming that municipalities are sensitive to tort awards, there is a need to explore with greater precision the ensuing consequences. It is conceivable that municipalities engage in injury-prevention activities to meet the potential threat of rising claims, but it is also possible that they engage in politically expedient reductions in services, or pass on most of the costs through revenue-raising measures.

Whatever the case, it is vital to know more about the mediating role of insurance. Are there systematic differences in the injury-reduction activities of insured municipalities as compared with self-insurers? Finally, if we are to develop a better understanding of the deterrence function of the tort system it is essential to gather more precise quantitative data on claims and costs, and to test a thesis that I regard as salient in virtually every area of perceived tort crisis: that the deterrence function has been seriously undermined in recent years not so much by dramatic changes in the number or substantive nature of claims made on the tort system as by a substantially higher degree of unpredictability in damage awards in serious injury cases.

Auto Accidents and Harm from Other Personal Activities

If one system-wide generalization can be made about the character of deterrence, it is that business conduct is more likely to be sensitive to the framework of tort rules than everyday personal behaviour. Whatever doubts one may raise about the actual impact of tort rules on business activities, there is strong intuitive support for the proposition that the deterrent role of tort in most personal liability situations is likely to be minimal.

Consider two illustrations from the California torts jurisprudence of recent years. In *Rowland v. Christian*,[44] the state Supreme Court scrapped the long-standing categories in land occupier cases that had limited the liability of owner-occupiers to social guests and trespassers. Instead, the court proclaimed that land entrants would be owed a general duty of care, limited only by traditional fault-based notions of foreseeability. It seems inconceivable that private owners and renters altered their behaviour in response to this decision (or that they were even aware of its existence), despite the fact that the new standard potentially brought a wide range of household activities within its ambit.

A second example is the recent case of *Taylor v. Superior Court*,[45] in which the California Supreme Court extended the action for punitive damages to cases of drunken driving that fell short of the pre-existing conception of 'actual malice.' Here too, as far as one can tell, the decision went virtually unnoticed by the driving public, in contrast to changes in the penal and regulatory law which appear to have had at least a short-term impact on driving behaviour.[46]

These cases are illustrative of a much broader phenomenon in every variety of cautionary personal tort rules. There is no reason to think that any substantial portion of the general population is aware of important tort law developments such as the shift from contributory to comparative negligence, the evolving defences to strict products liability, or the liberalization of recovery for emotional distress, despite the fact that many of these rules of conduct vitally affect the prospect of compensation in cases of accidental harm. In the circumstances, it seems quixotic to speak of the deterrent effect of tort law.

Public indifference to the rules of tort stems from a number of factors. Consider the example of automobile accidents. It seems highly unlikely that most drivers who fail to wear seat-belts do so as an expression of libertarian ideology. The explanation is more straightforward: drivers and passengers (and, for that matter, pedestrians) harbour – within bounds – illusions of omnipotence: the injury always happens to the next person. Moreover, drivers, by and large, are prototypical respectable citizens; they exercise a considerable measure of caution simply because they do not want to be hurt or to hurt others. This is in no way inconsistent with the hard reality of auto accidents, because, drunken driving to one side, most accidents arise out of the split-second hazardous situations that all of us face from time to time. Those who fail to avoid accidents in such situations probably fall into two classes: some are simply less lucky than the rest of us, and others are systematically slightly sub-par in their reactions to dangerous situations. Tort law is unlikely to have much of a deterrent effect in either case, particularly when one factors in the ubiquitous failure of insurers to engage in experience-rating in any meaningful sense. Indeed, the one class of drivers that might be most clearly exposed to the punitive impact of tort liability – the reckless and often intoxicated driver with little or no insurance coverage – almost certainly constitutes a high proportion of the risk-producing class that is immune to tort liability because of impecuniousness.

The auto-accident problem has been studied more than other areas of tort law, but much remains to be done.[47] Many of my assertions about driving behaviour rest on intuitions that could be confirmed by systematic study of the kinds of hazards that cause accidents and their respective susceptibility to deterrence pressure. More generally, it would be useful to analyse accident data so as to provide better information about the respective contributions of motor vehicle design, road-engineering, and driving conduct to the distressing record of highway carnage. And it would be a salutary development to generate better information about the comparative deterrent effect of third-party and first-party liability insurance systems.[48] On this score, the data on the impact of first-party no-fault auto compensation schemes have generated heated debate[49] – although, in my view, it seems inconceivable that no-fault can have a negative effect on cautionary behaviour as long as a complementary tort system remains in place for all serious accidents (as it does in every U.S. no-fault jurisdiction).

Conclusion

I have attempted to provide a succinct discussion of the uneasy case for the deterrent effect of tort liability. An underlying theme – in reality, an organizing principle – has been that deterrence is really many subjects rather than one; it plays out quite differently, depending on the characteristics of the class of actors to whom tort liability rules are addressed. But, no matter the class, the efficacy of tort law as a deterrence strategy is open to serious question. Even so, the logical follow-up question is this: deterrence through tort liability as compared with what alternatives? That is a subject beyond the scope of this paper. And in any event, if the efficacy of tort as a deterrence strategy is in serious doubt, the system almost certainly needs to be broadly reassessed, since the other principal goal of tort liability, compensating the injured, can almost certainly be achieved more efficiently and equitably by other means.

Notes

* A. Calder Mackay Professor of Law, Stanford Law School, Stanford University
1 O.W. Holmes, *The Common Law* (1881) 146–7
2 G. Calabresi, *The Costs of Accidents: A Legal and Economic Analysis* (1970)
3 On economic theories of tort law, see generally, I. Englard, 'The System Builders: A Critical Appraisal of Modern American Tort Theory' (1980) 9 *Journal of Legal Studies* 27; A.M. Polinsky, *An Introduction to Law and Economics* (1983) 37–49; W.M. Landes and R.A. Posner, 'The Positive Economic Theory of Tort Law' (1981) 15 *Georgia Law Review* 851.
4 See, for example, S.D. Sugarman 'Doing Away with Tort Law' (1985) 73 *California Law Review* 555; P. Huber, 'Safety and the Second Best: The Hazards of Public Risk Management in the Courts' (1985) 85 *Columbia Law Review* 277.
5 In addition to academic criticism, there has been a notable recent political impulse to reform the tort system, which has given rise to an outpouring of critical tort commission studies. See, for example, U.S. Attorney General's Office, *Report of the Tort Policy Working Group on the Causes, Extent and*

Policy Implications of the Current Crisis in Insurance Availability and Affordability (1986); *Report of the State of New York Advisory Commission on Liability Insurance*, vol. 1 (April 1986) and vol. 2 (July 1986); *Report of the ABA Action Commission to Improve the Tort Liability System* (December 1986).

6 Holmes, supra note 1, at 150–1
7 *Baltimore & Ohio Railroad Co. v. Goodman* (1927) 275 U.S. 66
8 *Pokora v. Wabash Railway Co.* (1934) 292 U.S. 98
9 See generally J.W. Wade, 'On the Effect in Product Liability of Knowledge Unavailable Prior to Marketing' (1983) 58 *New York University Law Review* 734, at 740.
10 For discussion, see J.A. Henderson Jr, 'The Role of the Judge in Tort Law: Why Creative Judging Won't Save the Products Liability System' (1983) 11 *Hofstra Law Review* 845, at 848.
11 *Cipollone v. Liggett Group Inc.* (1986) 785 F.2d 1108 (3d Cir.)
12 For a discussion of the dramatic growth in federal health and safety regulation beginning in the late 1960s, see R.L. Rabin, 'Federal Regulation in Historical Perspective' (1986) 38 *Stanford Law Review* 1189.
13 See, for example, *Ferebee v. Chevron Chemical Co.* (1984) 736 F.2d 1529 (DC Cir.) (federally approved herbicide warning label held not to preclude claim); *Hubbard-Hall Chemical Co. v. Silverman* (1965) 340 F.2d 402 (1st Cir.) (judgment for plaintiffs affirmed despite defendant's compliance with Congressional warning requirements); *Raymond v. Riegel Textile Corp.* (1973) 484 F.2d 1025 (1st Cir.) (nightgown manufacturer liable for plaintiff's injuries despite compliance with the federal Flammable Fabrics Act). Indeed, the cigarette ruling may be perfectly consistent with this approach, if the no-liability holding reflected the court's reaction to a warning aimed at *users* of the product – who, in this case, are cognizant of its risks – in contrast to the ordinary regulatory sanctions, which establish production or design standards for the benefit of unwary consumers and bystanders.
14 See Sugarman, supra note 4, 562–3.
15 See the discussion in R.A. Epstein, 'Products Liability as an Insurance Market' (1985) 14 *Journal of Legal Studies* 645, at 653; Polinsky, supra note 3, 54.
16 See Polinsky, supra note 3, 55.
17 See generally R.J. Pierce Jr, 'Encouraging Safety: The Limits of Tort Law and Government Regulation' (1980) 33 *Vanderbilt Law Review* 1281, at 1298–1300.
18 See generally Calabresi, supra note 2.
19 *United States v. Carroll Towing Co.* (1947) 159 F.2d 169, at 173
20 See R.A. Posner, *Economic Analysis of Law*, 3d ed. (1986).
21 See E.P. Bernzweig, *By Accident Not Design: The Case for Comprehensive Injury Reparation* (1980) 16–17.

96   Sanctions and Rewards in the Legal System

22 But it is important to note that from a distributional standpoint, the injurer bears the non-negligently incurred costs under a strict liability system, unlike the result in a negligence regime.
23 For a representative view, see Attorney-General's Interagency Task Force, *Report on Insurance Availabilty and Affordability* (1986).
24 Whether this perception is supported by the available data is another matter. The most systematic work on tort damage awards in the United States has been conducted by the Rand Institute for Civil Justice. On the question of 'runaway' damage awards, see Institute for Civil Justice, *An Overview of the First Six Program Years, April 1980–March 1986* (1986), discussing data that indicate increases in *average* monetary damage awards (in Cook County, Illinois, and San Francisco) between 1960 and 1985 of about 400 per cent. By contrast, although the *median* awards rose considerably in San Francisco, they actually declined in Cook County when measured in constant dollars. The significant increase in average tort awards in both jurisdictions appears to reflect major growth in a limited number of very large awards. For example, million-dollar awards constituted only 0.3 per cent of plaintiffs' verdicts in San Francisco during the 1960s (8 per cent of the dollars awarded), but rose to 2.3 per cent in the 1970s (50 per cent of the dollars awarded) by the latter half of the decade. In both jurisdictions, million-dollar awards constituted nearly two-thirds of trial court monetary awards by the 1980s. A caveat is necessary in evaluating data on trial court awards: the figures fail to reflect subsequent reversal on appeal, remittitur, inability to pay, and lower settlement in anticipation of appeal, among other things, as well as defence verdicts in the first instance. However, this caveat is as applicable to the 1960s data as to the later figures, and consequently has no apparent impact on the trend.

A later ICJ study, J. Kakalik and N. Pace, *Costs and Compensation Paid in Tort Litigation* (1986), finds an average annual rate of growth in average compensation per claim (settlements as well as court awards) of 12 per cent in auto cases and 17 per cent in non-auto accident cases over the five year period 1981–5. The consumer price index rose by an average of only 7 per cent during the same period. However, these figures do not separate the non-economic component of damage awards from economic loss.

With regard to punitive damages, there is reason to question seriously the perception of runaway awards in accidental injury cases. The published findings contemporaneous with the claims of tort crisis indicated substantial increases in the magnitude of punitive damages in intentional tort and insurance bad faith cases, but not in accidental injury cases. See M. Peterson, *Punitive Damages: Empirical Findings* (1987), and Daniels and Martin, 'Empirical Patterns in Punitive Damage Cases: A Description of Incidence Rates and Awards,' paper presented at Law and Society meetings, June 1987 (summary of an American Bar Foundation research project).

25 See generally J. Trauberman, 'Statutory Reform of "Toxic Torts": Relieving Legal, Scientific, and Economic Burdens on the Chemical Victim' (1983) 7 *Harvard Environmental Law Review* 177, at 197–201.

26 See, for example, A. Schwartz, 'Products Liability, Corporate Structure, and Bankruptcy: Toxic Substances and the Remote Risk Relationship' (1985) 14 *Journal of Legal Studies* 689 at 706–11.

27 P. Brodeur, *Outrageous Misconduct: The Asbestos Industry on Trial* (1985)

28 See J. Kakalik et al., *Costs of Asbestos Litigation* (1983).

29 For a discussion of current problems in toxic-tort-induced bankruptcies, see M.J. Roe, 'Bankruptcy and Mass Tort' (1984) 84 *Columbia Law Review* 846.

30 Trauberman, supra note 25, 180, 197–200; P.J. Strand, 'The Inapplicability of Traditional Tort Analysis to Environmental Risks: The Example of Toxic Waste Pollution Victim Compensation' (1983) 35 *Stanford Law Review* 575

31 For an example of such a study, see G.C. Eads and P. Reuter, *Designing Safer Products: Corporate Responses to Product Liability Law and Regulation* (1983).

32 Ibid., 108

33 Ibid., 106–10

34 Compare *Beshada v. Johns-Manville Product Corp.* (1982) 90 NJ 191, 447 A.2d 539 (assessing defectiveness by reference to the state of the art at time of trial) with *Feldman v. Lederle Laboratories* (1984) 97 NJ 429, 479 A.2d 374 (1984) (information about the product acquired post-distribution not to be taken into account). See also R.L. Rabin, 'Indeterminate Risk and Tort Reform: Comment on Calabresi and Klevorick' (1985) 14 *Journal of Legal Studies* 633 (arguing that there is no judicial trend toward ex post risk-benefit analysis).

35 See, for example, 'Fear of Malpractice Suits Leading Some Doctors to Quit Obstetrics' *New York Times*, 12 February 1985.

36 P. Danzon, *Medical Malpractice: Theory, Evidence, and Public Policy* (1985) 94, 129

37 Supra note 35, and 'Doctors Organize Battle to Reduce Malpractice Suits' *New York Times*, 15 February 1985

38 Telephone interview with P. Danzon, February 1986

39 *Tarasoff v. Regents of the Univ. of California* (1976) 17 Cal. 3d 425, 551 P.2d 334, 131 Cal. Rptr. 14. See T.P. Wise, 'Where the Public Peril Begins: A Survey of Psychotherapists to Determine the Effects of Tarasoff' (1978) 31 *Stanford Law Review* 165, and A.A. Stone, 'The *Tarasoff* Decision: Suing Psychotherapists to Safeguard Society' (1976) 90 *Harvard Law Review* 358.

40 See generally R.L. Rabin, 'Impact Analysis and Tort Law: A Comment' (1979) 13 *Law & Society Review* 987.

41 On this score, there are especially good data sources in the malpractice area because of the limited number of insurers and the 'captive' companies.
42 The failure to experience-rate can be clearly inferred from the wholesale cancellations and staggering premium increases for towns and communities across the nation. The inference is supported by personal interview reports from city attorneys in the San Francisco Bay area. See generally 'Lawsuits' Surge Strains Budgets of Many Cities' *New York Times*, 12 May 1985.
43 In the absence of systematic data collection, it is difficult to say how widespread the problem is. For a concrete illustration of the problem, see 'City Suit Figures Show L.A. Liability Tripled since 1980,' *Los Angeles Daily Journal* 23 April 1986.
44 (1968) 69 Cal.2d 108, 443 P.2d 561, 70 Cal. Rptr. 97
45 (1979) 24 Cal.3d 890, 598 P.2d 854, 157 Cal. Rptr. 693
46 See, for example, H.L. Ross, *Deterring the Drinking Driver* (1982) (changes in the penal law have a significant, albeit temporary, effect on drunken driving).
47 Recent studies include U.S. Department of Transport, *Compensating Auto Accident Victims* (1985); and Rand Corporation, *Automobile Accident Compensation* (1985). See also C.J. Bruce, 'The Deterrent Effects of Automobile Insurance and Tort Law: A Survey of the Empirical Literature' (1984) 6 *Law & Policy* 67.
48 See G. Calabresi, 'First Party, Third Party, and Product Liability Systems: Can Economic Analysis of Law Tell Us Anything about Them?' (1984) 69 *Iowa Law Review* 833.
49 See the discussion in the U.S. Department of Transport study, supra note 47, 159–66.

5 Methods for Measuring General Deterrence: A Plea for the Field Experiment

FRANKLIN E. ZIMRING*

> *[An] increase in the expenditure on police and courts in 1965 by $32 million could have reduced the loss from felonies by about $83 million.*[1]
>
> Isaac Ehrlich
>
> *One area ... received no preventive patrol. In the second area, police visibility was increased two to three times its usual level. In the third area ... normal patrol was maintained ... [T]he three areas experienced no significant differences in ... crime.*[2]
>
> Police Chief McNamara

The deterrent effect of criminal sanctions has long been a topic of debate, yet until recently very little systematic research on the impact of law enforcement and sanctions existed. Over the past fifteen years, however, social psychologists, sociologists, economists, and statisticians have used a wide variety of methodologies to assess the nature and extent of deterrence variables. Within the literature emerging from this new generation of deterrence studies, there are two quite different strategies for producing data on and insights into deterrence.

One approach is to gather aggregate data on crime and other social indicators and to study the variations in crime that occur between jurisdictions or over time. These researchers study changes that occur naturally, and attempt to control for all the other differences that occur in nature either between areas or over time to isolate the contribution of general deterrence to differences in noted crime rates. Statistical tools ranging from simple regression to complex simultaneous equations are used to analyse the data, and significant findings are frequently reported in the literature.[3]

The second approach attempts to assess the impact of changes in law enforcement or punishment policy by closely following what happens after particular policy shifts occur. Comparisons in reported crime rates are made before and after the policy change. In some studies, comparison or control areas are used to reduce the possibility that changes in the dependent variable (usually crime rates) are inaccurately attributed to the policy shift being examined. In general, the results reported in these 'real change' studies have been less exciting than the estimates of deterrent effectiveness derived from some of the cross-sectional and time studies.[4]

The Kansas City Preventive Patrol Experiment[5] falls squarely within the tradition of the second approach to studying deterrence through attempts to induce and analyse 'real' policy changes. The research is of special significance because the experiment used random assignment to produce control areas. Fifteen contiguous police beats were divided into three groups. The first group received intensive preventive patrol; the second group received its normal level of preventive patrol; and the third group received no preventive patrol. The Kansas City study is the most ambitious and successful field experiment of its type in law enforcement. For this reason, the experiment provides a suitable vehicle for discussing the uses and limits of experimentation in law enforcement, and for comparing the advantages of this approach with the quick and inexpensive insights of cross-sectional and time-series approaches. A more recent example, also funded by the Police Foundation, is the domestic violence experiment reported by Sherman and Berk.[6] Police in Minneapolis randomly assigned different outcomes in actual spouse-assault cases: arrest, ordering the offender to leave the premises for a period of time, or advice.

My own view is that policy experiments of this kind will gradually increase our modest knowledge of the impact of law enforcement crime rates. In the long run, this contribution will be more important than the knowledge base supplied by even the most sophisticated attempts to study natural variations.

To social scientists interested in rapid progress, this assessment will provide small comfort; those who recall with affection the parable of the hare and the tortoise may be more favourably disposed to it. In either event, the choices are of immediate importance in the design of future deterrence research in Canada and in the United States.

The Limits of Field Experimentation

Did the Kansas City experiment prove that preventive patrol has no value in reducing crime? The obvious answer to this question is no, but a restatement of what the Kansas City findings teach us is a useful introduction to the problems and limitations of field experimentation. My own version of the inference that can properly be drawn from the technical report of the study is this: increasing preventive patrol by a factor of two or more for twelve months in a car-patrolled area similar to those studied probably does not reduce the incidence of crime to a great extent. Each of the qualifications in this somewhat inelegant summary illustrates a limitation on the utility of the method.

To begin, my assessment of the results speaks only of the comparison between the 'proactive' (increased patrol) and 'control' areas. The degree to which the 'reactive' beats conformed to the conditions the researchers meant to produce is in some dispute.[7] Without taking sides in that dispute, I will say that the problem can be used to illustrate a general principle of great significance: no field experiment in criminal justice will ever be executed in total conformity to its plan. Kansas City is an example of modest deviation, and modest deviation is about the best we can expect from attempts to alter complex ongoing systems in predetermined ways.

My version of the Kansas City findings is limited to car-patrolled areas similar to those studied because there are great differences between areas and between car patrol and foot patrol that could lead to substantial differences in the impact of variations in patrol intensity. The problem of generalization is a persistent one in experimental science. Our capacity to generalize from particular experimental findings to broader behavioural conclusions depends on how much we know about the impact of other conditions. In law enforcement and crime control, we know very little. This knowledge gap hampers our capacity to generalize from experiments at the same time that it makes such experiments necessary.[8]

There are a number of good reasons for stating any conclusion from this field experiment in probabilistic terms. When crime rates are used as a dependent variable, they must be measured imperfectly. Crimes reported by the police are a partial sample of all offences, and may be influenced by a policy-oriented desire to see the experiment yield a certain result. For different reasons, surveys of victims are also imperfect measures of crime, and also introduce problems of sampling error at the same time that they make the experimental design relatively insensitive: decreases in offences must be fairly substantial before we can attribute any change to factors other than chance variation.[9]

All of these problems can be ameliorated, although the cures are neither quick nor inexpensive. Crime can be measured with both official and survey instruments, as was the case in Kansas City, and if both indicators perform consistently, confidence in the result can be increased. The experiment can and should be replicated. Experimental changes in foot patrols can be carefully measured.

Even more necessary is the replication of experiments when significant differences have emerged from the initial trial. The replication of the spouse-arrest studies is necessary to determine whether the reduction of subsequent domestic violence noted in Minneapolis after the increase in arrests and detention has persisted, and if so to what extent, and what elements of the treatment caused the result. An initial experiment is only the down-payment on a research program in deterrence. The more remarkable the results, the more necessary it is to replicate and refine the experiment.

But there are natural limits on the capacity to increase our knowledge of crime control through experimentation. Not the least of these is the high cost, in both money and time, of experimentation. There are also political and moral limitations on the conditions that can be varied in the name of experimentation. The political limits are obvious and substantial; imagine the fate of the brave researcher who would disarm the ghetto police so as to study the impact on injury and death rates. Putting police or citizens in potentially hazardous positions for the sake of research is also an obvious example of a situation in which moral constraints limit the range of true experimentation. The moral problems with experiments that entail upward variations on serious punishments are, to my mind, equally substantial.

The answer to these problems, to the extent that an answer exists, is to study those policy shifts that occur as a result of the political process. The rigour and reliability of such efforts are inferior to those of the controlled experiment; the degree of variance that can be observed will be limited by the political process. But if the evaluations are based on experimental logic, and if the results are reported with caution, such studies are probably the best technology available for examining issues not suited to true experiments.

The existing inventory of 'intervention' studies displays a wide variation in both methodological rigour and substantive conclusions. Field experimentation in law enforcement has rarely been undertaken. Quasi-experimental evaluations of topics as diverse as variations in police patrol, punishment for rape, the introduction of portable breathalyser tests, enforcement of drunken-driving laws, and crackdowns on speeders have produced decidedly mixed results.[10] This may be due in part to the insensitivity of rigorous interrupted time-series analysis to relatively small or gradual declines in offences or offence-related variables. It is clear, however, that if 'intervention' evaluations are to be the primary building-blocks for deterrence theory, progress will be slow and empirically justified generalizations will be difficult – a condition that is typical of social science.[11]

Do We Need Experimentation?

From a social policy standpoint, it would be unwise to make a substantial investment of resources in order to prove the obvious. There are a number of scholars who believe the effectiveness of deterrent countermeasures is not only obvious but has already been proved. Gordon Tullock, for one, finds that 'punishment will indeed deter crime,' because 'if you increase the cost of something, less will be consumed.'[12] Leaving aside the question whether he is reasoning by analogy or by deduction, the simple statement of that theorem has few policy implications, because one does not know by how much one needs to increase 'costs' to achieve palpable deterrent benefits. Tullock, I think, would agree that more than an axiom is needed to support major changes in punishment policy. But he argues that a large number of studies using multiple regression give substantial support to the deterrence hypothesis, and that since the economists and sociologists conducting these studies used 'statistical tools that were somewhat different,' the sociological studies 'can be taken as an independent confirmation of the economists' approach.'[13]

All of the studies Tullock refers to are statistical manipulations of the variation in crime and sanction rates that occur over time and between jurisdictions. Surprisingly, no study of a discrete, purposeful attempt to manipulate deterrence variables is mentioned in Tullock's article or in much of the rest of the emerging literature on deterrence.[14]

That does not mean Tullock lacks a bibliography. Since 1970 the cross-sectional study of crime and punishment using multiple regression has become a cottage industry. Almost all studies of variations in rates of imprisonment and rates of crime have noted a negative correlation between the two, and many (but not all) researchers reporting these results have attributed that relationship to the operation of the general deterrent effect of sanctions.[15] The relationship between the length of prison sentences and the crime rate is a more ambiguous matter. For most crimes, in most studies, there is no significant negative simple correlation between the average length of a prison sentence and the rate of crime. By the time additional control variables are added to the equation, weighted to the tastes of the researcher and processed through the sophisticated machinery of statistical analysis, the published results are in disagreement if not disarray.[16]

This is a relatively minor matter. The real problem is whether or not even the most sophisticated analyses of time-series and cross-sectional data can provide a scientifically rigorous test of the nature and extent of general deterrence. My scepticism about the use of sophisticated statistical methods over time and between areas as a mechanism of measuring deterrence derives from three problems:

1 The lack of information about, and the capacity to control for, other factors that influence variations in crime rates over time and between areas;
2 The problem of distinguishing between relatively high punishment rates as a cause of low crime rates and relatively low crime rates as a cause of relatively high punishment rates;
3 The fact that such studies shed no light on the issue of how systems that differ in punishment policy come to be different.

The first problem is well stated by Tullock: 'Statistically testing deterrence is not easy because the prospect of punishment obviously is not the *only* thing that affects the frequency with which crimes are committed. The crime rate varies with the degree of urbanization, the demographic composition of the population, the distribution of wealth, and many other circumstances.'

> Some statistical technique is necessary to take care of these factors – and such techniques are not available. Using multiple regression ... it is possible to put figures on each of these variables into the same equation and to see how much they influence the dependent variable, which, in this

case, is the rate of a specific crime. Although there are difficulties, this procedure will give a set of numbers called coefficients that are measures of the effect of *each* of the purported causative factors on the rate of commission of the given crime. If punishment deters crime, it will show up in these figures as a coefficient that is both significant and negative.[17]

The problem is that crime does indeed vary with circumstances. But we don't know what all of those circumstances are, or their predictive power under different social conditions. If one views a cross-sectional analysis as essentially a comparison of crime in South Dakota with crime in New Jersey, the question becomes whether or not it is possible to explain and measure all the differences other than criminal justice policy that account for differential crime propensities in those two states. If one views a time-series analysis as essentially a comparison of the United States in 1970 with the United States in 1960, the problem becomes one of identifying all the crime-related differences that have occurred over time, measuring these with precision, and allocating any residual effects to changes in criminal justice policy. In an important sense, one must know everything about the non-deterrence factors that influence crime before one can find out anything about deterrence from uncontrolled time and area comparisons. Even then it will be necessary to measure with some precision variables such as the moral structure of a community, which only the bravest of the computer experts would ever attempt to quantify.

I do not believe our present knowledge of the factors that influence variations in crime permits us to control statistically for differences between South Dakota and New Jersey, other than for differences in criminal justice policy. Instead, it is possible to use a great variety of different cross-sectional statistical 'controls,' and it is beginning to appear that the results one obtains at the 'residual' or deterrence end of the equation are heavily dependent on how the non-deterrence variables are selected, weighted, and measured.[18]

The second problem in interpreting studies of natural variation is that of separating causes from consequences. Assume that the total crime rate experienced by a society both influences and is influenced by criminal justice policy. In such circumstances, a higher crime rate may reduce the threat of imprisonment to a certain degree for reasons that have nothing to do with the weakening of general deterrence; at the same time, some increase in crime will occur that is attributable to less credible deterrent threats. Isolating that portion of the variation in the crime rate that is caused by changes in punishment policy does not seem possible if exclusively cross-sectional data are used. Whether or not some combination of cross-sectional and time-series studies can successfully deal with this problem is a matter for debate. But whatever one's final theoretical position on this issue, the existing inventory of studies falls far short of providing a satisfactory solution.

The third problem is that natural-variation studies shed no light on why punishment policy varies in real-world settings, and thus on how easy it would be to induce on a deliberate basis the kinds of policy changes that occur naturally. Although the study of discrete attempts at intervention teaches us the difficulties involved in changing policy, the natural-variation studies cannot investigate the causes of policy difference. One suspects that many of the characteristics that influence a society's punishment policy also influence its crime rates. Unless all of these factors can be controlled for, the observed statistical relationship between punishment policy and crime may be spurious. Of equal importance is the fact that many readers of the literature that is emerging from multiple regression research may be tempted to think of punishment policy as an easily manipulable independent variable that can be shifted from 'low' to 'high' with a flip of the public policy switch. Rarely is this the case in the real world.

Conclusion

I am not arguing that studies of natural variation are without value. They are useful, in my view, more to generate and refine hypotheses than to confirm them. Comparative and time studies can be a useful complement to other methods of increasing knowledge. My fear is, however, that over-reliance on manipulations of secondary data is competing with experiments rather than complementing them. And my guess is that as the number of non-intervention studies increases, the apparent clarity of the results will diminish. We are already observing deviant 'crime-generating' models leading to contradictory results. It is this guess about the econometric studies that leads me to the parable of the hare and the tortoise. The hare got off to a fast start, but encountered problems related to overconfidence. The tortoise, slow but steady, prevailed.

Yet in a deeper sense the parable is inappropriate. Methodologies and disciplines should mesh rather than clash; deterrence research should not become yet another example of what one observer called the 'cross-sterilization of the social sciences.' Our ignorance is vast; there is more than enough to go around. Humility in the use of a variety of imperfect methods gives the real hope of sustained progress in learning more about the impact of law enforcement on crime.

Notes

* Professor of law and director, Earl Warren Legal Institute, School of Law, University of California at Berkeley
1 Isaac Ehrlich, 'Participation in Illegitimate Activities: An Economic Analysis,' in G.S. Becker and W.M. Landis (eds), *Essays in the Economics of Crime and Punishment* (1974) 110
2 Police Chief McNamara, quoted in G. Kelling and A. Pate, *The Kansas City Preventive Patrol Experiment* (1974) iii
3 For a partial list of these studies, see G. Tullock, 'Does Punishment Deter Crime?' (1974) 36 *The Public Interest* 103; C.R. Tittle and C.H. Logan, 'Sanctions and Deviance: Evidence and Remaining Questions' (1973) 7 *Law and Society Review* 371; and P.J. Cook, 'Research in Criminal Deterrence: Laying the Groundwork for the Second Decade,' in *Crime and Justice: An Annual Review of Research*, vol. 2 (1980) 211.
4 See, for example, B. Schwartz, 'The Effect in Philadelphia of Pennsylvania's Increased Penalties for Rape and Attempted Rape' (1968) 59 *Journal of Criminal Law, Criminology, and Police Science* 509; H.L. Ross, 'Law, Science, and Accidents: The British Safety Act of 1967' (1973) 2 *Journal of Legal Studies* 1; F. Zimring, 'Firearms and Federal Law: The Gun Control Act of 1968' (1975) 4 *Journal of Legal Studies* 133 (a partial bibliography of intervention studies is in note 5, at 134); Mitre Corporation, *High Impact Anti-Crime Program: National Level Evaluation Final Report* (1978).
5 Kelling and Pate, supra note 2
6 Lawrence Sherman and Richard Berk, 'The Specific Deterrent Effect of Arrest for Domestic Violence' (1984) 49 *American Sociological Review* 261. See also Richard Berk and Phyllis Newton, 'Does Arrest Really Deter Wife Battery? An Effort to Replicate the Findings of the Minneapolis Spouse Abuse Experiment' (1985) 50 *American Sociological Review* 253. Other examples of 'real change' studies are the high-impact anti-crime program, the alcohol safety action program, and the 'Rockefeller drug law' program, which are described in F. Zimring, 'Policy Experiments in General Deterrence: 1970–1975,' in A. Blum-

stein, J. Cohen, and D. Nagin (eds), *Deterrence and Incapacitation: Estimating the Effects of Criminal Sanctions on Crime Rates* (1978), from which much of the material in this paper has been drawn.

7 For a dialogue on this topic between Richard Larson and the principal authors of the Kansas City report, see R.C. Larson, 'What Happened to Patrol Operations in Kansas City? A Review of the Kansas City Preventive Patrol Experiment' (1975) 3 *Journal of Criminal Justice* 267, and T. Pate, G.L. Kelling, and C. Brown, 'A Response to "What Happened to Patrol Operations in Kansas City?"' (1975) 3 *Journal of Criminal Justice* 299.

8 See A. Blumstein, J. Cohen, and D. Nagin (eds), *Deterrence and Incapacitation: Report of the Panel of Research on Deterrence and Incapacitation, National Academy of Science* (1978).

9 This problem is less serious in settings like Kansas City and in a high-impact program, where the amount of resources invested in prevention is great, than in cases where change occurs more gradually or is less costly. For a case study in which this issue is more troublesome, see H.L. Ross, 'The Scandinavian Myth: The Effectiveness of Drinking-and-Driving Legislation in Sweden and Norway' (1978) 4 *Journal of Legal Studies* 285, at 309–10.

10 Negative or inconclusive results are reported in all the analyses mentioned in note 4, except the Ross article. See also F. Zimring, 'Policy Experiment in General Deterrence 1970–1975,' in Blumstein, Cohen and Nagin, supra note 6.

11 See F. Zimring and G. Hawkins, *Deterrence: The Legal Threat in Crime Control* (1973) 339–67.

12 Tullock, supra note 3, 105

13 Ibid., 107

14 Ibid., 110–11. See also Ernest van den Haag, *Punishing Criminals* (1974) 133–42. Only one intervention study, a classroom experiment, is mentioned.

15 Jack Gibbs, a scholar whom Professor Tullock credits with the first published cross-sectional research in this field, is sceptical of the implications for deterrence. See Gibbs, *Crime, Punishment, and Deterrence* (1975).

16 Ibid., 145–88

17 Tullock, supra note 3, 104

18 Compare I. Ehrlich, 'Participation in Illegitimate Activities: A Theoretical and Empirical Investigation' (1973) 81 *Journal of Political Economy* 521, with B.E. Forst, 'Participation in Illegitimate Activities: Some Further Empirical Findings' (1976) 2 *Policy Analysis* 477. See also Blumstein, Cohen, and Nagin, supra note 6.

6 Sanctions and Rewards: The Approach of Psychology

JOAN E. GRUSEC*

One avowed purpose of the legal system is to facilitate compliance with the dictates of society. Through a system of rewards and sanctions – imprisonment, fines, deprivation of privileges, removal of licences, tax relief – society tries to mould the behaviour of its citizens so as to avert chaos and bring order to daily living. Psychology is a discipline that has addressed the issue of compliance at some length. Much research has been aimed at identifying the best techniques for gaining compliance from individuals and for modifying their behaviour. Although this has been the researchers' chief purpose, a closely related goal has been to understand the mechanisms underlying the manipulation of human behaviour so that people can be protected from the effects of persuasive agents who have anti-social intentions.

One must be under no illusion that the legal code of our society is perfect or that it represents the highest manifestation of an absolute morality. Any study of compliance must include an awareness of the importance of reasoned and thoughtful, rather than automatic, adherence to a set of values and rules. This issue has also been part of the psychological approach to the study of compliance.

Although the volume of which this paper is a part is addressed to both sanctions and rewards, it is probably safe to say that a substantial part of the legal system, and particularly the criminal justice system, maintains itself through the use of sanctions. Particularly when it comes to criminal acts, our society tends to assume that individuals should behave well 'naturally,' and that it is only when they cease to behave well that intervention is required. The major intervention is the imposition of punishment. For that reason much of this paper will be addressed to what psychology knows about the effectiveness of punishment as an agent of change.

The first section is concerned with what psychologists have learned about compliance. Because the study of compliance has been an extensive one, the initial discussion will centre on the discoveries psychological researchers have made about how to influence individuals to adopt what are considered to be appropriate standards of behaviour and how to deter them from unacceptable behaviour.

The second section turns from a consideration of the individual whose compliance is being sought to a consideration of the individual who seeks the compliance. Those members of society who have accepted societal norms are no less human than those who have chosen to reject those norms or those who are being encouraged to accept and internalize them. They have needs and proclivities that must also be considered if we are to understand the operation of the whole system. Do agents of social change have particular characteristics that make them more prone to use certain techniques of change, even if those techniques are not particularly effective? Does the system rely heavily on punishment because of the needs of society rather than because of the needs of the deviant member of society? If such is the case, then we must recognize that adequate understanding requires a consideration not only of the individual who is being censured (or, occasionally, encouraged), but also a consideration of those who create and enforce the system.

The third part of this paper is concerned with the issue of individual differences. It is a mistake to assume that, on the whole, all members of society are essentially similar, and that techniques that modify the behaviour of any one individual are techniques that will alter the behaviour of every individual. To some extent this is recognized by the legal system when attempts are made to tailor punishments to the perceived needs of the individual offender. The psychological research underlines the importance of this kind of individualized sentencing. Moreover, it suggests that punishment simply may not have the intended effect on certain people.

Techniques for Obtaining Compliance

What do psychologists know about how to gain compliance? The problem has been studied by social psychologists who have used mainly college students as their subjects, by developmental psychologists who have been concerned with the socialization of young children (that is, with the process whereby children come to take on, as their own, the values and attitudes of the society in which they are being raised), and by behavioural psychologists who have attempted to modify the deviant actions of neurotics, psychotics, aggressive children, and even, occasionally, lawbreakers. The focus in this paper will be most strongly on what developmental psychologists have had to say about socialization and compliance. Nevertheless, it should be realized that the social-psychological and developmental-psychological positions overlap to a great extent, and appear to reach essentially the same conclusions. There is some discrepancy in the approach to the study of conformity and in the conclusions, based on research findings, reached by social and developmental psychologists and by behavioural psychologists. Moreover, it is probably the position of the latter that has become best known in disciplines outside of psychology. For that reason it will be useful to try to understand why there are differences in the way compliance-getting is viewed by behavioural and by social and developmental psychologists, and to understand how differences between the two positions can be reconciled.

The Behavioural Approach

A position on reward and punishment that has had substantial impact on thinking both within and outside the discipline of psychology is that of the behaviourist B.F. Skinner.[1] Skinner argues that government, narrowly defined, is the use of the power to punish. He indicates that punishment consists, in the case of the government, of such events as the removal of positive reinforcers (dispossession of property, fines, punitive taxation, incarceration, or banishment), or the presentation of negative reinforcers (flogging, threat of injury or death, hard labour, and so on). Skinner argues that this system is wrong because punishment does not work. He believes that governments should control through positive reinforcement, using their ability to influence the behaviour of citizens through economic means: people can be induced to act legally through subsidies and bonuses for good behaviour, rather than being deterred through punishment from acting illegally.

A second approach Skinner espouses is the educational control of legal behaviour. Presentation of information about why a particular behaviour is desirable can be substituted for punishment and rewards. A soldier, rather than being induced to fight by threats of imprisonment or death if he refuses to go into battle, should be educated about the importance of defending one's country from invaders, protecting one's country from alien and undesirable influences, and defending freedom and liberty. People who go through stop signs can be deterred from further behaviour of this kind not by punishment, but by learning about the connection between reckless driving and its consequences – injury or death.

According to Skinner, the advantage of a more positive approach to inducing conformity – either the manipulation of positive reinforcement or education – is that it produces governments that are seen as just, and it leads to feelings of freedom in citizens (even though, it should be noted, they are no less controlled than they are in a system that uses punishment) and to greater feelings of security.

The Evidence

Skinner's beliefs about punishment were easily accepted because they had an intuitive appeal and because they argued for an apparently more positive and humane approach to behaviour modification. Unfortunately, however, they were based on flawed conclusions. Skinner derived his position from the results of early research conducted by himself[2] and by his student, William Estes.[3] Both of them trained rats to press a lever for a food reward. After the lever-pressing response had been learned, it was followed by punishment – a slap or an electric shock applied to the foot. Although punishment successfully suppressed the bar-pressing response as long as it reliably followed it, once the punishment was discontinued the bar-pressing response reappeared. On the basis of this evidence Skinner concluded that although positive reinforcement produces permanent alterations in behaviour, punishment results in only temporary suppressive effects.

The conclusion is a curious one. It is true that once the punishing stimulus is removed, the punished organism, if it does not have an alternative way of gaining reinforcement, will revert to the formerly punished behaviour. It is also true, however, that when positive reinforcement that has been made contingent on a response like bar-pressing is removed, responding decreases – the learned response is just as 'temporary' as it is in the case of punishment. Both punishment and positive reinforcement, then, have transient effects. One is no better than the other in its effectiveness. Later research has shown that punishment is indeed capable of suppressing unwanted behaviour, and that the more or less temporary suppression of that behaviour makes it possible, in the meantime, to teach the organism alternative techniques for gaining reinforcement. (This research is described at length by Walters and Grusec.)[4] The conclusion is that moderate levels of punishment, administered by a humane and caring agent so that the contingency between the individual's behaviour and the aversive outcome is clear, are just as effective in controlling behaviour as is the use of positive reinforcements such as food, water, and money.

Side-Effects of Punishment

Some people who have accepted that punishment is an effective control technique have nevertheless argued that its use has undesirable side-effects which the use of positive reinforcement does not have. It is argued that punished organisms experience an increase in aggressive propensities which they direct toward the punishing agent or displace to another person or object.[5] There are data that support this contention, although the results can be explained in terms other than the arousal of aggression after punishment. We know that frustration of any kind (for example, removal of a positive reinforcer), not only that induced by punishment, leads to an increase in the organism's arousal, and that this produces an increased vigour in responding which observers may label aggressive.[6] The important thing to note is that this increased vigour in responding occurs in a variety of situations, not just those involving punishment.

It can also be argued that punishment provides a model of aggressive behaviour, and that the strong human propensity to imitate means that the recipient of punishment will use that model to guide his or her own behaviour. Indeed, this is a serious criticism of the use of punishment. Punishment is a coercive form of control that relies on the superior strength of the parent, the state, or whoever is administering it. Yet our legal and moral system says that it is not permissible to take what we want through the use of force. It seems counter-productive to use as a technique of control the very behaviour one is trying to eliminate. Although the form of deviant behaviour might be altered somewhat, the occasion of punishment becomes one of informing the recipient that force is an acceptable and useful control technique. Nor can it be argued that people would be reluctant to model aggressive behaviour when they themselves had been its victim. For example, consider the literature on child abuse. It is frequently observed that parents who abuse their children were themselves abused when they were children.[7] Although this happens in a minority of cases, it is evident that being abused as a child does put one at some degree of risk for becoming abusive.[8] Even though they have experienced firsthand the unpleasantness of abuse, some individuals nevertheless direct it toward their own unfortunate offspring.

Other deleterious side-effects of punishment may be less serious. It has been suggested that punishment causes the organism to escape from the punitive situation.[9] Children or adults who experienced aversive consequences contingent on a specific behaviour would be expected to remove themselves from further contact with the source of punishment. If the punishing agent is also a source of reinforcement, however, this becomes a less viable alternative. Only agents who dispense punishment and nothing else will produce escape behaviour. Punishment is supposed to lead to neurotic behaviour. But so-called demonstrations of this phenomenon[10] have been misleading. Animals placed in situations where there is no correct response, and where aversive outcomes occur regardless of how they behave, display 'abnormal fixations': they develop perseverative responses even when the problem is ultimately made soluble. But if the problem is soluble from the beginning, the use of punishment for an incorrect response does not appear to produce abnormal responses. Finally, it is argued that punishment can produce an inappropriate suppression of related responses.[11] A favourite example is that of the child who is punished for masturbating and who, it is said, will have difficulty engaging in socially acceptable sexual activities in adulthood. Again, however, the evidence suggests this need not be the case. Moderate levels of punishment, *administered so that the contingency between response and outcome is clear*, do not produce inappropriate levels of generalization.

The Social and Developmental Approaches

Developmental and social psychologists diverge somewhat from Skinner's position on punishment and reward. They argue that control by *either* punishment *or* reward is ineffective. For developmentalists the goal of behaviour control, or socialization, is to get children to conform to the rules of society in the absence of external surveillance. Rules, values, and behaviours must be internalized; that is, they must be accepted by the individual as his or her own. In the end, socially acceptable behaviour should be performed not because it produces certain external consequences, but because of self-administered approval and disapproval. The notion of conscience is more central in this conception. We should tell the truth, not be aggressive toward others, and be honest, not in order to avoid punishment or to gain reward, but because we truly believe this is the best way to behave. Unlike Skinner, many social developmental psychologists argue that we do not want to maintain behaviour by having to provide positive reinforcement. Honesty, for example, must be its own reward.

How is internalization achieved, then, if reliance on externally imposed rewards and punishments is ruled out? Skinner's third technique of control – education – becomes important. Developmentalists refer to it as 'reasoning.' Internalization is also achieved through the process of identification, whereby children take on the values of society through becoming like the exemplars of those values, usually their parents. Each of these approaches will be discussed.

The Use of Reasoning

Although all kinds of reasoning are believed to be useful in the promotion of internalization, one form has been singled out as particularly important. This is 'empathic reasoning,' or reasoning that points out to children the effect of their behaviour on others. Martin Hoffman has argued that children whose deviations are responded to in this way will be those who best internalize the standards of society.[12] The best response to a child who assaults a playmate is not to hit her in retaliation, not to send her to her room, and not to pat her on the back, praise her, or give her her favourite food when she plays non-aggressively, but to explain to her that hitting people is not an appropriate behaviour because it hurts them and it makes them feel bad. Hoffman maintains that empathic reasoning is advantageous for several reasons. First of all, it does not provide a model of undesirable behaviour as does punishment. Second, it does not produce anger and reactance (that is, the tendency of people who feel coerced to engage in behaviour that is the opposite of what is being required). Nor does it lead to high levels of arousal, which can be generated by punitive consequences and which interfere with effective learning. Finally, empathically oriented reasoning does not necessitate continued surveillance by agents of socialization. The use of external contingencies as techniques for gaining compliance means that someone must always be on hand to administer them. But the knowledge of having harmed others is always present, since it is self-generated: it can never be escaped. And this knowledge leads to feelings of guilt – feelings that deter the individual from future repetitions of the anti-social act.

Data relevant to these assertions are provided by Hoffman and Saltzstein.[13] They measured the morality of seventh-grade children in a variety of ways. First, they used a 'projection' technique in which children were asked to complete a story about a child who had transgressed (in one story a child's negligence had contributed to the death of a younger child; in another a child cheated in a swimming race and won), telling what the central character felt and thought and what happened afterward. Responses to stories were coded for guilt (extreme guilt, for example, was coded if the protagonist underwent a personality change or committed suicide). Next, children were asked to make judgments about several hypothetical transgressions. Those judgments were coded for an orientation toward control by fear ('You can go to jail for that') or control by internal means ('It's wrong to violate someone's trust in you'). Behavioural reactions to transgression were assessed by asking the children's teachers and mothers to describe how the child typically reacted after wrongdoing. In order to relate the children's morality to the compliance techniques used by their parents, Hoffman and Saltzstein asked the parents to imagine four concrete situations involving a child's misbehaviour – delayed compliance with a parent's request, careless destruction, talking back, and academic failure – and to select, from a list of possible disciplinary techniques, a means of responding.

Hoffman and Saltzstein found that frequent use of 'power assertion' by the mother – physical punishment, deprivation of material objects or privileges, application of force, or the threat of any of these things – was consistently associated with weak moral development in the child. The use of empathic reasoning was consistently associated with advanced moral development, and 'love withdrawal' – ignoring the child, isolating her, or showing dislike – did not relate strongly to moral development. No consistent set of relationships emerged between paternal training and the child's moral development.

Although the direction of relationship obviously cannot be determined from such a correlational study (better-behaved children, for example, may require only gentle techniques such as reasoning to induce them to comply, while those less well-developed morally may need stronger forms of intervention from their parents), Hoffman and Saltzstein's investigation certainly provides support for the contention that the use of empathically oriented reasoning, at least by mothers, can be effective in promoting compliance. As well, a number of other studies have demonstrated a significant correlation between the use of reasoning by mothers and the moral development of their children. These studies have been summarized by Hoffman.[14] In another study, Hoffman found that mothers who used empathic reasoning (in contrast to parents who relied on withdrawal of love) were also inclined to use power-assertive techniques when their children failed to comply.[15] This finding will be discussed below.

The use of empathic reasoning has other virtues besides the promotion of moral development. An adequate approach to understanding compliance should include a consideration of the promotion of reasoned and thoughtful, rather than automatic, adherence to society's norms. Hoffman dealt with this issue in an analysis of the production of guilt during socialization.[16] Recall that Hoffman and Saltzstein found no relationship between parental withdrawal of love and moral development. Although reasoning and withdrawal of love are both compliance techniques that produce an internal moral orientation, they differ in the form this internalization takes. From an analysis of responses to projective tasks, Hoffman observed that children of reasoning parents were humanistic in their approach, and demonstrated empathy and identification with parents who were responsive to extenuating circumstances and sensitive to the importance of considering others. Their guilt after deviation was benign, with a potentially constructive effect on personality (in the sense that concern for the condition of others might be heightened). In contrast, children whose parents withdrew love tended to demonstrate a conventional approach of rigid adherence to institutional norms regardless of consequences and circumstances. Guilt in these children was less constructive than in the humanistic children, and was sometimes even destructive, consisting as it did of a withdrawal of parental love turned inward and a heightened arousal occasioned by dread of abandonment. The heightened arousal, according to Hoffman, makes the child unaware of or unable to attend to the plight of others, and so empathic sensitivity to others is blunted. We can conclude, to the extent that Hoffman's analysis has merit, that an approach to socialization and induction of compliance that involves sensitizing individuals to the impact of their behaviour on others will also lead to flexibility in thinking and the ability to think constructively about one's own adherence to societal norms.

Attribution Theory

A different theoretical approach to the understanding of compliance is provided by attribution theory, which finds its roots in social psychology.[17] Its conclusions about the most effective compliance technique are not markedly different from those of Hoffman, even though most of the early research on attribution was conducted with adults. According to attribution theory, people are always looking for explanations for their own behaviour and the behaviour of others. If the server at dinner compliments me on my choice of wine, I tend to wonder why she did it. I may attribute her behaviour to her genuine admiration of my knowledge and good taste, or to her desire for a large tip. The attribution will, of course, have some effect on my subsequent behaviour, including the size of the tip I leave. More important for present purposes are self-attributions – that is, the explanations individuals have for their own behaviour. Of particular relevance to the notion of internalization are the concepts of 'insufficient justification' and 'overly sufficient justification.'[18] If people perceive that they have behaved in a certain way because of strong external pressure to do so, their value systems will not change to conform with that behaviour as much as they would if they were unable to perceive any external pressure. It is suggested that children and adults who perceive that they have been coerced into conformity should be less likely to internalize moral standards (that is, to behave in accord with societal dictates in the absence of surveillance) than should those with less consciousness of having been coerced.[19] Techniques that minimize feelings of coercion include persuasion, education, and reasoning. Individuals who are induced to conform through education or reasoning can find little external justification for their behaviour, and so they come to believe that they have conformed with the wishes of agents of socialization because it is the 'right' thing to do.

The importance of minimal force in the induction of compliance is demonstrated in a study by Lepper.[20] Children were brought into a laboratory where they were induced not to play with an attractive toy by being threatened either mildly ('If you play with it, I will be a little bit annoyed with you') or severely ('If you play with it, I will be very upset and angry with you'). Three weeks later the children were placed in a situation where they had the opportunity to cheat. Fewer children in the mild-threat group cheated than in the severe-threat group. Lepper suggests that children who had been mildly threatened were more likely to attribute compliance with the experimenter's instruction not to play with the forbidden toy to internal causes, because there was little obvious external justification for this compliance. This presumably led to a change in their own value systems, and they continued to behave in accord with their changed value system in a new situation by cheating less. Indeed, Lepper found that children in the mild-threat group, when asked to fill out an adjective checklist, rated themselves as more honest than those in the severe-threat group, which suggests that their perceptions of themselves had been somewhat altered.

The attributional approach does require a major refinement to the picture of the most effective control technique as that based on education, persuasion, reasoning, and, particularly, empathically oriented reasoning. If children are to make internal attributions about their behaviour, and thereby internalize the standards of society, it is necessary for them to perform the behaviour in the first place. Indeed, it is imperative that pro-social, not anti-social, behaviour be elicited from them. Internal attributions about anti-social behaviour could have devastating consequences. But how does one ensure that socially acceptable behaviour is exhibited? This is accomplished only by the threat of punishment for unacceptable behaviour or the promise of reward for acceptable behaviour, approaches that mitigate against internalization. How is the seeming paradox to be resolved? The attributional analysis suggests that the salience of external consequences must be reduced by their being paired with persuasive educational techniques. In Hoffman's study, parents who used empathically oriented reasoning were often inclined to pair that reasoning with punishment. Hoffman suggested that in these cases the punishment was necessary for the voice of reason to be attended to. The attributional analysis suggests that reasoning is necessary in order that punishment be less attended to.

Research Support

Two different theoretical approaches argue for essentially the same approach to inducing compliance. We have already seen that correlational evidence exists to support Hoffman's thesis about the importance of reasoning. Another major study of the relationship between child-rearing practices and the internalization of standards has also provided evidence for the proposition that reasoning paired with firm consequences for failure of obedience is the most effective approach to socialization. Baumrind carefully observed children and parents in the home, and interviewed parents about their disciplinary practices and attitudes.[21] On the basis of these observations and interview responses, she identified three types of parenting practices – authoritarian, authoritative, and permissive. *Authoritarian* techniques are used by parents who see obedience as a virtue and believe in restricting the child's autonomy. Preservation of order is valued as an end in itself. Authoritarian parents do not encourage give-and-take, and they are punitive. *Authoritative* parents direct their children's activities in a rational and issue-oriented manner. They set standards for conduct and they value compliance with reasonable rules, but they also respect the child's autonomy and individuality. *Permissive* parents were affirmative, accepting, and benign toward their children and their children's behaviour. The behaviour of permissive parents was characterized by an absence of restraint.

After classifying the three styles of parenting, Baumrind attempted to determine how effective each was in promoting socialization. Children from authoritative homes showed greater social responsibility (including such things as achievement orientation, friendliness toward peers, and co-operativeness toward adults) than children from authoritarian or permissive homes. The authoritative parents appeared to use a combination of external pressure and persuasion, discussion, and reasoning. The external pressure of these parents – what Baumrind referred to as firm control – was different from the restrictive, punitive control of authoritarian parents. This firm control involved consistency in enforcement of rules, structuring of the child's activities, the parent's sense that she was in control of the child's activity, and actual success on the part of the parent in gaining compliance from the child. Gentle but firm pressure, combined with a willingness to be flexible, marked the successful agent of socialization.

Implications for the Legal System

Both the child-socialization literature and the social-psychological literature addressed to adult conformity appear to lead to the same conclusions, which have implications for the general issue of compliance and the legal system. A striking difference between the legal system and the socialization system is the differential emphasis on education, reasoning, and persuasion rather than punishment. The research on socialization suggests that punishment, while necessary, must not loom large in the process of gaining compliance. The legal system, and particularly the criminal justice system, rests solidly on the presence of punishment. If at least one goal of the legal system is to modify behaviour, it goes about achieving that goal in quite the wrong way. The system must include external contingencies. People need to be motivated to adhere to society's demands. But psychology tells us that there should be an overlay of education aimed at acquainting non-conformers with the effects of their misdeeds. Convicted and potential drunken drivers should be made aware of the consequences of their thoughtless behaviour not only for themselves but for the well-being of others. The image of innocent victims and of the grief of bereaved loved ones should permeate their consciousness. Family violence may be curtailed not only by the presence of punitive consequences, but also by the offender's sensitization to the effects of violence on spouse and children. It is interesting to note that the educative function of law is possibly stressed more in the Soviet system than in our own.[22] That system has mechanisms to promote a sense of moral and legal responsibility among its citizens, including opportunities to remedy bad situations.

It must be emphasized that the psychological research shows clearly that unacceptable behaviour cannot be suppressed in the absence of real and tangible consequences. It is wrong to suppose that education programs should be administered as a substitute for punishment. It would be quite ineffective, for example, to ask drunken drivers with suspended licences to sit through a series of lectures about the effects of their behaviour on others if the reduction of punishment (for example, early reinstatement of the suspended licence) were made contingent on such an educational experience. The punishment must be real. The education must help the individual understand why the punishment is justified and modify her values accordingly.

The Prevention of Deviation

An adequate theory of socialization must deal not only with the suppression of undesirable behaviour, but with ways of preventing transgression in the first place. This preventive approach in the legal system is advocated, for example, by Ross in the case of drunken driving.[23] Prevention also plays an important role in child socialization. The most extensively studied approach to the prevention of deviation is the use of modelling.

Other techniques, such as structuring the environment so as to reduce the likelihood of deviation or non-compliance and attributing of pro-social characteristics to the child, will be discussed briefly.

Modelling

Through the process of identification, or incorporation of parental values, children adopt as their own the moral system of society. We have already seen how an adult's style of discipline provides an example for the child's attempts at eliciting compliance from others. Parents who rely on power assertion, for example, are teaching their children that compliance is best obtained through force. Parents who rely on reasoning and persuasion are teaching their children that compliance is best obtained through discussion and negotiation. A great deal of psychological evidence attests to the strength of adult and peer example in promoting pro-social (and anti-social) behaviour in young children.[24]

Many studies have shown that children will imitate adults who share, who help others in distress, and who set high standards of achievement for themselves. The situation with more passive forms of moral behaviour (for example, resistance to temptation) is somewhat more complex, although recent research lends strong support to the conclusion that modelling is an important ingredient in the inculcation of self-control.

Typically, studies in this area have been experimental. Children are usually asked to engage in a boring task, or not to play with an attractive toy. They then observe a 'model' who either complies with the same request, or yields to temptation and plays with the toy or fails to perform the boring task. The subject's subsequent willingness to comply with the experimenter's request when the experimenter is absent and the child is alone is assessed. It has been assumed to be important that the test of resistance to deviation occur when the child is not under surveillance, so as to achieve an adequate measure of internalization.

In one study, four- and five-year-old children were asked to sort a large collection of cards neatly according to colour.[25] While they did this they were left alone with 'Charlie,' a talking table who repeatedly tried to lure them away from their boring task to play with him and the attractive toys he had. Children in one experimental condition had previously observed an adult model who, when tempted by Charlie, told him she would like to play with him but could not because she had to work. In another condition, children observed a model who stated that playing with Charlie's toys was more fun than sorting cards and who subsequently gave up sorting cards and played with the toys instead. In a control condition Charlie did not tempt the model, so the child had no opportunity to witness someone either resisting or yielding to temptation. The outcome of these manipulations was that children who saw the model resist temptation took longer to yield to Charlie's tempting, and yielded for a shorter time, than did those in the control condition. Children who saw the adult set an example of self-indulgence yielded more quickly and for a longer time than did those in the control condition.

In addition to demonstrating that individuals will imitate models who resist temptation, researchers have also shown that the consequences of models' behaviour affect the willingness of observers to imitate them. Children who see another child punished for aggression are less likely to imitate the aggression than if they see the behaviour go unpunished.[26] This finding has implications, then, for the issue of general deterrence. The psychological literature certainly suggests that observing offenders being punished should keep people from engaging in the punished acts themselves: if they see deviant behaviour go unpunished, the probability that they will perform similar acts themselves on some future occasion may increase.

Structuring the Environment

Successful parents do not make demands for compliance without taking into account the likelihood that their demands will be met. The wisdom of this approach is clear from earlier arguments made in the discussion of attribution theory: a child who fails to comply will make attributions that are not helpful in the promotion of internalization. The research suggests that even before their children possess the cognitive capacities to make attributional inferences, however, mothers who are best at obtaining compliance are those who make sure their child is in a position to give it. Structuring the environment so as to promote pro-social behaviour may have its effect through other mechanisms than those of altering attributions.

Shopping with a young child in the supermarket can be the source of much aggravation for a mother. Holden observed mothers of two-and-a-half-year-olds in this setting to see how they dealt with the problems posed by it.[27] Those who were most successful at avoiding demands for ice cream and candy or unwanted motor activity (such as pulling packages off shelves) made frequent use of 'proactive controls': they distracted their children's attention from the temptations of the supermarket shelves by engaging them in conversation (often about shopping) or in some other activity such as eating, looking at books, or holding the shopping list. In interviews the mothers said that they felt they should 'childproof' their children's environments; one mother expressed the sentiment in the following words: 'I guess I'm a great avoidance person. I try to never let it happen. I try to anticipate and therefore fix it so we don't run into a lot of confrontations.'[28] Schaffer and Crook report similar attempts by mothers to structure environments for their children.[29] They noted that mothers who were able to induce their young children to play with a wide variety of toys in an experimental laboratory (in response to a request made by the experimenter) were those who oriented the child's attention to the toys before requesting that they play with them, or who waited until the child was spontaneously oriented to the toy, thus making it easier for the children to comply.

Character Attribution

In the discussion of attribution theory it was assumed that children were making inferences about their own behaviour. It is possible, however, for others to make attributions about a child's behaviour, a procedure that also produces modifications in subsequent behaviour. In one investigation psychologists had teachers and the principal of a school tell children that they were the kind of people who are neat and clean. In contrast to children who had been exhorted to be neat and clean, and to a control group that received no intervention, those who had neatness attributed to them subsequently littered less.[30] The technique, of course, requires that the character attribution be believable. It would tax the credibility of a socializing agent were he to argue that a demonstrably belligerent individual was actually peace-loving. Character attribution requires that pro-social behaviour actually be elicited, and in a way that minimizes external coercion. If the behaviour can be attributed to the external coercion, it will not be attributed to an internal, or character, disposition.

The usefulness of this line of reasoning is demonstrated in an experiment by Grusec, Kuczynski, Rushton, and Simutis.[31] They induced children to donate winnings from a game to poor children either by having them watch someone else do it (an ambiguous inducement) or by instructing them to do so (an unambiguous coercion). After they had shared the winnings, the children's donation was attributed either to a personal characteristic of generosity ('You must have shared because you're the kind of person who likes to help others') or to external coercion ('You must have shared because you thought I expected you to'). In a subsequent test of generosity, conducted when the children were alone, those who had been given the character attribution shared more than those whose behaviour had been attributed to external pressure, but only when their initial sharing had been induced by observing a generous model. For those who were originally instructed to share, their attribution condition made no difference. Presumably they knew why they had donated and were less receptive to, or less in need of, the suggestion of the experimenter.

Implications for the Legal System

Modelling, structuring the child's environment, and character attribution are all ways of trying to prevent the initial occurrence of anti-social behaviour. Given that successful parents are probably those who rely on these approaches to as great an extent as possible, one could argue by analogy that a successful society would be one that attempted to reduce temptation for its citizens, provided examples of pro-social behaviour, and attributed good behaviour on the part of its citizenry to their own desires rather than to fear of external consequences. An example of the official use of modelling in the legal system is provided by Berman.[32] He notes that many Soviet writers are concerned that respect for law among the masses cannot be achieved unless officials show the same respect for the law in their actions. In our own country a similar concern is evidenced in the Charter of Rights and Freedoms, which provides that evidence against an individual shall be excluded if its admission would bring the administration of justice into disrepute.[33] This provision is an acknowledgment of the potentially dangerous effects of deviant examples on the behaviour of those who see them.

The Function of Punishment

In our society we tend to believe that a major function of punishment is to deter law-abiding individuals from crime and to reform those who have failed to abide by society's rules. In the preceding pages of this paper discussion has focused on how the legal system can most effectively promote reform and resistance to temptation. But an additional function of punishment and the legal system may be one we are less willing to recognize, although that makes it no less real. Society may want retribution for crimes committed against it. An adequate analysis of the legal system requires consideration not only of the needs of the deviant individual but of the needs of society. A consideration of recent trends in research on child development and parent-child interaction, and of social psychological theories that suggest that people need to see justice served, is instructive here.

New Trends in Socialization Research

Traditionally, the socialization process has been studied predominantly from a unidirectional perspective in which the child was assumed to be a passive recipient of the parent's influence. The goal was to understand how general styles of parental influence (for example, permissiveness and authoritarianism) determine certain personality characteristics of the child (such as aggressiveness and conformity). Certainly, parents have an effect on their children's behaviour. But psychologists have increasingly come to recognize that children also have an effect on their parents' behaviour. It is true that parents are in an advantageous position because they are more powerful than their children. (The legal system is also in a more advantageous position because it is more powerful than individual citizens.) But parents are human. They respond emotionally; they have needs and desires that come into play in any discipline situation.

A number of variables have been shown to have an impact on parents' behaviour. Among these are the physical attractiveness of the child, the child's reaction to punishment, and the nature of the misdemeanour in which the child has engaged.

Attractiveness of the child as a determinant of adult perceptions and behaviour. Dion gave female college students a brief description of a child's transgression, and showed them a picture of the so-called perpetrator.[34] Half of the subjects saw a picture of an attractive child, half a picture of an unattractive child. Those who believed the misdeed had been committed by an unattractive child evaluated the transgression as more undesirable than those who believed it had been committed by an attractive child. Unattractive transgressors were also rated as more dishonest and more unpleasant than their attractive counterparts. In the case of severe transgressions, such as injuring a dog by throwing stones at it, unattractive children were also more likely to be perceived as anti-social in disposition. Attractiveness influenced adults' assumptions about the child's character as well as evaluations of the transgression.

Attractiveness also influences an adult's behaviour. In another study, college students monitored the videotaped task performance of an attractive or an unattractive child and administered penalties for incorrect responses. Women were more lenient in their administration of punishment with an attractive boy than they were with either an attractive or an unattractive girl. Men were not influenced by either the sex or the attractiveness of the child.[35]

The child's response to her misdeed as a determinant of adult behaviour. Parents often modify their disciplinary actions in response to the child's own reaction to her misdeed. In an experimental demonstration of this phenomenon,[36] female college students were shown a videotape of a supposedly 'live' display of anti-social behaviour by a seven-year-old boy who pushed another child's workbook off his desk. The boy responded in one of four ways both before and after punishment had been administered by an adult who had witnessed the transgression: he offered to pick up the book (an attempt at reparation); he pleaded with the adult for leniency; he ignored the adult by turning his back; or he acted defiantly ('It was a dumb book anyway'). Defiance and ignoring caused the subjects observing these events to recommend more punishment than did attempts at reparation on the part of the child. In fact, reparation tended to elicit a mild reward.

Nature of the misdeed. No theory of socialization maintains that particular disciplinary techniques will be more effective than other disciplinary techniques in suppressing certain misdeeds but not others. The assertion that reasoning and punishment together are favoured behaviour-modification techniques does not carry a caveat stating that it applies only to particular misdeeds. And yet a number of recent studies strongly indicate that parents, in reality, are selective in the techniques of discipline they use in response to a variety of misdeeds.

This selectivity was first demonstrated in a study in which mothers of four- and seven-year-olds heard tapes depicting a child engaging in several different kinds of misdemeanours (not coming to dinner when called, breaking a vase by bouncing a ball in the house, fighting with another child, refusing to share, and making fun of an elderly man).[37] Each mother was asked to imagine that it was her own child in the tape, and to describe how she would respond to the child's behaviour. Misdeeds typically elicited the use of more than one disciplinary technique, with a variation in types of techniques depending on the misdeed. Acts that produced harm to persons – either to the child or to someone else – caused mothers to describe rules or explain the physical or emotional consequences of the child's behaviour for the child or for others. Disobedience and damage to physical objects elicited power-assertive techniques such as physical punishment, withdrawal of privileges, and making the child engage in appropriate behaviour. Often these interventions were paired with some kind of reasoning. It appears that mothers may use reasoning when they feel it important to promote the internalization of a universal norm (you do not hurt other people's feelings, you do not steal, you do not endanger your life by running into the street without looking), and that they employ power-assertive techniques when the goal is to establish immediate control over the child's behaviour.

Evidence that mothers tailor the discipline to the misdeed has also been provided by several other researchers. Zahn-Waxler and Chapman asked mothers to keep records of actual misdeeds engaged in by their young (one- to two-and-a-half-year-old) children and to describe how they responded to them.[38] In a real-life setting they found results that paralleled those cited above. Mothers reported that they would talk to their children about the meaning or consequences of an act or engage in dramatic enactments of distress when the misdeed involved harm against people (such as pinching the baby). Transgressions involving property destruction (drawing on the couch with marking pens) or lack of self-control (spitting in one's milk) elicited both power assertion, such as physical punishment or restraint, and withdrawal of love, such as sending the child to another part of the house. The researchers suggested that parents may attempt to make children aware of the consequences of their behaviour for others so as to sensitize them to the reactions of others, and because they believe that power assertion may transmit a contradictory message to the child about the acceptability of aggression toward others. Property destruction and lack of self-control are particularly inclined to provoke anger in mothers, and thus may lead to aggression on their part. The separation from the child that often accompanied power-assertive techniques may be a way of protecting the child from further anger, which could result in harmful levels of punishment (for example, physical abuse).

Another study that demonstrates the matching of misdeed and parent reaction is one by Grusec, Dix, and Mills.[39] Mothers were read short descriptions of children's misdeeds, and then asked to show, by role-playing, how they would respond if the children in the story were theirs. In this case misdeeds fell into two general categories: anti-social acts such as lying, stealing, and aggression, and failure to engage in pro-social acts such as helping, showing concern for others, and sharing. Following are two examples of the stories used:

> You are in the habit of leaving loose change in a bowl on your dresser. One day you see your child playing with a new toy he (she) has been begging for, which you know costs three dollars. It turns out that he (she) took the money from the bowl on your dresser. (Anti-social act.)
>
> Your child is waiting impatiently to be picked up by his (her) friend's family who are taking him (her) to the country for a picnic. Suddenly he (she) remembers that he (she) has promised to bring his (her) frisbee along. You are holding the baby, so your friendly neighbour rushes in to get it for him (her). As she comes out the door with the frisbee, your child calls, 'Hurry up! They're here!' In her excitement the neighbour trips on the step and falls, landing in a heap at the bottom. Your child ignores the fact that she might be hurt and says, 'Quick, give me the frisbee!' (Failure to engage in a pro-social act.)

Again, discipline depended on the nature of the misdeed. Anti-social acts were dealt with more punitively than failures to be pro-social, possibly because anti-social acts reflect violations of more universally agreed-upon norms. In our culture there is some ambivalence about the display of pro-social behaviour – sometimes, for example, we discourage sharing or excessive sacrifice for others in the interest of the individual's own rights. The researchers also found that mothers were more punitive when they, rather than a neighbour or a peer, were the victims of the child's misdeed. The anger aroused by being not only an observer but a recipient of misdeeds may simply intensify the punitive response.

Studies of the effects of child variables and characteristics demonstrate that a number of these affect the punitiveness of intervention on the part of agents of socialization. There is often no 'logical' reason for the effect.

Reactions to misdemeanours are affected by the nature of the misdemeanour, for example, although there is no evidence that this matching is particularly facilitative of behaviour change. It seems reasonable to propose, however, that such things as the amount of anger aroused by a misdeed, the sureness that the agent of socialization feels about the correctness of her position, the physical attractiveness of the wrongdoer, and the reaction of the deviant individual to threats of punishment all have an effect on the punishing agent that is apparently unrelated to a desire to modify behaviour.

To be added to these variables is the need of individuals to see the world as fair and wrongdoers as having been suitably penalized. This need has been the object of inquiry by social psychologists, and we shall turn to it now.

Belief in a Just World and Equity

People believe in a 'just world' in which individuals get what they deserve and deserve what they get.[40] They expect that goodness will triumph and evil will be vanquished. Such a belief serves an important psychological function because it allows the individual to see the world as a safe, stable, and reasonably predictable place; she can lead her life confident that things will go well. Although much research that demonstrates the importance of belief in a just world focuses on attitudes to victims (who, for example, are often denigrated so that their suffering is seen as 'just'), it is clear that the need to view the world in this manner also leads to a need to punish perpetrators of injustice whenever possible. If we are to lead lives free of anxiety, we must know that those who are evil will suffer.

Equity theory contains the same notions.[41] It suggests that individuals strive to maintain equal ratios of effort and reward both for themselves and for others. Victims of injustice who find themselves in a situation of inequity can attempt to restore equity in a variety of ways. One way is to deny that they have suffered, or to minimize their own suffering, but this usually happens only when there appears to be little hope of changing the inequitable situation.[42] When the situation *can* be changed, actual equity can be restored either by seeking compensation from the exploiter or by seeking retaliation. We see, then, that there are good psychological reasons for expecting society to seek revenge.

131 The Approach of Psychology

We do not know how universal is the need to restore equity or to believe in a just world. There may well be a biological predisposition to this need, or the need may be a culturally determined one. Even if the need does occur in all cultures, the nature of what is considered suitable revenge may differ from society to society.

Implications for the Legal System

Psychological research and theorizing attest to the fact that agents of socialization are human beings with emotions and needs that affect their attempts at gaining compliance. Those emotions and needs may not always be conducive to the use of the most effective compliance techniques. Anger frequently leads to power-assertive tactics, which, in the extreme, can produce child abuse. Some transgressions – for reasons we can only speculate about – elicit greater anger, and possibly a greater need for revenge, than others. If the legal system is to be modified to increase its effectiveness, it must take into account the needs of society as well as the needs of the law-breaker. Some crimes may be considered more repugnant than others (either universally or by virtue of a particular society's attitudes toward them), and any attempts to make their consequences less punitive may require changing society's attitudes. Behaviour-modification programs, for example, which call for the rewarding of good behaviour, may be difficult to institute when the public's belief is that criminals should not be 'coddled' or provided with more than the minimal necessities of life. In the final analysis, the punitiveness of our legal system may exist more for the sake of society than for the sake of the law-breaker.

Individual Differences in Responsiveness to Sanctions and Rewards

Developmental psychologists have recently begun to realize that there are large individual differences in how children react to the same events. The study of child temperament, pioneered in the work of Thomas, Chess, and Birch,[43] is the event that has chiefly oriented researchers to these differences. The evidence indicates that children differ from birth in fussiness, activity level, ease of adaptation to sleeping schedules, distractability, and attention span. Moreover, some children have a preference for orienting to people rather than to inanimate objects, and other children tend to be insensitive to painful events. The basis of these temperamental differences is assumed to be biological, because there is some evidence for their heritability and because they appear very early, before differential experience could have had an effect on child behaviour.[44]

One of the effects of individual differences in temperament is to make children differentially responsive to parental discipline. Children who are prone to orient to people, for example, may be easily influenced by social approval and disapproval of their behaviour; such an approach may work less well for children who are less socially oriented.[45] The problem has been addressed in the work of Gerald Patterson.[46] Patterson and his colleagues observed the mutual encounters of aggressive and non-aggressive boys with their parents and siblings in the home, and looked at moment-by-moment interactions. Although Patterson had originally believed that aggressive children behaved as they did because they were rewarded for aggression in the home, he found no evidence for this belief. Instead, he found that aggressive children were different from non-aggressive children in their reaction to punishment. Non-aggressive children were less likely to continue their aggressive behaviour when they were punished for it, and aggressive children were more likely to continue. The aggressive children appeared insensitive to punishment.

Implications for the Legal System

The developmental research points to the differential effect of the same event on individuals. It emphasizes the importance for the legal system of individualizing sanctions: a technique that might be successful in modifying the behaviour of one law-breaker might be quite unsuccessful in modifying the behaviour of another. (The ultimate example of this is the individual who breaks windows in order to be put into jail so he will have a roof over his head and some food to eat. In these circumstances, jail is a reward, not a sanction.) In order to produce appropriate changes in behaviour, the system must be able to provide a solution for each individual by looking at her response to punishment in the past. It does little good simply to process people through the system, with little thought given to individual characteristics and responsiveness.

Conclusion

The research and theory of developmental psychologists concerned with the socialization of children provides several general principles for an understanding of the use of sanctions and rewards in the legal system. First, it suggests that education should play a more prominent role in the system than sanctions, and that education should go hand in hand with sanctions. No system of behaviour modification should be geared at producing obedient automata who thoughtlessly adhere to the rules. As long as the rules are imperfect, there must be room for questioning and negotiation. Some of the approaches discussed in this chapter are intended to produce that kind of flexibility. Second, the work of psychologists indicates that society itself has certain needs when it deals with those who have broken the law, and that these needs must be taken into consideration in any attempt at reform. Although we tend to criticize retribution as a part of the system, for example, it may be a necessary component. The legal system exists for the victim of transgression and for all members of society who witness the transgression, as well as for the perpetrator of the crime. The final principle discussed in this paper has to do with the issue of differential susceptibility to sanctions and rewards. Attempts to influence behaviour must be tailor-made to the individual being trained. It cannot be assumed that the same event has the same meaning to every individual.

A final word of caution is in order. One is ill-advised to generalize directly from principles developed in one domain, such as that of child socialization, to the domain of adult behaviour and the legal system. Nevertheless, those principles may offer some helpful guidelines for considering the function and usefulness of present and future systems.

Notes

* Professor, Department of Psychology, University of Toronto
1 B.F. Skinner, *Science and Human Behavior* (1953) chapter 22
2 B.F. Skinner, *The Behavior of Organisms* (1938)
3 W.K. Estes, 'An Experimental Study of Punishment' (1944) 57 *Psychological Monographs* no. 263
4 G.C. Walters and J.E. Grusec, *Punishment* (1977)

5 S. Feshbach, 'Aggression,' in P.H. Mussen (ed.) *Carmichael's Manual of Child Psychology*, 3d ed., vol. 1 (1970) 159
6 A. Bandura and R.H. Walters, *Social Learning and Personality Development* (1963)
7 J. Belsky and L.D. Steinberg, 'The Effects of Day Care: A Critical Review' (1978) 49 *Child Development* 929
8 J. Kaufman and E. Zigler, 'Do Abused Children Become Abusive Parents?' (1987) 57 *American Journal of Orthopsychiatry* 186
9 See, for example, R.S. Woodsworth and H. Schlosberg, *Experimental Psychology* (1955).
10 N.R.F. Maier, *Frustration: The Study of Behavior without a Goal* (1949); J.H. Masserman, *Behavior and Neurosis* (1943)
11 A. Mauer, 'Corporal Punishment' (1974) 29 *American Psychologist* 614
12 M.L. Hoffman, 'Moral Development,' in Mussen, supra note 5
13 M.L. Hoffman and H.D. Saltzstein, 'Parent Discipline and the Child's Moral Development' (1967) 5 *Journal of Personality and Social Psychology* 45
14 See Hoffman, supra note 12
15 M.L. Hoffman, 'Conscience, Personality and Socialization Techniques' (1970) 13 *Human Development* 90
16 Ibid.
17 H.H. Kelley, 'Attribution Theory in Social Psychology,' in D. Levine (ed.), (1967) 15 *Nebraska Symposium on Motivation* 192
18 R.E. Nisbett and S. Valins, *Perceiving the Causes of One's Own Behavior* (1971)
19 Walters and Grusec, supra note 4. See also M.R. Lepper, 'Intrinsic and Extrinsic Motivation in Children: Detrimental Effects of Superfluous Social Controls,' in W.A. Collins (ed.), (1981) *14 Minnesota Symposia on Child Psychology* 155.
20 M.R. Lepper, 'Dissonance, Self-Perception, and Honesty in Children' (1973) 25 *Journal of Personality and Social Psychology* 65
21 D. Baumrind, 'Current Patterns of Parental Authority' (1971) 4 *Developmental Psychology Monographs* no. 1, part 2; Baumrind, 'The Development of Instrumental Competence through Socialization,' in A. Pick (ed.), (1973) 7 *Minnesota Symposia on Child Psychology* 3
22 H.J. Berman, 'Foreword,' in *Soviet Education* (1972) 14
23 See H.L. Ross, 'Sociology and Legal Sanctions,' elsewhere in this volume.
24 See, for example, A. Bandura, *Social Learning Theory* (1976). Bandura, of Stanford University, has been the strongest proponent of the importance of imitation or modelling in the development of behaviour.
25 J.E. Grusec, L. Kuczynski, J.P. Rushton, and Z.M. Simutis, 'Learning Resistance to Temptation through Observation' (1979) 15 *Developmental Psychology* 233

26 A. Bandura, 'Influence of Models' Reinforcement Contingencies on the Acquisition of Imitative Responses' (1965) 1 *Journal of Personality and Social Psychology* 589
27 G.W. Holden, 'Avoiding Conflict: Mothers as Tacticians in the Supermarket' (1983) 54 *Child Development* 233
28 Ibid., 238
29 H.R. Schaffer and C.K. Crook, 'Child Compliance and Maternal Control Techniques' (1980) 16 *Developmental Psychology* 54
30 R.L. Miller, P. Brickman, and D. Bolen, 'Attribution Versus Persuasion as a Means for Modifying Behavior' (1975) 31 *Journal of Personality and Social Psychology* 430
31 J.E. Grusec, L. Kuczynski, J.P. Rushton, and Z.M. Simutis, 'Modeling, Direct Instruction, and Attributions: Effects of Altruism' (1978) 14 *Developmental Psychology* 51
32 See Berman, supra note 22.
33 Canadian Charter of Rights and Freedoms, part 1 of the Constitution Act, 1982, s. 24(2)
34 K.K. Dion, 'Physical Attractiveness and Evaluation of Children's Transgressions' (1972) 24 *Journal of Personality and Social Psychology* 207
35 K.K. Dion, 'Children's Physical Attractiveness and Sex as Determinants of Adult Punitiveness' (1974) 10 *Developmental Psychology* 772
36 R.D. Parke, 'Punishment in Children: Effects, Side-Effects, and Alternative Strategies,' in H.L. Hom Jr and P. Robinson (eds), *Early Childhood Education: A Psychological Perspective* (1976)
37 J.E. Grusec and L. Kuczynski, 'Direction of Effect in Socialization: A Comparison of the Parents' versus the Child's Behavior as Determinants of Disciplinary Techniques' (1980) 16 *Developmental Psychology* 1
38 C. Zahn-Waxler and M. Chapman, 'Immediate Antecedents of Caretakers' Methods of Discipline' (1982) 12 *Child Psychiatry and Human Development* 179
39 J.E. Grusec, T. Dix, and R. Mills, 'The Effects of Type, Severity and Victim of Children's Transgressions on Maternal Discipline' (1982) 14 *Canadian Journal of Behavioural Science* 276
40 M.J. Lerner, *The Belief in a Just World: A Fundamental Delusion* (1980)
41 J.S. Adams, 'Inequity in Social Exchange,' in L. Berkowitz (ed), (1965) 2 *Advances in Experimental Social Psychology* 267
42 E. Walster (Hatfield), G.W. Walster, and E. Berscheid, *Equity: Theory and Research* (1978)
43 A. Thomas, S. Chess, and H. Birch, *Temperament and Behavior Disorder in Children* (1968)
44 R.Q. Bell and M.F. Waldrop, 'Temperament and Minor Physical Anomalies,'

in Ciba Foundation Symposium 89, *Temperament Differences in Infants and Young Children* (1982)
45 R.Q. Bell, 'A Reinterpretation of the Direction of Effects in Studies of Socialization' (1968) 75 *Psychological Review* 81
46 G.R. Patterson, *Mothers: The Unacknowledged Victims* (1981)

7 Sanctions and Rewards: An Organizational Perspective

HUGH J. ARNOLD*

Most adults in our society spend a considerable part of their lives occupying various roles in formal organizations of which they are members. The nature of the organizations, the quality of their management, and the character of their systems of sanctions and rewards have a significant impact upon their members' feelings, attitudes, actions, and effectiveness. We are also heavily influenced by the nature of organizations with which we come into contact. The quality and effectiveness of those organizations determines the quality of our education, our health care, our legal services, our government services, our cultural life, and so on. Formal organizations are a ubiquitous component of modern society, and have a pervasive impact upon the nature and quality of our lives. The extent to which that impact is favourable is largely determined by the quality of the management of those organizations, and, as we shall see in what follows, the quality of management is itself largely dependent upon the way in which managers make use of sanctions and rewards.

In a fundamental sense, the role of management is to manipulate the behaviour of members of the organization. The term 'manipulation' is not used here in a pejorative sense, nor is it meant to imply that managers necessarily induce organization members to engage in activities against their will, or in activities to which they may object in any fundamental moral sense. Management's role is to ensure that members of the organization engage in the types of behaviour that management has deemed necessary or desirable if the organization is to meet its goals, accomplish its mission, and, at the most basic level, continue to exist.

Since behavioural manipulation is at the core of management, the issue whether this task is best accomplished through the use of sanctions, rewards, or some combination thereof has occupied an important place in organizational research for many years. In what follows I will first explore alternative assumptions that managers may make about the motivation of organization members, and the implications of these assumptions for the design of organizational systems of rewards and sanctions. I will then discuss the empirical research that has focused on the impact of various organizational systems of sanction and reward upon a variety of aspects of employee behaviour, such as absenteeism, adherence to safety regulations, and performance effectiveness. The paper concludes with a general discussion of the implications of the results of organizational research for the use of sanctions and rewards in the manipulation of the behaviour of individuals in organizations.

Assumptions and Their Implications

In 1960 Douglas McGregor published *The Human Side of Enterprise*. In that book he outlined two opposing sets of assumptions that managers hold about people in organizations. He labelled these two sets of assumptions Theory x and Theory y. Theory x managers assume that people are essentially lazy and that they dislike work. They further assume that people, on average, have little to contribute to their organizations, and little desire to contribute anything above and beyond the minimal requirements laid out for them by the organization. The Theory x assumption that workers are fundamentally lazy and recalcitrant leads to the view that the role of management is to force people, against their natural instincts, to work hard and do a good job. In order to prevent people from reverting to their natural state of sloth, management must construct a complex system of controls and sanctions. The outcome is an approach to management that emphasizes tight control, close supervision, and the development of elaborate systems of rules and regulations designed to prevent reversion to what are assumed to be natural patterns of behaviour which would be dysfunctional for the effectiveness of the organization. Since the role of management is seen as the *prevention* of dysfunctional behaviour patterns, there is a strong emphasis upon the development of sanctions and various forms of punishment designed to prevent people from manifesting their natural response tendencies.

In contrast to Theory x, Theory y managers assume that people have a great deal to contribute to their organizations, that people can and do enjoy working hard and doing things well, and that if given the opportunity people will take initiatives and contribute effectively to the success of the organization. The Theory Y assumptions lead to a very different set of implications for the role of management and the design of organizational control systems. Instead of designing elaborate monitoring and control systems to prevent the manifestation of people's naturally occurring dysfunctional behaviour patterns, the role of management becomes one of *encouraging* and *rewarding* the functional behaviours that individuals will naturally engage in if given the opportunity. The manager is not a policeman hired to prevent the manifestation of proscribed behaviours, but rather a supportive coach whose job is to encourage and reward people for engaging in the effective behaviours that come naturally to them.

McGregor argued that although Theory X assumptions had been widely prevalent in the design and management of organizations, the assumptions had remained untested, and were incorrect. It was his contention that the Theory Y assumptions represented a more accurate picture of the nature of human beings in relation to organizations. He further argued that the implementation of organizational management and control systems based upon Theory X assumptions has a variety of dysfunctional consequences for organizations and their members, consequences that are avoidable if Theory Y assumptions are made.

Dysfunctions of the Theory X Approach

Theory X assumptions lead to the design of organizational control systems that heavily emphasize proscription, prevention, and punishment. The organization must clearly tell people that the things they would naturally like to do are unacceptable, take steps to prevent their occurrence, and ensure that people understand that they will be punished for doing what is assumed to come naturally. The result is the development of an elaborate system of rules, regulations, and procedures that outline in detail what people must *not* do – for example, arrive late, leave early, take too much time on their breaks, go to the washroom too often, or talk to colleagues while they are working. In order to ensure that the elaborate regulations are observed, people must be closely supervised and their supervisors must be given the power to impose sanctions for violations of the rules – reprimands, warnings, suspensions, fines, and ultimately termination.

There are three sets of fundamental dysfunctions associated with this approach to management.

The Self-Fulfilling Prophecy

The first dysfunction has to do with the creation of a self-fulfilling prophecy.[1] The term 'self-fulfilling prophecy' refers to a series of events wherein a false premise causes an individual or individuals to engage in behaviour which subsequently causes the false premise to become true. For example, when a bank that is perfectly solvent is assumed to be insolvent by depositors (a false premise), the incorrect assumption (of insolvency) causes depositors to withdraw their funds, thereby causing a liquidity crisis that results in the actual insolvency of the bank. Numerous examples of the self-fulfilling prophecy have been documented from educational and work settings.[2] One of the best-known examples involved an experiment in which elementary-school teachers were told that certain students in their classes were intellectual 'late bloomers' who would show significant gains in IQ during the academic year.[3] Although the students so identified were chosen at random, they showed significantly greater gains in IQ scores and other standardized measures of intellectual attainment at the end of the experimental period than the other students in the class. Comparable performance effects have subsequently been demonstrated with adults in a variety of job-training situations.[4]

The implications of the self-fulfilling prophecy in the case of Theory X assumptions about people in organizations are clear. The assumption that people are lazy, untrustworthy, and lacking in initiative leads to the adoption of patterns of managerial action, as well as the design and implementation of organizational control systems, that treat people *as if* they were lazy, untrustworthy, and lacking in initiative. When people are treated in this fashion, they soon come to behave *as if* they possessed these characteristics, regardless of whether they actually do. The Theory X assumptions, though invalid at the outset, can become self-fulfilling as organization members respond to being treated in such a fashion.

Emphasis on Process Controls

Regardless of the assumptions made about people and their motives, organizations require control mechanisms in order to ensure co-ordinated actions on the part of their members in the pursuit of the organization's goals. A variety of different types of organizational control mechanisms are available, however, and the types of control mechanisms chosen are influenced strongly by the assumptions made by managers. A distinction can be drawn between control systems that focus upon work *processes* and those that focus upon work *outcomes*.

'Process controls' are mechanisms that attempt to control or influence the behaviour of organization members by specifying and measuring the actual work processes and activities that people engage in on the job. People are told in great detail what they are supposed to do and how they are supposed to do it, as well as what they are not supposed to do. Monitoring and control mechanisms are put in place to ensure that people engage in the prescribed behaviours and avoid the proscribed behaviours. 'Outcome-based controls' are mechanisms that attempt to control or influence the behaviour of organization members by specifying the outcomes, or results, that people are responsible for achieving, as opposed to the processes or activities that they engage in to attain those results. People are told what they are responsible for accomplishing, but are given considerable freedom and latitude in determining how to go about achieving the expected results.

Theory x assumptions lead organizations to rely strongly upon process controls as a means of influencing the behaviour of their members. Theory x assumes that people are both unwilling and unable to achieve results without being closely monitored and watched. This leads to a high level of specification, formalization, and monitoring of what people are doing at all times. The precise work processes and activities that people are to engage in are specified in great detail, as are the forbidden activities. Job behaviour is closely monitored, and deviations from specified activities are punished.

Process controls are much more cumbersome and expensive to design, implement, and operate than outcome controls. Organizations become bureaucratized as they develop elaborate job descriptions, complex policies and procedures, and strict supervisory and disciplinary systems. Equally detrimental is the diminution in the initiative and innovation among organization members who are repeatedly told not only what to do but precisely how to do it. Finally, the reliance of process control systems on the punishment of departures from specified work processes and activities generates a number of undesirable side-effects in and of itself.

Side-Effects of Punishment

Theory X assumptions lead to the design of control systems that rely heavily upon punishment and threats of punishment. Punishment as a control technique in organizations has been shown to cause a variety of undesirable side-effects.[5]

First, the use of punishment has a tendency to create resentment, anger, and hard feelings toward the punishing agent and the organization in general. These feelings may subsequently manifest themselves in a variety of dysfunctional behaviours, such as uncooperativeness, unwillingness to contribute beyond minimal requirements, or sabotage.

Second, the effectiveness of punishment as a deterrent to proscribed forms of behaviour is effective only so long as the potential punishing agent, or some independent monitoring device, is present to observe behaviour. The development of such monitoring and control systems can be extremely time-consuming and expensive, and hiring additional supervisors is similarly costly. Further, no monitoring or control system will be capable of monitoring *all* of the behaviour of *all* of the members *all* of the time; individuals will always be able to engage in some of the proscribed behaviours some of the time. In addition, the more elaborate the control and monitoring systems, the more people may come to see beating the system as a challenge to be overcome; the organization thus inadvertently encourages the very behaviour the system was originally designed to reduce or prevent.

The third key problem with the use of punishment is the failure to indicate to the individual being punished what it is that the organization wants the person to do. Punishment sends the message that what the person has done is undesirable, but does nothing to clarify or explain what is desired. Organization members are left with a clear perception of what is considered to be poor or unacceptable performance, but are given no guidance regarding what is considered to be acceptable or outstanding performance.

The assumptions made by management regarding the motivation and ability of organization members have a strong and direct impact upon the tendency of the organization to rely upon sanctions or rewards in manipulating behaviour. Theory X assumptions lead to heavy reliance upon punishment; Theory Y assumptions are more likely to lead managers to develop mechanisms for rewarding effective performance. Further, Theory x assumptions can be seen to have a variety of dysfunctional consequences, some of which are direct (such as the self-fulfilling prophecy effect), and some of which may operate through the negative outcomes of the use of punishment.

Empirical Results

A considerable body of empirical evidence demonstrates the effectiveness of rewards in generating high levels of performance in organizations and, conversely, the dysfunctions of reliance upon punishment. We will examine the results of research investigations that have focused upon a variety of categories of job-related behaviour.

Absenteeism

Absenteeism is costly to organizations. When an employee is absent, some of the work of the organization does not get performed, resulting in poorer overall organizational performance. If absenteeism does not generate performance decrements, then the organization is overstaffed and therefore less efficient than it might be.

The classical organizational approach to dealing with absenteeism has been rooted in Theory x assumptions about organization members. If it is assumed that employees don't like to come to work and prefer to stay at home, then it becomes necessary to ensure that methods of punishment are put in place to discourage people from engaging in their preferred course of action. As a result, many organizations require independent evidence of the reason for an absence, usually in the form of a medical certificate. Employees who are chronically 'voluntarily' absent are closely monitored and threatened with suspensions, demotions, or discharge. Absenteeism is viewed as a disciplinary matter.

An alternative approach to viewing absenteeism as a problem to be discouraged by punishment is to view regular attendance at work as desirable behaviour that is to be encouraged by rewards. A number of studies have demonstrated the effectiveness of this approach using different types of rewards and diverse occupational groups. In these studies, rewards for attendance, punishment for absenteeism, or a combination of both has been introduced.

Rewarding Attendance

A manufacturing organization implemented a lottery incentive system to improve attendance among 215 hourly employees at a manufacturing/distribution facility.[6] Employees in four adjoining plants served as comparison groups. Baseline data on absenteeism were collected from all five groups for a period of thirty-two weeks. A lottery system using a poker game was then introduced at the plant. Each day that an employee came to work and was on time, he was allowed to choose a card from a full deck of fifty-two cards. His choice was then recorded by his supervisor and entered on a large score-chart that listed the names of all the employees in the department and the cards that they had drawn for that week. At the end of each week the person with the best poker hand in each of the eight departments in the plant won a $20 prize. The more cards one had, the greater one's chances of winning. Those with perfect attendance for the week would have five cards in their hands, and those who had been absent during the week would have fewer cards. This system was continued for a period of six weeks. For a subsequent ten-week period, a lottery was held every second week instead of every week. After the conclusion of the program, absenteeism data continued to be monitored in all five plants for a subsequent period of twenty-two weeks.

The initial baseline absenteeism rate in the experimental group was 3.01 per cent. During the sixteen-week experimental period, this rate demonstrated a statistically significant 18.27 per cent decrease to 2.46 per cent. The lower rate remained relatively steady regardless of whether the lottery was run every week or every two weeks. After the lottery system ended, absenteeism showed a statistically significant increase of 30.08 per cent to 3.02 per cent. During the experimental period absenteeism rates remained constant at three of the four control plants, and increased slightly at the fourth.

In another study, two financial reward systems were used in a hospital setting to reduce absenteeism among nurses, ward clerks, and nursing assistants.[7] Six nursing units were randomly selected from the nursing department of a large private hospital in the southeastern United States. Three units were randomly assigned to one of two reward systems. System A permitted subjects to become eligible for cash prize drawings of $20 if they were not absent during a three-week period. System B allowed subjects to become eligible for the drawings if they were not absent on eight dates randomly selected from the three-week period. Baseline absenteeism data were collected for a period of three weeks prior to the experimental treatment and two weeks following it.

Under System A the pre-treatment absenteeism rate of 4.84 per cent dropped to 3.57 per cent during the experiment, and rebounded to 6.70 per cent following the treatment period. A similar pattern emerged under System B, where the pre-treatment absenteeism rate of 4.19 per cent dropped to 2.65 per cent during the experimental period, and rose to 5.17 per cent following the treatment. Under both systems the absenteeism rates during the treatment were significantly lower than the rates observed prior to and following the treatment. The absenteeism rates during the experimental period under the two systems were not significantly different from one another.

Finally, Nord has reported on the results of incentive programs introduced by two organizations with the goal of reducing absenteeism.[8] Although these examples were not controlled experiments, they do provide further data on the impact of incentive systems on absenteeism. In the first example, a hardware company with six outlets used a plan whereby monthly drawings for prizes were held for those who had perfect attendance and punctuality during the month. There was approximately one prize for every twenty-five employees, and every six months a drawing was held for a major prize (a colour television). As a result of this program, sick-leave payments decreased 62 per cent and absenteeism and tardiness were down 75 per cent during the first sixteen months. In the second example, a metropolitan school system was experiencing a high rate of teacher absenteeism, and therefore was incurring high substitution costs. The school system introduced a bonus plan whereby all teachers who had not been absent for an entire semester were rewarded with a small cash bonus. The school system reported decreased teacher absenteeism and a reduction in substitution expenses.

Punishment of Absenteeism

In general, there have been fewer systematic investigations of the impact of punishment on absenteeism. One such study examined the impact of a disciplinary program that monitored all sick time taken, required a physician's letter, and used other punitive and aversive methods to control absenteeism.[9] The program came to symbolize something broader to employees, who apparently viewed it as evidence of a management strategy of mistrust, surveillance, and a general attempt to clamp down on workers. The result of this program was an increase in lost time.

Punishment and Rewards

Several studies have evaluated the impact upon absenteeism of programs that combine punishment for absence with rewards for good attendance. One study used positive reinforcement in the form of non-monetary privileges for good attendance and punishment in the form of progressive discipline for excessive absenteeism in two industrial organizations.[10] Results showed substantial reductions in absenteeism. Along similar lines, Kopelman and Schneller used both reinforcers and punishers to control the incidence of overtime and unscheduled absences in a medical centre.[11] The system resulted in a 54 per cent reduction in average annual overtime leave, an arrest of the sharp upward trend in costs of paid sick leave, and employee satisfaction with the new program.

Job Performance

Researchers have studied the impact of reward and punishment systems on a variety of different components or aspects of employee performance.[12] I will briefly examine the results of a few representative studies.

Logging Productivity

Latham and Baldes implemented a system of goal-setting and verbal praise with the drivers of thirty-six logging trucks in six logging operations in Oklahoma.[13] The drivers were all unionized company employees who were paid by the hour. Before the experiment the drivers were told to 'do their best' in loading their trucks to the maximum legal weight. A detailed analysis of the performance of each logging operation revealed that the trucks were frequently falling far short of the maximum weight.

A 94 per cent truck net weight was decided upon as a difficult but attainable performance goal. The drivers were told that this was an experimental program, that they would not be required to make more truck runs, and that there would be no retaliation if performance suddenly increased and then decreased. No monetary rewards or fringe benefits were offered for improving performance. Supervisors were simply instructed to give specific verbal praise to the drivers for meeting or exceeding their goals, and to withhold negative comments when the goal was not met.

The net weights of the logging trucks were recorded for three consecutive months prior to the goal-setting. The results of the goal-setting and the verbal praise were then monitored for nine consecutive months. During the three months prior to goal-setting and praise, the drivers were averaging approximately 60 per cent of the legal net weight. During the first month of the program the figure jumped to over 80 per cent. From the third month onward of the experimental program, performance stabilized at over 90 per cent. The company estimated that without this increase in efficiency, it would have spent $250,000 for the purchase of additional trucks in order to deliver the same quantity of logs to the mills. This figure does not include the cost of the additional diesel fuel that would have been consumed or the expenses of recruiting and hiring additional drivers.

Occupational Safety

Many organizations rely upon threats of punishment in order to influence their employees to obey safety regulations. Employees are threatened with reprimands or suspensions if they engage in unsafe work procedures, fail to wear safety equipment, etc. An alternative approach is for the organization to define clearly what constitutes safe work procedures and then to reward or reinforce employees who follow those procedures.

Evidence of the efficacy of this approach is found in a study of a wholesale bakery.[14] The researchers began by working with members of the organization to identify and define specific, observable examples of safe behaviour. Independent observers then regularly coded the incidence of safe and unsafe work practices during baseline periods ranging from five to thirteen weeks in two different departments. During this period 70 per cent of the incidents observed in one department were performed safely, and 78 per cent were performed safely in the second department.

Following this baseline measurement period, employees were provided with training in safe work behaviour. The tenor of the training sessions was very upbeat, and positive expectations were set for the employees. It was stressed that they already were performing safely more than two-thirds of the time, and their attention was drawn to the areas in which safe behaviour was already occurring. The value of improved safety was described in terms of the workers' own protection, the decreased costs for the company, and the improvement in the plant's safety ranking within the larger corporation (it had been ranked last). A 'safe-performance' goal of 90 per cent was suggested and agreed to by the employees. The employees were told that their safety behaviour would continue to be observed, and that the results of each set of observations (in terms of the percentage of safe behaviours observed in each department) would be displayed on a large, prominently displayed graph, which also contained the data collected during the baseline period. In addition, supervisors were trained to give recognition and verbal reinforcement to employees observed engaging in safe work practices.

These interventions were followed by immediate dramatic improvements in safety behaviour. During the eleven weeks that the program was in place, 95.8 per cent of observed behaviours in one department were carried out safely. In the second department the safety rate was 99.3 per cent. In order to better assess the impact of the program, the intervention phase was followed by a reversal phase during which observations were not taken or posted. During this reversal phase the 95.8 per cent safety rate dropped to 70.8 per cent, and the 99.3 per cent rate dropped to 72.3 per cent. Following this reversal phase of the research, the company decided to institute the program on an ongoing basis. After the program was reinstated, the plant's injury rate fell to ten lost-time accidents per million hours worked, the lowest such rate in the entire company. Before the program was implemented, the plant's injury rate had been the worst in the company – fifty-four lost-time accidents per million hours worked.

Salespersons' Performance

Luthans, Paul, and Baker introduced a system of positive reinforcement in a well-designed field experiment conducted with salespeople in a large department store.[15] The researchers began by working with store personnel to define key dimensions of effective sales performance. Five such dimensions were identified, and detailed operational methods of measuring the incidence of these behaviours by direct observation were developed.

Of the approximately one hundred departments in the store, four were randomly selected for inclusion in the experimental group, and four others were randomly assigned to a control condition. The experiment consisted of a four-week baseline measurement period, a four-week intervention period, and a four-week post-intervention period. Two observers operated continuously throughout the twelve weeks of the study; they made two observations per hour per day of each of the sixteen work groups, resulting in a total of 15,360 observations.

The intervention consisted of establishing a series of rewards to individuals who attained various standards of performance. People who attained the standards could receive time off with pay or equivalent cash, in addition to an opportunity to compete in a drawing for a company-paid one-week vacation for two. The results of the program, which were immediate and dramatic, are summarized in figures 1 and 2. Figure 1 graphs data on 'aggregate retailing behaviour,' which is the average of three of the five dimensions of performance measured. The average level of performance on aggregate retailing behaviour increased by 17 per cent during the intervention period. Figure 2 graphs the average of the remaining two performance dimensions (absence from the work station and idle time), which showed a 21 per cent improvement during the intervention period. The authors argue that the failure of the experimental groups to return to baseline levels of performance in the post-intervention period may be due to the fact that the work environment itself contained sufficient existing natural reinforcers (for example, supervisor's praise, favourable customer reactions, the feeling of a job well done) to maintain the higher levels of performance once they had been established.

Conclusion

A number of conclusions follow from this discussion. First, there is a considerable and growing body of systematic empirical scientific evidence demonstrating the efficacy of a variety of reward systems in establishing and maintaining effective performance from organization members. Data on the effectiveness of rewards have been drawn from a wide variety of different types of organizations, industries, locations, and employees. The examples presented in this paper are a representative sampling of existing studies, and in no way approximate an exhaustive review of the relevant research.

While the data regarding the impact of rewards on effective performance continue to grow, the existing empirical research on the effects of punishment in organizations is much less extensive and conclusive. A recent review of the use of discipline in organizations stated that it does not appear possible to draw clear conclusions about the effects of pun-

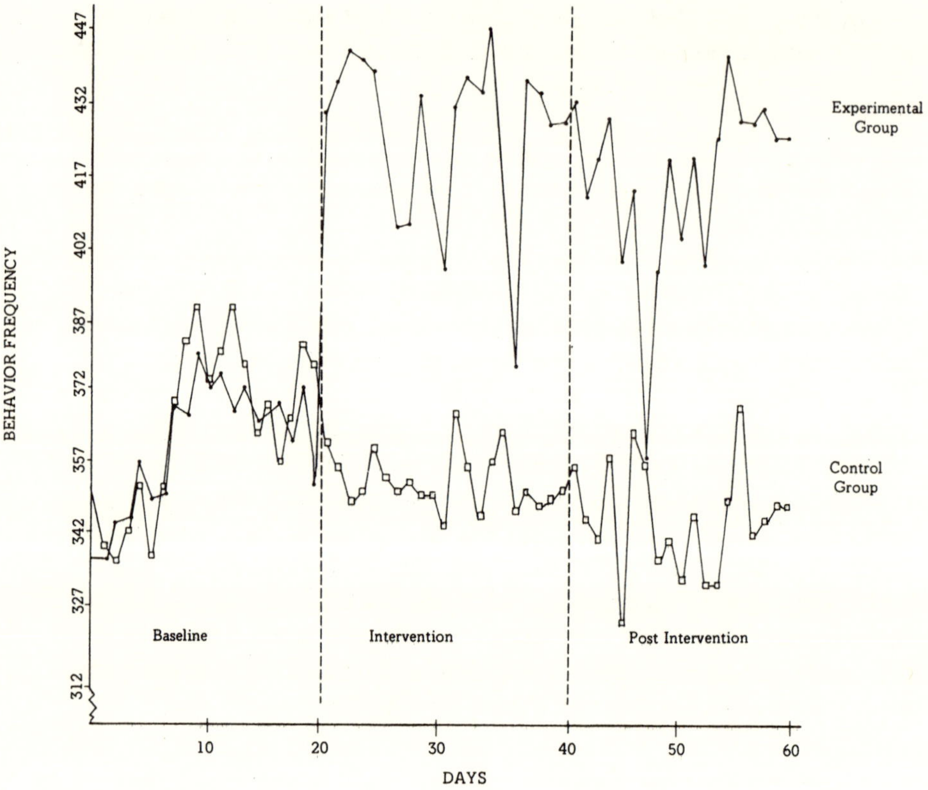

Figure 1. Aggregate retailing behaviour (From F. Luthans, F. Paul, and D. Baker, 'An Experimental Analysis of the Impact of Contingent Reinforcement on Salespersons' Performance Behavior' (1981) 66 *Journal of Applied Psychology* 314. Copyright © by the American Psychological Association. Reprinted by permission of the publisher and authors.)

151 An Organizational Perspective

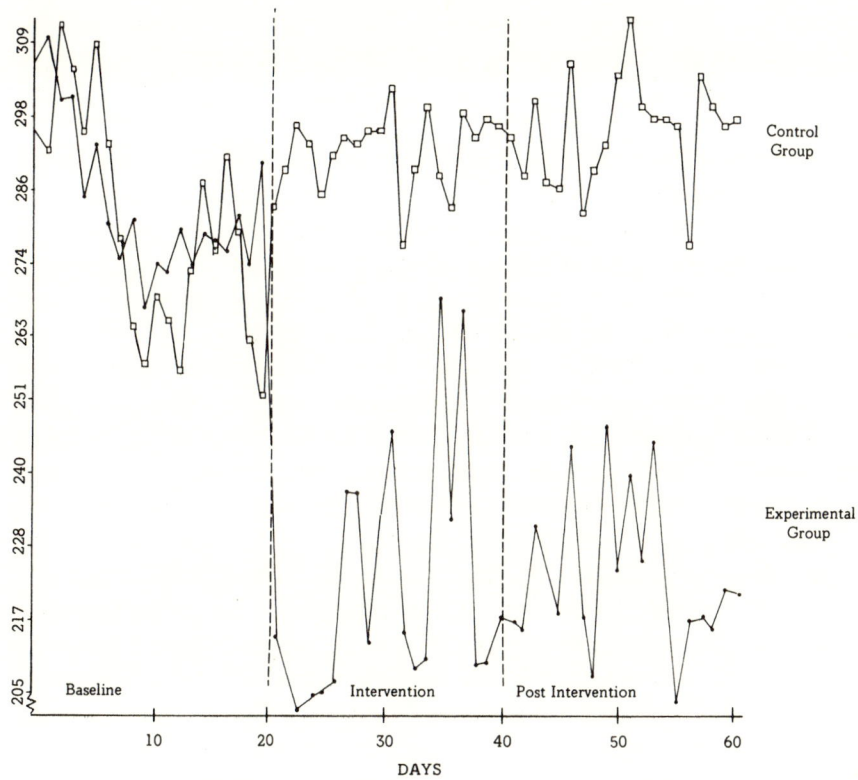

Figure 2. Absence from the work station and idle time (From F. Luthans, R. Paul, and D. Baker, 'An Experimental Analysis of the Impact of Contingent Reinforcement on Salespersons' Performance Behavior' (1981) 66 *Journal of Applied Psychology* 314. Copyright © by the American Psychological Association. Reprinted by permission of the publisher and authors.)

ishment on job performance;[16] studies have suggested positive effects, negative effects, and no effects. A number of possible explanations have been put forward for these confusing findings, including different frequencies in the use of punishment and reward in different organizations, differences in the nature and level of the samples studied, and the influences of a variety of moderating variables such as the timing of punishment and the role ambiguity of job incumbents.

Does this then lead to the conclusion that research in organizational behaviour implies that organizations need rely only upon rewards to influence the behaviour of their members and that they should do away with sanctions altogether? Clearly not. First, although the research results regarding the impact of punishment on behaviour in organizations are mixed and somewhat inconsistent, there is no doubt that punishment can and does have an impact on employee behaviour.[17] None the less, there is emerging consensus that the effects of punishment on performance are not as strong as the influences of reward, and that punishment may be more effective in influencing the frequency of highly specific target behaviours as opposed to more general criteria of performance effectiveness.

Clearly, there are and will continue to be various specific forms of behaviour that organizations will find intolerable and hence subject to sanction – theft of property, gross negligence, etc. But the overwhelming implication of both the theoretical and the empirical research in organizational behaviour is that the set of behaviours requiring formal organizational sanction is usually extremely small. Beyond this small set, it appears much more efficient and effective for the organization to attempt to influence the behaviour and performance of its members through the use of rewards.[18]

It is important to note, however, that the effective manipulation of employee behaviour, whether by rewards or punishments, is dependent upon two conditions. First, the organization must be capable of identifying with some specificity the types of behaviours or outcomes that it does and does not desire. This is not always a straightforward task, particularly when rewarding effective performance. Second, the organization must develop methods for measuring these behaviours and effectively tying them to appropriate rewards and sanctions.[19] Any manager who has ever carried out a performance appraisal knows the difficulty and ambiguity involved in assessing the performance effectiveness of organization members.

It is not at all difficult to find examples of organizational reward systems that claim to be rewarding certain types of behaviour while in fact encouraging quite different types of behaviours. Some of the most common examples are recounted in an article entitled 'On the Folly of Rewarding A, while Hoping for B.'[20] A common example has to do with innovation and risk-taking. Many senior managers today will say that their organizations encourage innovation and risk-taking among managers. In many organizations that espouse risk-taking, however, managers who take risks and fail are severely punished with demotions, transfers into dead-end jobs, or termination. The espoused message is "Take risks and you will be rewarded,' but the behaviourally communicated message is 'Avoid failure or you will be punished.' The surest way to avoid failure is to avoid taking risks. Thus, while the organization hopes for risk-taking behaviour, it rewards conservative risk avoidance.

Finally, we return to the fundamental assumptions made by managers about the nature of people in organizations. Theory X assumptions lead to the development of complex systems of sanctions and performance controls in order to prevent dysfunctional behaviour. As we have seen, heavy reliance on sanctions is ineffective and inefficient in fostering high levels of performance among organizational members. Theory Y assumptions are much more likely to lead to the development of reward-based organizational systems and procedures, which empirical research increasingly indicates to be more likely to generate high levels of employee performance.

Notes

* Magna International Professor of Business Strategy, Faculty of Management, University of Toronto
1 R.K. Merton, 'The Self-Fulfilling Prophecy' (1948) 8 *Antioch Review* 193; R.A. Rosenthal and D.B. Rubin, 'Interpersonal Expectancy Effects: The First 345 Studies' (1978) 3 *Behavioral and Brain Studies* 377; D. Eden and A.B. Shani, 'Pygmalion Goes to Boot Camp: Expectancy, Leadership, and Trainee Performance' (1982) 67 *Journal of Applied Psychology* 194
2 D. Eden, *Pygmalion in Management: Productivity as a Self-Fulfilling Prophecy* (1986)
3 R.A. Rosenthal and L. Jacobson, *Pygmalion in the Classroom: Teacher Expectation and Pupils' Intellectual Development* (1968)
4 D. Eden and G. Ravid, 'Pygmalion versus Self-Expectancy: Effects of Instructor- and Self-Expectancy on Trainee Performance' (1982) 30 *Organizational Behavior and Human Performance* 351

5 H.P. Sims Jr, 'Further Thoughts on Punishment in Organizations' (1980) 5 *Academy of Management Review* 133
6 E. Pedalino and V.U. Gamboa, 'Behavior Modification and Absenteeism: Intervention in One Industrial Setting' (1974) 59 *Journal of Applied Psychology* 694
7 T.A. Stephens and W.A. Burroughs, 'An Application of Operant Conditioning to Absenteeism in a Hospital Setting' (1978) 63 *Journal of Applied Psychology* 518
8 W.R. Nord, 'Improving Attendance through Rewards' (1970) 33(6) *Personnel Administration* 37
9 N. Nicholson, 'Management Sanctions and Absence Control' (1976) 29 *Human Relations* 139
10 R.W. Kempen and R.V. Hall, 'Reduction of Industrial Absenteeism: Results of a Behavioral Approach' (1977) 1 *Journal of Organizational Behavior Management* 1
11 R.E. Kopelman and G.O. Schneller IV, 'A Mixed-Consequence System for Reducing Overtime and Unscheduled Absences' (1981) 3 *Journal of Organizational Behavior Management* 17
12 P.M. Podsakoff, W.D. Todor, and R. Skov, 'Effects of Leader Contingent and Noncontingent Reward and Punishment Behaviors on Subordinate Performance and Satisfaction' (1982) 25 *Academy of Management Journal* 810; P.M. Podsakoff, W.D. Todor, R.A. Grover, and V.L. Huber, 'Situational Moderators of Leader Reward and Punishment Behaviors: Fact or Fiction?' (1984) 34 *Organizational Behavior and Human Performance* 21; H.P. Sims Jr, 'The Leader as a Manager of Reinforcement Contingencies: An Empirical Example and a Model,' in J.G. Hunt and L.L. Larson (eds), *Leadership: The Cutting Edge* (1976) 121
13 G.P. Latham and J.J. Baldes, 'The "Practical Significance" of Locke's Theory of Goal Setting' (1975) 60 *Journal of Applied Psychology* 122
14 J. Komaki, K.D. Barwick, and L.R. Scott, 'A Behavioral Approach to Occupational Safety: Pinpointing and Reinforcing Safe Performance in a Food Manufacturing Plant' (1978) 63 *Journal of Applied Psychology* 434
15 F. Luthans, R. Paul, and D. Baker, 'An Experimental Analysis of the Impact of Contingent Reinforcement on Salespersons' Performance Behavior' (1981) 66 *Journal of Applied Psychology* 314
16 R.D. Arvey and A.P. Jones, 'The Use of Discipline in Organizational Settings: A Framework for Future Research,' in L.L. Cummings and B.M. Straw (eds), (1985) 7 *Research in Organizational Behavior* 367
17 R.D. Arvey and J.M. Ivancevich, 'Punishment in Organizations: A Review, Propositions, and Research Suggestions' (1980) 5 *Academy of Management Review* 123; see also Arvey and Jones, supra note 16, R.T. Keller and

A.D. Szilagyi, 'Employee Reactions to Leader Reward Behavior' (1976) 19 *Academy of Management Journal* 619, and Sims, supra note 5

18 A. Bandura, *Social Learning Theory* (1977)
19 E.E. Lawler III, *Pay and Organizational Effectiveness* (1971), and E.E. Lawler III, *Pay and Organization Development* (1981)
20 S. Kerr, 'On the Folly of Rewarding A, While Hoping for B' (1975) 18 *Academy of Management Journal* 769

8 An Anthropological View of Sanctions and Rewards

PIERRE MARANDA*

Introduction

Many people draw a distinction between the 'natural sciences' and the 'social sciences.' Their position is that social facts cannot be approached with either the same rigour or the same brutal coolness as physical facts. Yet many long for the day when neurophysiological psychology and the social sciences will have rendered human behaviour amenable to 'real scientific treatment.' In the meantime, somewhat like quantum physicists, we keep looking for probable outcomes. Wittingly or not, we formulate hypotheses on others' responses – on the basis of previous experiences – so as to find our bearings and act properly.

Don't we think we know somebody intimately if we can predict that person's behaviour? Don't we think we fit well in our peer groups if we know what is expected of us? *Prediction, expectation*, and *conformity* (which ensures predictability) are key terms in social interaction. We need 'rules,' 'patterns,' 'norms,' and 'normality' so that we can define and consolidate 'regulations' and thus steer acceptable courses of action. Human beings need to know when recurrences become patterns, when patterns become acceptable, and when widely acceptable patterns are prescribed as norms. Consumers' associations, anti-smoking sentiment, sex education programs in schools: all are examples of recurrences gathering momentum to stand up as patterns that can eventually be enforced through laws. And compliance with laws yields conformity (that is, social homogeneity), which in turn allows for sound expectations, so that one can predict outcomes and feel good because of a sense of 'belonging.'

Now, that works well on the level of abstract principles, and even on

157 An Anthropological View

the grass-roots level since, as we say in anthropology, all cultures tend to be imperialistic: the members of all human societies look down upon foreigners, as they need to do in order to consolidate their self-respect.[1] Human cultures have to offer uncontrovertible semiotic charters[2] to their members – charters that will give people 'social contracts' enabling them to 'belong': to communicate with each other in trust, within relatively well-defined and stable parameters. Further, semiotic charters make people believe in themselves enough to think it worthwhile to reproduce themselves. And since societies exist only to reproduce themselves, laws must guarantee cultural incontrovertibility. In other words, there must be absolute taboos and prescriptions; violating the former must be punished and complying with the latter must be rewarded.

Some people, however, derive their rewards from getting away with taboo violations; by the very fact that they try to secure obedience, do societies fail to engage their 'smartest' members? Or does that depend on types of legal systems and on the relative importance given to sanctions as opposed to rewards within a legal system?

A jurist turned anthropologist has suggested a distinction between legal systems in technological societies and more 'human' ones.[3] Our legal system would be characterized by codified and rigid sets of laws that are mostly repressive; that of other, simpler societies, by flexibility and fluid adaptation emphasizing rewards.[4] (It is interesting to note that the title of this volume reflects, in its word order, the emphasis of our conception of law: first, 'Sanctions,' and second, 'Rewards.') Our own system would be essentially conservative, while that of other societies would be essentially amenable to socially variable conditions (would demographers say that conservativeness is correlated with population size?). And to Pospisil's New Guinea data we can add further evidence from several cultures in Africa and elsewhere.[5]

To be more specific: in some cultures, litigation contributes to joyful social life instead of building up tensions. The very judicial process is a reward in itself, not a grim fight. Let me quote one example, from a well-documented ethnography of the Subanum of the Philippines, where the legal process is a most convivial form of social interaction.

> Litigation [in that society] cannot be fully understood if we regard it only as a means of maintaining social control. A large share, if not the majority, of legal cases deal with offenses so minor that only the fertile imagination

> of a Subanum legal authority can magnify them into a serious threat to some person or to society in general ... A festivity without litigation is almost as unthinkable as one without drink.
>
> In some respects a Lipay trial is more comparable to an American poker game than to our legal proceedings. It is a contest of skill ... accompanied by social merrymaking, in which the loser pays a forfeit. He pays for much the same reason we pay a poker debt: so he can play the game again ...
>
> Along with drinking, feasting and ceremonializing, litigation provides patterned means of interaction linking the independent nuclear families of Lipay into a social unit.[6]

We do not see trials as social feasts and we do not joke with or about the Law. Stolid citizens advocate it as the corner-stone of their stolidity. What the Subanum achieve through spirited and lively litigation processes, we aim at through solemn and severe tribunals. For us, at least in authority circles, social homogeneity is a cause to promote and consolidate. But don't our cities and even our villages comprise many subcultures, each with its own code of ethics, of etiquette, of love, of parental behaviour? Multiculturalism, 'racial integration' policies, and minority rights go against monolithic views of society. Must we conclude, in the best relativistic tradition, 'to each its own norms'? Is the cause of social homogeneity a delusion or even a mystification? And shouldn't our predictions rest on a different basis from our stern conception of law? Shouldn't we revise that basis to accord with notions of norms and expectations? This leads us to focus on the notion of 'norm.'

This paper consists of a general and partial anthropological overview of law. The following section begins with law as a social fact, to set it in a holistic perspective; sanctions and rewards are then approached from the standpoint of social norms and inertia (conservativeness), and a sketchy statistical framework is provided for their analysis. In the third section, sanctions and rewards are cast in terms of regulation mechanisms acting on the imagination. A brief account of our correlational analysis of car-driving and sexuality is presented in the fourth section; five testable hypotheses on the topic are proposed. The final section suggests three outlooks related to legal sanctions and rewards: semiotic capital, terrorism and martyrdom, and creativity. In conclusion, the ideology of social reproduction is set in the context of the ratio of sanctions to rewards.

Law as a Social Fact

Anthropologists define 'law' as a 'social fact.' The term comes from Emile Durkheim;[7] British anthropologists use 'institution' for the same concept. For us, social facts are the sets of behavioural frames, resting on more or less fuzzy rationales, that a society deems essential to its perpetuation. Examples of social facts are kinship systems, monetary systems, religions, art, and politics. We consider any single social fact to be intertwined with all others in the social fabric. Consequently, our approach to law or any other social fact is 'holistic.' Sometimes this leads us to unexpected investigations: for example, in a recent study on car-drivers, we were led to take pornography into consideration. Anthropology is like landscape photography; one may focus on a component, but one cannot ignore the rest of the grounds.

All societies have regulation mechanisms. Taboos are such a mechanism: their violation entails 'metaphysical' or social sanctions. All societies have compensation mechanisms as well: the costly consequences of wrong behaviour can be neutralized through some form of expiation or redemption. Rewards also work as regulatory devices. They provide incentives. We argue that sanctions and rewards are society-specific and designed on the basis of statistical norms, and that their function is to maintain social inertia.

Social inertia is as fundamental in social life as gravity is in the physical world. Inertia maintains collective identity and enables the members of a society to predict the consequences of actions. One crosses a street when the traffic light is green on the assumption that, in all probability, cars will respect the interdiction signified by a red light and will not run pedestrians down. One can predict the results of an act of kindness, a smile, or a tantrum because social inertia has consolidated types of responses to such stimuli. Social inertia is a sort of gyroscope that keeps a society set on a given course and provides its members with mental and psychological security. It even goes as far as shaping 'common sense.' Social inertia can be defined as the commonality vector structuring the thought and behaviour of most people in a given society. In this respect, it is obviously describable in statistical terms. Social inertia carries human lives in the ruts more or less clearly marked by norms.

On the one hand, norms can be elicited from behaviour patterns. Expectations are then based on 'belonging' to the peer group, to one's subculture. Norms will be situational and will result from implicit widespread consensus: a statistical inference. And a political authority that wants to be acknowledged by its subjects must consolidate those norms emerging from social pragmatics. On the other hand, norms can also be defined from the top, by being imposed by some authority – a curfew, censorship, abolition of the death penalty, whatever the authority thinks it can get away with, whatever it can impose on its subjects without being overthrown. Here, belonging will be defined as conformity to an abstract group, the homogeneous nation, or the dominant culture. Conformity to both types of norms will be required and rewarded, and deviance will be punished. And both types are teleological; that is, their function is to ensure social perpetuation.

I do not want to belabour the point; I urge readers familiar with anthropology to skip the following paragraphs, and those familiar with statistics to skip the curves that come after.

The following excerpt is from an introductory textbook in cultural anthropology that is already twenty years old. It shows what undergraduates learn in our field about norms and expectations.

> The reader may well ask whether the concepts of norms and expected behavior are not identical ... A refined analysis of social organisation requires that they be logically distinguished. The status of a religious specialist in our society, a minister or a priest, will serve to illustrate this distinction. The expected behavior associated with this status includes the most exemplary conduct ... abstention from gambling and drinking, dignified demeanor, etc. However, the minister who serves a sophisticated congregation may find it necessary to keep close to his people through such devices as moderate social drinking, laughing agreeably at off-color stories ... Such behavior may actually become the norm for ministers in a given community without altering expectations of more exemplary conduct (expected behavior) ...
>
> What is the value of this distinction? Principally, it contributes to understanding social organization as a dynamic process. Social structure would be a static concept without the essential ingredient, action. Real action departs from expected action for any status or structural position in a society. Such departure, however, is never a disorganized or haphazard process. Even the departures occur within specified limits and may become

normative in themselves. Thus, in the example above, ministers or priests may behave closely in accordance with community expectations. In this case, the norms and the expected behavior will be nearly congruent or coincidental. Where social factors favor a more relaxed attitude on the part of the clergy, expectation action and normative action will diverge. But clergymen will, under these circumstances, tend to depart from expected behavior in similar directions, thereby establishing a new pattern or norm. This is one way in which new norms come into being: when actual behavior shows a general shift away from an established pattern. Such a process goes on continuously in any society. Isolating the cause for such shifts is an important part of the study of culture change.[8]

A Sketchy Statistical Framework

Let me illustrate this anthropological view with some basic statistical representations. They are purposely simplistic, in order to make the point unambiguously.

The following curves sketch profiles of compliance, with the horizontal axis representing degree of compliance, and the vertical axis representing the number of persons that comply more (+ tail) or less (− tail).

Curve 1 represents a 'tightly knit' society, such as Quebec before the Quiet Revolution;[9] here, inertia is very high, and there is only one dominant culture (imposed from above, in the case of pre-1960 Quebec, through the collusion of church and state). Curve 2 depicts a 'loosely knit' society, one that is more tolerant and less monolithic than that represented by curve 1. Here, inertia is low. Curve 3 shows a society on its way to a major split: it is pulled apart by two competing polarities. In that case, inertia is polarized by two different vectors. Established authority is in conflict with a subculture that has gathered momentum to the point of 'establishing a new pattern or norm,' in Schwartz and Ewald's terms. A curve 2 society may be on its way either to type 1 from type 3 or to type 3 from type 1, depending on inertia dynamics – that is, the interplay of centrifugal and centripetal forces.

For the sake of these illustrations, let us divide the curve into three segments, a main area and two tails. The main area gives the profile of the majority. Its shape is indicative of the degree of solidarity. A flattened curve depicts diffuse solidarity. In contrast, in a curve like the first one, social solidarity is intense; average, means, and mode coincide. In a

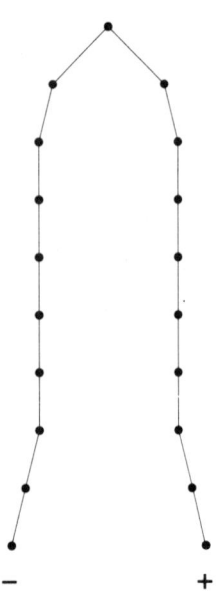

Curve 1   A tightly knit society

curve like the third one, the two modes signify a lack of solidarity. Divisive factors are such that means and average are mental constructs rather than adequate factual representations.

We will label the right-hand tail 'positive.' There stand the people who are the supreme embodiments of social ideals – heroes, saints, martyrs, charismatic leaders. At the left-hand tail of the curve are found supremely deviant people: assassins, rapists, terrorists, dictators – whatever types of deviants are deemed the most reprehensible in a given society.

The overwhelming majority of the members of the society represented by curve 1 gather around similar values; their opinions and behaviour are stereotyped; they tend to be submissive, intolerant, self-righteous, law-abiding, and severely punitive of deviants. In this type of society, there is almost no room for normal standard deviation: it would take very strenuous efforts to pull away from the pack. Only simple categories of exceptionality are possible: outcasts and saints. Sanctions and rewards will be equally drastic and fundamental – for

163 An Anthropological View

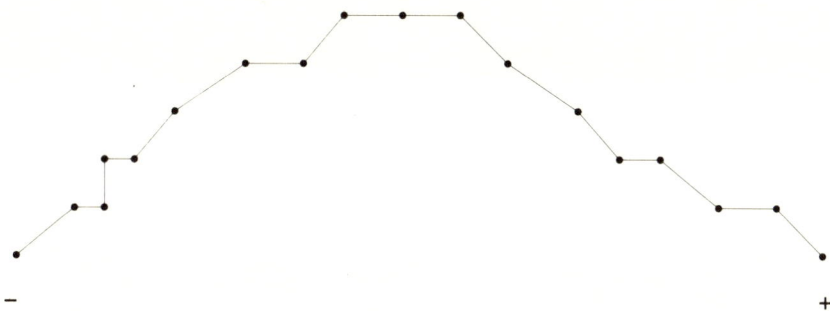

Curve 2   A loosely knit society

example, the death penalty as well as canonization will be regular enforcement mechanisms.

A society whose profile could be represented by curve 2 is much more permissive than those sketched in curves 1 and 3. It is not strongly homogeneous; it is relatively easy for people to move out of the centre of inertia to the tails of the curve. Both sanctions and rewards will be moderate – the death penalty as well as canonization will be avoided. As the number of people may accrue toward one or the other tail, however, the society may evolve in one direction (toward generalized compliance), in the other direction (toward generalized dysfunction), or in both directions at the same time. Curve 2.1 shows a move toward generalized compliance; curve 2.2 shows a move toward social rebellion. Curve 3 sketches the result of a move in both directions, which may result in a deep social split yielding two subsocieties, each of the type represented in curve 1.

Curve 2.1 is skewed toward the right. It means that most of the population it represents is much closer to the positive tail than to the negative tail; it is the curve of a population of strongly law-abiding citizens. Its long negative tail indicates that the population also comprises a much higher component of deviants than the population represented by curve 1.

In curve 2.2, the left-skewedness indicates a society in which a majority is reluctant to abide by its leaders' decisions. Whereas curve 2.1 is typical of people 'pulled forward' by a common incentive, curve 2.2 is a display

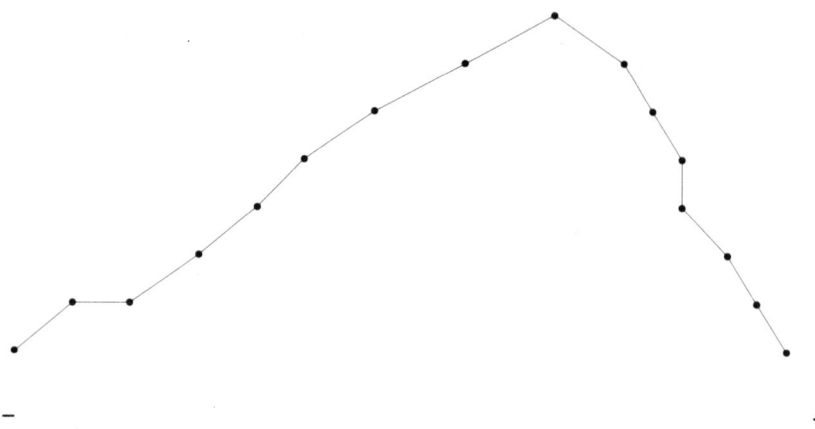

Curve 2.1 A society moving toward conservative solidarity

of people 'held back' near the negative tail end, by inertia, lack of adhesion, or lack of commitment. This type of society could be dominated by some form of tyrannical or dictatorial power consolidated mainly by fear or indifference.

In curve 3, we have a bi-modal curve; that is, a curve with two equally important peaks. People in the valley between the two peaks are at the same time situated on the negative tail of mode A and on the positive tail of mode B. Their 'schizophrenic' status will become more and more excruciating as the pull increases toward social split. But should centripetal force become powerful enough, (+) and (−) would be resorbed gradually, the mean and the average would shift to the right or to the left, and the curve would become similar to curve 2.1 or curve 2.2.

Sanctions and Rewards: The Major Regulation Mechanisms of Inertia

The two main regulation mechanisms of inertia are fear and seduction. Both operate on imagination as the *faculté* of anticipation. The threshold of fear is relatively low, that of seduction much higher. In other words, a little fear goes a long way toward affecting people's behaviour, but it takes a lot of seduction power to achieve the same results. This facility

Curve 2.2 A society moving toward social rebellion

of fear may be the reason our legal system relies more heavily on sanctions than on rewards.

Fear and seduction thresholds can be measured. On the basis of studies in communication and marketing,[10] we can state that the impact of fear on a person or group will have to be around 10 per cent of the system's inertia[11] to be effective as a factor of change. Seduction will have to score about 40 per cent to 50 per cent on the same scale to trigger a response strong enough to override inertia. Think of marriage stability motivated by fear of divorce; of anxiety motivations underlying investments in insurance policies versus investments in the stock market; of brand loyalty; of the results of Quebec's sovereignty-association referendum; and of the semiosis of marketing on the whole. Psychography, semiography, and applied semiotics provide tools for quantifying these momenta.

In comparative studies of the people of Quebec City's Upper and Lower Town, we were able to pin-point differential vulnerabilities.[12] Through the collection of data with specialized protocols, we produced semiographies,[13] on the basis of which we could build probabilistic models of inertia and of the differential effects of threats and rewards on the two populations. We were able to show that inertia and fear are typical of family-centred people (the 'private man'), and innovative behaviour and

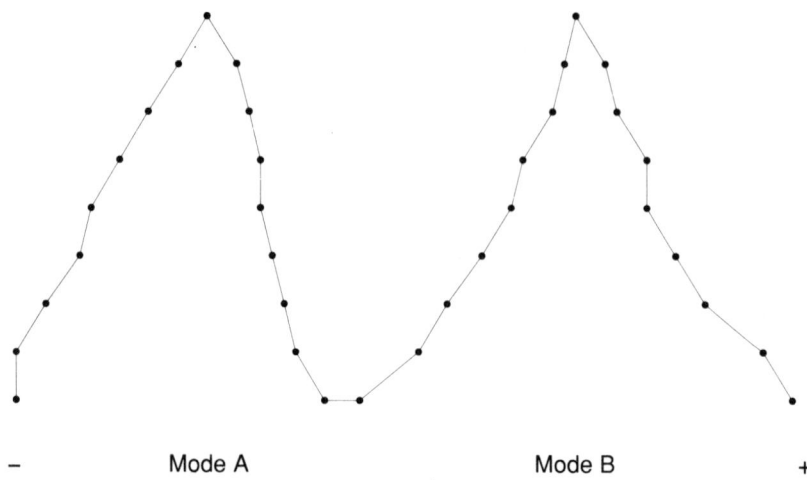

Curve 3 A strongly polarized society

quests for rewards are typical of career-oriented people (the 'social man').

Accident-Proneness and Pornography

Recently, we conducted a study of the three 'pornographic' magazines with the highest sales in Canada: *Penthouse*, *Playboy*, and *Hustler*.[14] (I use the word 'pornographic' to mean 'sexually explicit' but not necessarily illegal.) In the framework of a previous study of male car drivers between eighteen and twenty-five years of age,[15] we had been led to consider a correlation between the use of pornography and driving behaviour. We found corroboration of the hypothesis that men tend to 'metaphorize' vehicles as women. Both provide 'trips.' And one can infer accident-proneness, among young male drivers, from the way they view women; correlatively, one can infer the type of pornography consumed from driving styles. Why are these two dimensions related? A brief general semiotic exposition is required to answer the question.

Cars and Mates

One may go as far back as *The Song of Songs* in the Bible, where a woman is compared to 'a mare of Pharaoh's chariots.' Women have long been 'metaphorized' as horses in our western symbolic systems. Then cars came along and superseded horses. A carry-over took place – that is, a transduction along a semiotic inertia vector. A new thing (car) fulfilling an old function (transportation) is named after the former signifier; car engines are rated by their 'horsepower.' Transduction inspires many car-makers when they give names to their products: Mustang, Bronco, Pinto, Pony. And a maker's fleet of Formula 1 racing cars is called his 'stable.'

Cars, the new 'horses,' have kept the latter's signifier value: they can be used as an idiom to 'metaphorize' women. In other words, a newly derived signifier became available for an ancient signified. Figures 1 and 2 illustrate this.

The French semiotician Roland Barthes, and the exuberant and tremendously popular French writer of pseudo-mystery stories, San-Antonio, both commented in the same terms on the Citroën DS, pronounced '*déesse,*' or 'goddess.' The automobile is the modern man's goddess.[16] Indeed, the young drivers in the random sample tended to structure the connotations of women and of cars along the same semiotic vectors. Our sample was divided into two groups of 100 male drivers each, ranging in age from eighteen to twenty-five; all were products of the same general social conditions. Group 1 had had car accidents while driving, and group 2 had had none. A combination of Word Association Tests and Plot Association Tests[17] was used to elicit connotations of three stimuli ('automobile,' 'woman,' 'man') and to have the respondents invent a story with the same three stimuli.[18]

Drivers who had had no accidents predicated the same attributes of their women and of their cars: trustworthy, reliable, thrifty, very dependable though somewhat sedate and slow in responding, and requiring good care. Those young men already saw themselves as socially established fathers, responsible citizens whose lives gravitated toward a domestic pole. In fact, their self-images were those of men approximately ten to fifteen years older.

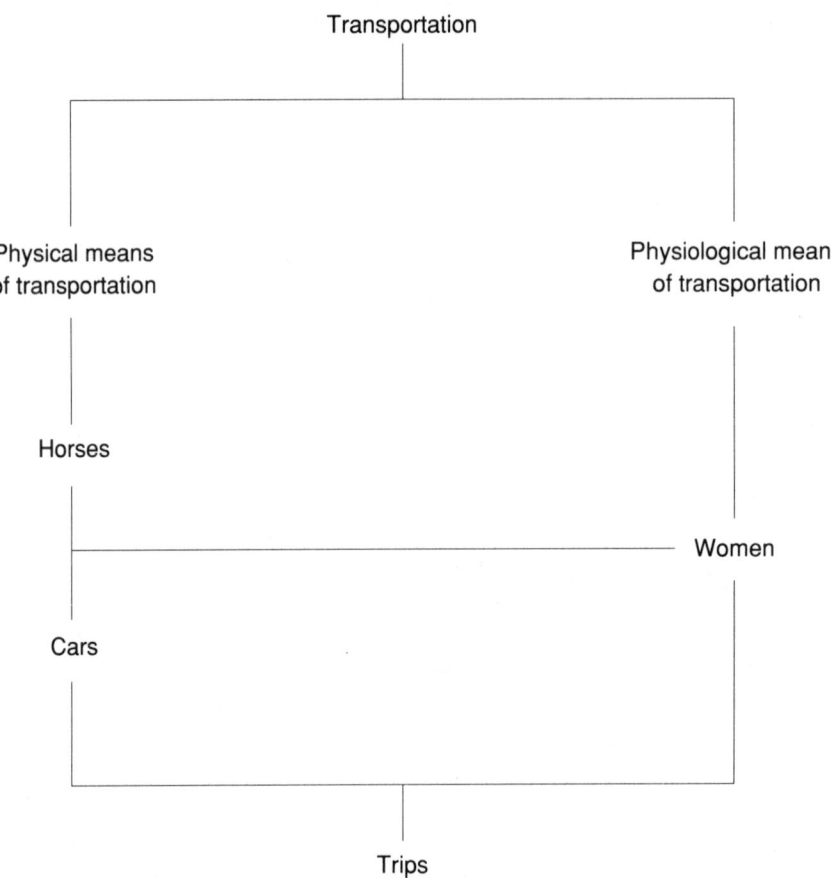

Figure 1 Horses, cars, and women: semiotic transduction

Drivers who had had accidents also predicated the same attributes of their women and of their cars, but the attributes differed from those of the other group. Both 'instruments of pleasure' had to be exciting, challenging, dashing. They were to be given little care, yet must be flashy. They had 'nerve' and quick responses, and they could 'drive you nuts' in the positive sense of the idiom. Immediacy of pleasure and short-time orientation were strong components of those connotations by accident-prone drivers, who did not share in the long-term visions of themselves specific to the group I subjects.

An Anthropological View

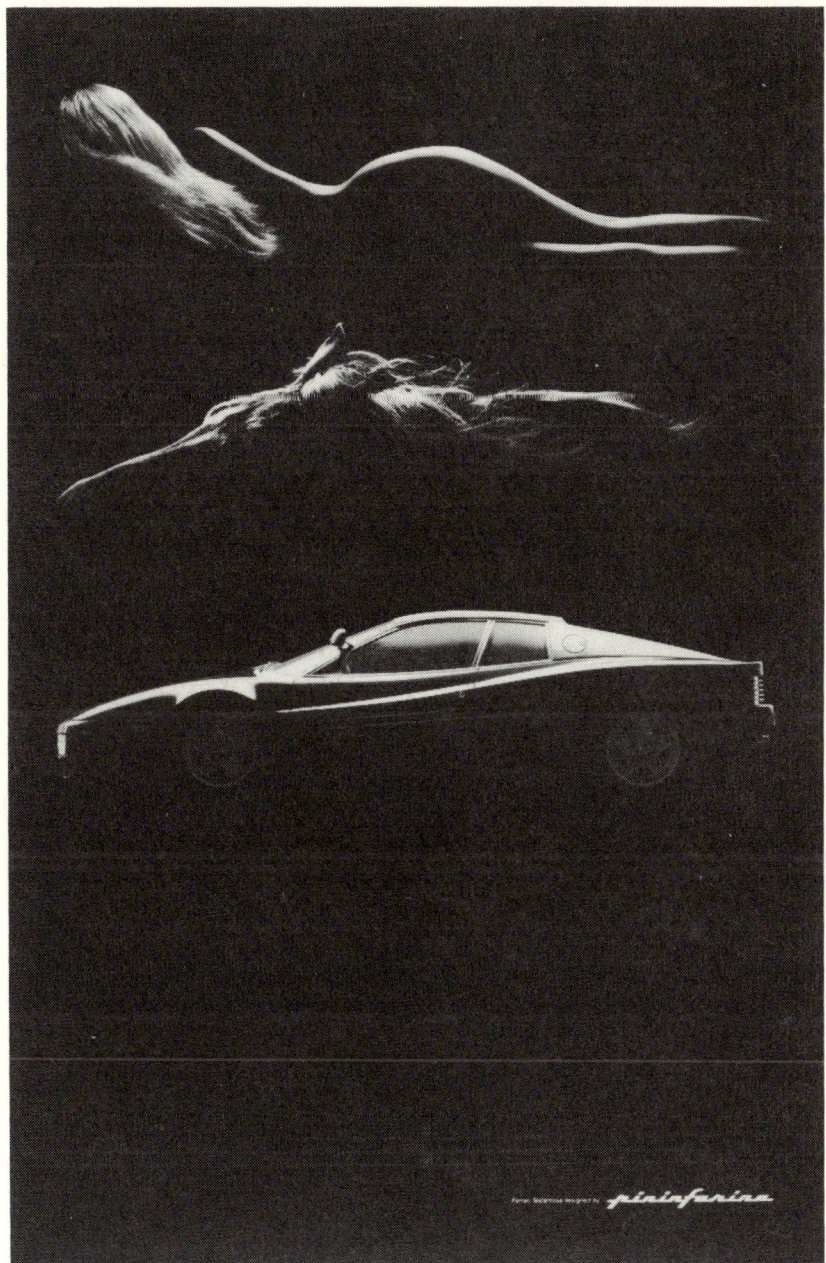

Figure 2. Horses, cars, and women
Reprinted with permission of *Road & Track* magazine

Driving and Pornography

What, then, of pornographic magazines? The least pornographic of the three publications analysed was *Playboy*. It was also the one in which there were the most car advertisements. The most pornographic magazine in the sample, *Hustler*, contained no car advertisements at all. *Penthouse* fell in between. An interesting correlation: the pornographic contents of *Playboy* increased over the last twenty years; congruently, the number of car advertisements went up, from an average of two per issue in 1965 to an average of eight in 1985 (with a peak of fifteen in 1980). But the increase in pornographic content lagged considerably behind that of *Penthouse* and *Hustler*.

The types of cars advertised in *Playboy* were mostly of the middle-range variety, with occasional trends toward higher-performance models but very seldom approaching the true sports machines. *Playboy*'s cars remained sedate, like its bunnies. It was a magazine for dreamers (and safe drivers) rather than doers. In contrast, *Penthouse* featured motorcycles. And although *Playboy* occasionally advertised radar-detectors, it did so in the ratio of 0.25 to car advertisements; *Penthouse*'s ratio was 1.8 times.[19] In other words, the ratio of car to radar-detector advertisements was 7.2 times higher in *Penthouse* than in *Playboy*, and *Penthouse* was clearly more pornographic than *Playboy*. Is it significant that *Hustler* published neither car nor radar detector advertisements?

To tackle the issue from a slightly different angle: safe drivers will buy *Playboy*; they will look for mild excitement – soft-core porn and sedate cars. Risk-prone drivers will buy *Penthouse*, and they seem to offer a better market than *Playboy* readers for radar-detectors. They want more than allusions, more than just convenient performance. *Hustler*'s readers do not 'metaphorize' women into cars, or vice-versa: the ads in the magazine are for all sorts of sex gadgets. Whereas the readers of the two other magazines fantasize and metaphorize, *Hustler*'s readers seem to have no need for figurative meaning; they want the thing itself, in its literal meaning.

Of course, our examination of car-driving and pornography still leaves a great many issues unexplored. Like all studies, it ends with more questions than answers. So far, the limited data enable us only to suggest such hypotheses as the following five. (Remember that only males between the ages of eighteen and twenty-five are under consideration.)

Hypotheses on Relationships between Driving and Sexuality

1. *An active sex life correlates positively with low accident rates.* In Quebec City, ten regular patrons (average age: 30.47 years) of an Upper Town brothel do not consume pornography ('Why would we? We've got the real thing!' they said in answer to our questions), and they have had fewer car accidents than consumers of pornography.

2. *The use of hard-core pornography correlates positively with high accident rates.* Hard-core pornography consumers are more prone to car accidents than soft-core pornography consumers. These consumers tend to be doers rather than dreamers. They tend to take risks, sometimes only for the sake of risk. They like to live dangerously, to take chances. Their driving behaviour is congruent with their general attitude to life.[20] Their psychodynamics are stereotyped by images of forcefulness, power, challenge, domination, prestige, and the need to succeed.[21]

3. *The use of soft-core pornography correlates positively with average accident rates.* Soft-core pornography consumers are dreamers rather than doers; they live more in imagination than in reality: their imagination constitutes a kind of buffer-zone that enables them to distance themselves from stress and frustrations. Since they compensate in imagination rather than in fact, they are less aggressive than hard-core pornography consumers, who need action more than dreams and who compensate in ways that may be aggressive.

4. *Abstention from pornography correlates positively with high accident rates.* Consumers of soft-core pornography might be less prone to car accidents than non-consumers because the latter are more timid and subject to greater stress without escape mechanisms; they would accordingly be less sure of themselves and more prone to erratic driving.

5. *The efficacy of publicity for safe driving correlates positively with the skilful use of images of women.* When life-size cardboard or plastic 'policemen' are set up by the roadside in Italy, they arouse fear in drivers. In Belgium, there are large posters showing a shapely woman admonishing drivers that 'fast driving is as stupid as fast love-making'; they are a form of seduction.[22] My hypothesis is that of these two deterrents, the poster of the woman has proved more effective in the long term and has exerted a stronger influence.

Risk Behaviour and Marginality

Radar-detectors, motorcycles, and hard-core pornography are popular among risky drivers; safe drivers prefer sedate cars and soft-core pornography. The former are hard on their women and on their cars; the latter are soft on both. Isn't the idea of radar-detectors analogous to the mental device used by a spouse having a secret affair? To that of a taxpayer trying to outsmart Revenue Canada? To that used by anybody who wishes to overstate his personality through some form of marginalization? Think also of the lengths to which some individuals will go to assert themselves in their fashions, and think of all common forms of boasting.

Inertia is important to many because it offers a strong security factor. But the desire to belong may be in conflict with inertia, as may the need to assert oneself. Most people adjust their aspirations and imagination so as to experience a 'goodness of fit,' to use a statistical metaphor, which will enable them to merge with the majority of the group in which they seek or wish to keep membership. Those people will go as far as to buy *Playboy* but not *Penthouse*, let alone *Hustler*. There are people positioned near the 'negative' end of the curve – that of non-conformity – who will do as much as possible to escape from the 'pack': their ambition is not to fit in; they want to feel creative. In order to achieve such a state of grace, they opt for marginality. Narcotics, 'trips,' and 'speeding' in all forms provide them with the feeling of living intensely. Those ways of being actually promise and often give them vertigo, which Caillois viewed as related to the experience of the sacred,[23] and which young children attain by spinning around until they collapse, or by riding on faster and faster merry-go-rounds in amusement parks.

Three Outlooks on Sanctions and Rewards

Semiotic Capital and Inertia

Inertia level is determined (1) by the 'semiotic capital' or 'mental stocks' owned by individuals and societies alike, and (2) by their management strategies ('network density' and 'channel capacity', or multiplexing power).[24] Sanctions and fear will have a much greater effect on people with fewer resources; conversely, rewards will have more impact on people with greater resources, who are less easily threatened – for example, white-collar crooks. In this context, it is worth mentioning the profound modification of Quebec society engineered by the former finance minister Jacques Parizeau through his REAQ program:[25] seduction power has overriden traditional fear for over 500,000 Quebecois. Instead of investing in personal insurance out of fear, as they used to do, they are now putting their money into the stock market because the rewards have reached an economic level that allows them to recover substantial amounts of the income tax deducted at source from their pay-cheques.

Terrorism and Martyrdom

Terrorism acts on fear, and is based on a kind of reward that is akin to political 'power trips': a very small group of people can threaten a whole nation. In this respect, terrorism can be seen to be related to martyrdom, in which people put themselves in such a position that punishment (by their societies' enemies) will be their ultimate reward. Both are forms of 'heroism,' which is in turn a form of marginalization: to carve for oneself a place in the tail of a normal distribution curve is a stimulating, rewarding endeavour.[26]

Deviation and Creativity

McLuhan has defined creativity as 'whatever one can get away with'[27] – and this applies to deviant behaviour as well as to poetry or music. Law-making and law enforcement face this 'creativity problem.' Will innovative trends prevail over conservative forces? How much mafia can a social system tolerate without collapsing? This goes back to the types of social dynamics illustrated by the curves earlier in this paper. Marginalization and creativity are rewards in themselves. They provide vertigo. In order to be creative, a legal system has to offer positive incentives that outweigh sanctions; to offer only inertia consolidation through sanctions might be enough for the rank and file, but this is tantamount to underestimating one's own fellow citizens and is akin to élitist and oligarchic philosophies of authority.

Conclusion: Law and Social Reproduction

The preservation of *social* identity is necessary for people to have *personal* identities – this was Althusser's classical contribution to the analysis of *appareils d'état*.[28] To paraphrase him: a society's inertia can call people by their names because it has given them their names. The French anthropologist Augé has developed the thesis; what he calls the 'ideo-logic' of a society is its semiotic charter, in which people inscribe and save their identities.[29] Sanctions and rewards play a fundamental role in that preservation process.

But what are the grounds of that process? We say that human societies, like animal species, exist only to perpetuate themselves. The difference between us and other mammals is that we have 'culture' – a deliberate mechanism to ensure 'pro-*creation*' (social reproduction), an essential part of which is a set of values implemented through a program of sanctions and rewards. We punish those who undermine our self-confidence and reward those who enable us to consolidate our power and social comfort. We can thus believe that our society is worth perpetuating.

The legal systems of technological societies are more repressive – that is, conservative and inert – than productive of creativity. Could the ratio of inertia to creativity be changed? Could our legislators and judges look forward instead of walking backward like lobsters? The answer is clearly yes. It is a question – a major one – of restructuring our conception of law to centre on rewards rather than sanctions. This is a task for semiotic engineering, for it implies revamping mentalities. Could we hope for such a conversion? Could we aim at operating mentally and emotionally like Malinowski's Trobrianders? Can we envisage, and work for, a new society in which enthusiasm would override meanness, and where it would be so rewarding to dwell that sanctions would become a rarity? Optimistically, yes.

Think of what Parizeau did recently to traditional Quebec business pusillanimity and inertia with the REAQ legislation. Is it not time to reexamine our conception of law and to act on the basis of a creative rather than a repressive model? For example, could not the car insurers return, but much more boldly, to the incentives (too timid in the past) of lowering premiums for good drivers? Rates would go down, year after year and substantially, for drivers who were accident-free over a continuous period, and they would increase substantially with each accident for other drivers. Of course, insurance companies would make less money. But should the rationale of legislation be based on the profitability of insurance companies?

When we learn to use rewards (positive incentives) rather than sanctions (fear and deterrents), we will have come a long way toward a much more dynamic and productive society, a society that will want to reproduce itself for better reasons than just inertia. We can envisage a nation in which law would be inspiring and ahead of the times instead of being stifling and trying clumsily to catch up with events generated by imaginative freaks.

Notes

* Professor, Department of Anthropology, Laval University
1 See C. Levi-Strauss, *La Pensée Sauvage* (1962) 118–19, 220.
2 A semiotic charter is a set of implicit propositions (some anthropologists, like Hoebel, call them 'cultural axioms') providing common semantic grounds to the members of a society. Those common semantic grounds are interpretation grids, and they are shaped in clichés, proverbs, sayings, stereotypes, prejudices, and postulates, as expressed in folk-tales, popular songs, religious beliefs, novels, films, etc. A semiotic charter is generally acquired through enculturation during childhood and is more or less consolidated over the years. Such charters enable people to have the impression that they understand each other when they communicate. Semiotic charters are culture-specific and form the basis of 'common' sense. Their basic components and dynamics can be analysed by semiography (see infra note 13).
3 L. Pospisil, 'Law and Order,' in J.A. Clifton (ed), *Introduction to Cultural Anthropology* (1968), 201
4 Witness an unimpeachable authority in ethnography, B. Malinowski; he commented as follows on 'law' in Trobriand society: 'Here we come at last to the most important point – there exists a class of binding rules which control most aspects of tribal life, which regulate personal relations ... There is no religious sanction to these rules, no fear, superstitious or rational, enforces them, no tribal punishment visits their breach, nor even the stigma of public opinion or moral blame ... The binding forces of Melanesian civil law are to be found in the concatenation of the obligations, in the fact that they are arranged into chains of mutual services, a give and take extending over long periods of time and covering wide aspects of interest and activity. To this there is added the conspicuous and ceremonial manner in which most of the legal obligations have to be discharged. This binds people by an appeal to their vanity and self-regard, to their love of self-enhancement by display. Thus the binding force of these rules is due to the natural mental trend of self-interest, ambition and vanity, set into play by a special social mechanism into which the obligatory actions are framed' (Malinowski, *Crime and Custom in Savage Society* [1961] 66–7; see also 31–2). Another British anthropologist, M. Gluckman, objected to Malinowski's use of the term 'civil law' to cover 'the mechanisms of social

control which operate positively to induce people to fulfil their obligations':
Gluckman, *Politics, Law and Ritual in Tribal Society* (1965) 205; see also
196–206. In contrast, the American sociologist-cum-anthropologist G. Homans
readily used the notion of 'control through effective integration' to account
for similar mechanisms: Homans, *The Human Group* (1950) 288.

5 For evidence on Africa, see, for example, John Mensah Sarbah, *Fanti Customary Laws* (1968) 22; Max Gluckman, *The Judicial Process among the Barotse of Northern Rhodesia* (1955) 350; and John Beattie, *Bunyoro, an African Kingdom* (1960).

6 C.O. Frake, 'Litigation in Lipay: A Study in Subanum Law,' in *Proceedings of the Ninth Pacific Science Congress of the Pacific Science Association* (Bangkok 1963) 3: 221

7 See *Sociology and Philosophy* (1953), a collection of Durkheim's later essays (at 24) and his essay 'Value Judgments and Judgments of Reality' in the same volume (at 80–97).

8 B.M. Schwartz and R.H. Ewald, *Culture and Society: An Introduction to Cultural Anthropology* (1968) 189–90

9 M. Rioux, *La Question du Québec* (1969)

10 For example, O.E. Klapp, *Opening and Closing: Strategies of Information Adaptation in Society* (1978), and C. Cossette, *Les Images Demaquillées* (1985)

11 System inertia is measured through applications of digraph theory and probabilistic network analysis. Along related lines, on the basis of information theory, Klapp (supra note 10) distinguishes between positive inertia and negative inertia – in his terminology, 'good' versus 'bad' redundancy. The former maintains social stability and consolidates a semiotic charter; it also provides some immunity against fear and is more readily open to seduction. The latter does the opposite. This is not the place to enter into an exposition and discussion of marketing techniques, psychography, applications of communication theory, and related contributions to the understanding of social facts. It is enough to mention that the figures given rest on empirical case studies – unpublished analyses of voting intentions at the time of the Quebec referendum – and on theoretical derivations from information theory on the amount of information one can process without threat ('channel capacity').

12 See P. Maranda, 'Sémantographie du domaine "travail" dans la haute-ville et dans la basse-ville de Québec' (1978) 20 *Anthropologica* 249.

13 'Semiography' is the name of a set of technical tools for the operational description of meaning and of its generative matrices; see P. Maranda, 'Semiography and Artificial Intelligence' (1985) 1 *Toronto International Spectrum* 1. Our approach rests on dynamic network theory. It consists in identifying major images, symbols, or 'concepts' in a population by eliciting the bundles of connotations that give them effective meaning; then, by measuring their diffrac-

tion and condensation properties in a network, a 'map' can be sketched of the main constituents of a 'mentality.' Social inertia is a function of semiographic network density. The higher the number of interrelations between the nodes of a network, the stabler the network will be and, consequently, the less open to change. The types of rewards and sanctions that will be effective on a given population will be a function of the types of nodes as well as of network density – that is, of the 'notions' whose connotations are mapped in the network and on the interrelationships between those notions.

14 Our sample included three issues a year, every five years from either 1965 (for *Playboy*) or from the first year of publication for the other two magazines. See P. Maranda, *Analyse de contenu et de discours des trois revues à caractère sexuel les plus répandues au Canada* (Ottawa: Ministry of Justice 1986).
15 P. Maranda, *Connotations de l'automobile chez un échantillon de jeunes Québécois* (Quebec: Régie de l'Assurance Automobile du Québec 1985)
16 R. Barthes, *Mythologies* (1973) 88–90
17 P. Maranda, *Introduction to Anthropology: A Self-Guide* (1974) book 10
18 The protocol comprised several additional steps: see Maranda, supra note 15, for details.
19 In our sample, 1980 magazine issues do not advertise radar-detectors. The figures are only for the issues contained in the sample slice of 1985.
20 For field observations of faulty driving in Quebec City, see J. Herickx, 'Les Manoeuvres des Conducteurs Québécois' (1986) 3 *Repères* (Régie de l'Assurance Automobile du Québec) 2.
21 Ibid. 3
22 One might suggest, to increase efficiency and achieve still deeper conditioning, the addition of two more posters. They would both still feature the same shapely woman. The first one's caption would read: 'Are you a competent lover?' and the text of the last of the three would be: 'Answer: look at your speedometer!'
23 R. Caillois, *Les Jeux et les Hommes – Le Masque et le Vertige* (1967)
24 These strategies rest effectively on operating conditions such as 'network density' – which means the ratio of actual connections between things over the number of possible connections; 'channel capacity' means the actual quantity of information that can be conveyed through one channel (the mind of a person, a telephone line, a telegram) without being garbled; 'multiplexing power' adds to 'channel capacity' the notion of parallel transmission of different sets of data without function entropy.
25 REAQ stands for Régime d'Epargne Actions du Québec (Quebec Stock Savings Plan). The program enables residents of Quebec to deduct from their income, for income tax purposes, sums they invest in corporations whose headquarters are in the province. The scheme has had a momentous impact on Quebec mentality.

It can be seen as a second phase in the opening of traditional 'peasant economics' to the monetary system and risk-taking.
26 For related observations, see M. Augé, *Pouvoirs de Vie, Pouvoirs de Mort* (1977).
27 M. McLuhan and Quentin Fiore, *The Medium Is the Massage* (1967) [unpaginated]
28 L. Althusser, 'Idéologie et Appareils Idéologiques d'Etat' (1971) 151 *La Pensée* 3
29 See Augé, supra note 26.

9 Achieving Compliance with Collective Objectives: A Political Science Perspective

CAROLYN TUOHY*

In considering how compliance with collective objectives can and ought to be achieved, the contributors to this volume raise issues that are of central concern to political scientists. I welcome this opportunity to suggest how my discipline can contribute to the project, and vice versa. At the same time, I must begin with a disclaimer. This paper will present not 'the' political science perspective on these issues, but rather *one* perspective – that of mainstream North American liberal pluralism. It will not deal with classical theories of the just state and their implications for appropriate compliance mechanisms. Nor will it present a Marxist or neo-Marxist analysis of rewards and sanctions as instruments of class conflict and struggle. Nor will it adopt the phenomenological perspective of critical theory, though it will make brief reference to the symbolic dimensions of compliance mechanisms.

The first section of this paper presents a theoretical analysis of the distinctive competencies and incompetencies of three pure types of social control when measured against fundamental economic and political criteria. The second section treats more practical considerations, recognizing that the choice of a compliance mechanism in practice never involves the selection of a pure type but rather involves changes to an existing mix of rewards and sanctions in an established political and economic context.

Types of Control Mechanisms

From the perspective of political science, mechanisms for achieving compliance with governmental objectives can be classified according to three general types: command, exchange, and persuasion. Those familiar with

Lindblom's *Politics and Markets* will recognize a marked similarity between these types and the three elemental mechanisms of social control, which he terms authority, exchange, and persuasion. The difference is largely one of terminology: I believe that the term 'command' better expresses the concept Lindblom terms 'authority'.[1]

These basic mechanisms can be conceptualized as follows, with reference to two actors: one, A, who seeks to have the other, B, comply with A's objectives.

Under the *command* mechanism, B complies with A's objectives simply because A tells him to do so. B's compliance is based on a superior-subordinate relationship with A, which may be grounded in either force or consent, and which may be more or less limited in its scope (that is, in the range of matters with respect to which A can command B's compliance). Its major institutional manifestation is the apparatus of law-making, application, and adjudication – legislatures, bureaucracies, and courts.[2]

Under the *exchange* mechanism, B's compliance with A's objectives is voluntary and is obtained at a price. A induces B to comply by offering something of value in return. The exchange mechanism's major institutional manifestations are the market and the negotiating table.

Under the *persuasion* mechanism, B complies with A's objectives because A adduces arguments or principles that lead B to agree with the objectives. An institutional manifestation is less easily identified here than in the other two mechanisms (the educational system may be the best analogue).

Each of these pure types has its own distinctive competencies and incompetencies, which can be assessed against three criteria: technical efficiency, allocative efficiency, and democratic accountability and participation. The first of these criteria, technical efficiency, refers in this context to the minimizing of the cost of achieving compliance with a given objective – 'transaction' costs, or, more specifically, 'enforcement' costs in economic language. The second criterion, allocative efficiency, involves the achievement of the *optimal* level of compliance so as to maximize social welfare, and implies that society should invest in achieving compliance with its objectives up to the point at which the marginal cost of achieving compliance equals its marginal benefit.

The third criterion, democratic accountability and participation, requires some elaboration. It reflects the fundamental respect for individual autonomy that characterizes the liberal democratic tradition. In liberal democratic thought, mechanisms of social control are consistent with individual autonomy only to the extent that they rest on the free and informed consent of the individuals forming the society. This fundamental tenet takes a number of formulations in twentieth-century liberalism, variously emphasizing the need to ensure the *accountability* of decision-makers to affected interests, or the *participation* of affected interests in decision-making.[3] For John Rawls, the just distribution of rewards and sanctions (and the just process for determining the distribution of rewards and sanctions) is that which would be consented to by free and informed individuals from behind a 'veil of ignorance' of their individual positions in the distribution.[4] Moving from the realm of Rawlsian discourse to the realm of political action, Carole Pateman argues that there is democratic value in participation per se – individuals develop habits of democracy through participation in the decisions that affect their lives, and democratic political cultures develop as a broad base of the populace participates in such decisions.[5] Aaron Wildavsky focuses not so much on the significance of participation in the promotion of social justice or the formation of democratic individuals and political cultures as on its role in producing 'intelligent' decisions. Wildavsky distinguishes two modes of public policy-making, which he terms 'cogitation' and 'interaction.'[6] The cogitation mode, he argues, assumes erroneously that individual preferences with respect to public policy exist independently of the process through which they are aggregated: the decision-maker is to discover society's objective function and to adopt those policy instruments which maximize social welfare. A more appropriate model of the policy process, for Wildavsky, is the 'interaction' model, which recognizes that preferences are shaped as well as discovered through a process of interaction among affected interests. Furthermore, the definition of 'problems' and 'solutions' requiring collective action is not a sequential but a reciprocal process: 'Policy analysis is an activity creating problems which can be solved.' And this activity must be interactive: 'The truth [that analysts] have to tell is not necessarily in them, nor in their clients, but in what these cerebral prestidigitators often profess most to despise, their give and take with others whose consent they require, not once and for all, as if the social contract were forever irrevocable, but over and over again.'[7]

There are limits, however, in Wildavsky's view, to the amount and type of interaction that is conducive to intelligent decision-making. Elsewhere, he points to the potential for paralysis as the number of 'clearance points' through which a decision must pass increases,[8] and to the potential for distortion when selectively increased participation leads to increased imbalance in the representation of interests in the political arena.[9] In this respect, Wildavsky's writings reflect the unresolved issue of the appropriate mix of accountability and direct participation within democratic theory. (Indeed, Wildavsky's recognition of the difficulty of resolving these issues has led him increasingly to advocate an exploration of the capacity of market as opposed to governmental mechanisms for aggregating preferences in particular arenas.)

Furthermore, it has been argued that different ideas regarding the appropriate mix of accountability and participation are reflected in the political cultures of particular liberal democratic nations. Some political scientists have distinguished between 'subject' and 'participant' political cultures, and have placed Canada in the 'subject' category: 'Historically, the norms of Canadian citizenship emphasize a subject rather than participatory competence in government and politics – obedience to recognized authority, preservation of hierarchical organizations, acceptance of social inequalities, deference to power elites.'[10]

Whatever the divergences within the vast literature on democratic accountability and participation, there is one general point of agreement that is of significance in this context: accountability itself rests on a base of rewards and sanctions; that is, a decision-maker can be effectively accountable only to those who have the ability to reward or sanction him.[11]

Having set out the various types of compliance mechanisms and the criteria against which their respective competencies and incompetencies are to be assessed, we can now proceed to that assessment.

Command

Command mechanisms vary, in theory as well as in practice, in the extent to which they rely upon legislative, bureaucratic, or judicial instruments for the specification and enforcement of legal requirements and the resolution of disputes regarding those requirements. The ways in which command mechanisms measure up against our evaluative criteria depend upon the balance of legislative, bureaucratic, and judicial elements. A full treatment of alternative systems and their respective merits and demerits is not possible here; none the less, some illustrative comments can suggest the relevant types of considerations.

Legislative-Bureaucratic Instruments

The implication for technical efficiency of a heavy reliance on legislative-bureaucratic instruments is a matter of spirited academic debate. Lindblom has argued that the establishment of a hierarchy of control minimizes marginal enforcement costs. Once the relationship has been established, the superior has only to command and the subordinate obeys. Depending on the degree of recalcitrance among subordinates, however, it may be necessary continually to reinforce the command structure through police or audit functions. The conditions under which various organizational designs do in fact minimize transaction costs are the subject of continuing theoretical speculation and empirical research.[12]

The implications of command structures for allocative efficiency are also a matter of dispute. On the one hand, it is argued that the fundamental problem of hierarchies lies in knowing *what* to command. Legislative prescriptions at best represent the outcome of the interaction of a variety of mechanisms (notably political parties and interest groups) for articulating and aggregating social preferences at a given time. At worst, these organized groups, each advancing its own subset of interests, can together generate a kind of 'institutional sclerosis' thwarting the adoption of efficiency-enhancing measures.[13] Furthermore, the bureaucratic structures that administer and elaborate legislative prescriptions have been criticized as having 'strong thumbs but no fingers';[14] they lack the flexibility to adapt to and manipulate changing environmental conditions. They possess no inherent mechanism for equilibrating marginal costs and benefits in particular cases; and they may enhance co-ordination at the expense of innovation.

On the other hand, Herbert Simon argues that it is only through (well-designed) hierarchies that human rationality and hence allocative efficiency can be maximized: what is at issue for him is not the need for hierarchy but the flexibility and intelligence with which its decision rules and information-processing capacity are designed.[15] In the public policy arena, an important design principle for Simon is ensuring that decisions with a high 'value' content rest with legislators, and those with a high 'factual' content rest with administrators. This insistence upon fact/value or politics/administration distinctions is an enduring and problematic feature of the literature of public administration.[16]

Finally, with respect to democratic accountability and participation, command mechanisms score well only to the extent that they rest on the consent of the governed, and that the governed possess the ultimate ability to reward or sanction those in command. The possibility of reconciling the legislative-bureaucratic apparatus of the modern state with these democratic principles is one of the most difficult issues in modern political science, and the literature is too vast to be discussed here. What is at issue, essentially, is the domination of decision-making in these structures by organized interests and/or bureaucratic decision rules. The arguments range from those which emphasize that the predictability provided by such organizations is a pre-condition for democratic accountability in complex decision-making systems[17] to those which hold that bureaucratization and/or concentrations of power pose a great threat to democratic decision processes.[18] In the mid-range are numerous contributions emphasizing the importance of alternative institutional designs in the resolution of this tension.[19]

In concrete instances, these debates resolve into questions such as the following: Are product standards developed by bureaucratic agencies more likely to serve the interests of producers or of consumers? Do producers, with their superior information resources, possess a greater ability to influence bureaucratic decision-makers than do consumers, who must rely on their ability to reward or sanction the bureaucrats' 'political masters' at the polls? Does the relative influence of producers and consumers differ depending upon whether the bureaucratic agency is a 'line' department under the direct authority of a cabinet minister or a 'semi-independent' agency with a more attenuated relationship to the political executive?

Judicial Instruments

The degree of emphasis to be placed on judicial mechanisms in the legislative-bureaucratic-judicial mix of command mechanisms is also a matter of theoretical dispute. In terms of technical efficiency, the laborious and time-consuming requirements of the adjudicative model do not score well. The elements of this model have been summarized elsewhere as follows:

1 Each party must have the opportunity to present proofs and reasoned arguments for a decision in his favour to the decision-maker.
2 The decision-maker must be impartial and must attend to, and be capable of comprehending, those arguments.
3 The decision-maker should normally answer those arguments in explaining his decision.
4 The decision should be strongly responsive to the parties' proofs and arguments in the sense that it should proceed from and be congruent with those proofs and arguments and should not be based on principles, facts, or arguments not presented by the parties themselves.

> This general model comprises a number of variants, of relative degrees of formality. All entail rights to notice and hearing by an impartial judge; most entail rights to counsel and rights to cross-examine adverse witnesses; and the more formal entail the keeping of a written record against the possibility of subsequent review and increasingly strict rules of evidence.[20]

If this time-consuming mechanism of information-gathering and decision-making results in a full scanning and an impartial balancing of the relevant interests and facts, the transaction costs may be outweighed by gains in allocative efficiency. But the constraints of the model limit the likelihood of a full scan of the relevant information, especially regarding 'polycentric' problems:

> Adjudication appeals to precedent in what has been called the 'gradual tracing out of the full implications of a system already established' (Fuller, 1978: 377); and it is ill-suited to finding innovative solutions to conflicts between interests which have not been resolved even in general terms through a contract or through an accommodation of interests at the legislative level.
>
> These shortcomings may well be outweighed by the power of the adjudicatory process to clear through adversarial presentations to a core of established fact and to maintain the role of principle as opposed to power balance in the operation of the state. But it is likely to do so only to the extent that the issues do indeed resolve around a firm core of established fact, implicate principles of 'right' and 'wrong,' and affect a range of interests which is capable of being captured in a single dispute.
>
> ... Milton Eisenberg [1978] has argued that the 'norm of strong re-

sponsiveness' inherent in the adjudicative model (that is, its requirement that the judge's decisions proceed from the arguments, and only from the arguments advanced by the parties appearing before him) makes it ill-suited for the resolution of 'polycentric' problems. Polycentric problems are those involving complex interactions among a large number of interests, such that different solutions may implicate different sets of interests (or, put another way, different solutions may change the parameters of the problem). Fuller [1978] analogized the polycentric problem to a spider web, which is 'many centered – each crossing of strands is a distinct centre for distribution of tension.' To limit the focus of decision-making (through the norm of strong responsiveness) essentially to two opposing interests in a given dispute – in Fuller's analogy, to a single 'crossing of strands' – ignores the overall structure of the problem, the complex web of interactions.[21]

It is with regard to liberal democratic principles of accountability and participation that an adjudicative model appears most attractive, in a limited but important context. Within those categories that are caught by its rules, it protects individuals against the arbitrary exercise of state authority and against private wrongs, in theory without regard to concentrations of political and economic power. Furthermore, it allows individuals a form of 'participation' in the decisions that affect their lives by giving them an opportunity to hear and to make reasoned arguments.

The strengths and the weaknesses of a heavy reliance on an adjudicatory model are well illustrated by the U.S. experience with the control of toxic substances. Civil liability suits against asbestos manufacturers, for example, have been enormously technically inefficient as compensation mechanisms. By 1983, the Rand Corporation reported that asbestos victims had been awarded $236 million through civil liability suits: lawyers had received fees totalling $164 million; and fees for defence lawyers for the asbestos and insurance industries had reached $600 million.[22] The negative implications for allocative efficiency of the heavy reliance on civil liability suits in the United States to provide, in effect, compensation from the 'deepest pockets' has also received much criticism.[23] The deterrent effect of these suits in encouraging compliance with social objectives of risk-reduction cannot be known, but it is arguable that they are inefficient mechanisms by which to achieve compliance as well as compensation. It is doubtful, however, that the information about asbestos exposure and corporate culpability generated by these suits would have come to light under any other mechanism.

The advantages of the adjudicatory model are perhaps better exhibited by the 'judicialized' process of regulation-making and enforcement regarding toxic substances in the United States. Although the formal notice and comment procedures followed by regulatory agencies and the almost inevitable judicial review of standard-setting have been criticized as technically inefficient in comparison with less formal Swedish, West German, and British processes yielding roughly similar results, the same commentators laud the openness of the U.S. process and its ability to generate and disseminate vast amounts of information (to the advantage of free riders such as Canada).[24]

Exchange

It is the essence of the exchange mechanism that each transaction is voluntary. Compliance is voluntarily exchanged for something of value to the one complying; conversely, compliance is 'bought' in each instance on a quid pro quo basis. (This contrasts with the command mechanism in which, though entry into the continuing superior-subordinate relationship may be voluntary, obedience in particular instances is not.) For the purposes of analysis, it is possible to distinguish two major categories of exchange-based compliance mechanisms – one focused at the level of individuals or individual firms, and one at the level of social groups.

'Price'-Based Mechanisms

In the first category are mechanisms that set a 'price' for compliance or non-compliance. 'Enforcers' decide how much compliance to purchase, and 'targets' decide how much to supply. Differential health insurance premiums for smokers and non-smokers are one example of price-based compliance mechanisms. More common in the public policy arena, however, is the incorporation of price mechanisms within a command-based system, as in the case of systems of 'emission charges' for the control of environmental pollutants. Instead of establishing legal limits on emissions and imposing fines and jail sentences for the violation of those limits, the state levies fees based on the amount of pollutant emitted; polluters can emit as much pollutant as they are prepared to pay for.

Such price-based exchange mechanisms can be evaluated against each of our three criteria. In the first place, to the extent that the mechanisms are voluntary, they may be less technically efficient than mechanisms of command. As Williamson and Ouchi have argued,[25] one major reason for the establishment of hierarchical mechanisms is to reduce the transaction costs of monitoring and enforcing voluntary agreements. This supposed advantage of hierarchy, however, needs closer theoretical specification and empirical support.

With respect to allocative efficiency, exchange mechanisms are in theory the most attractive of the three types. They encourage individuals and groups to make cost-benefit trade-offs. The individual who is paid to comply (or who may pay to avoid compliance) will presumably comply up to the point at which, for him, the marginal cost of non-compliance equals its marginal benefit. Whether these individual decisions yield socially optimal results depends upon a number of factors. In the first place, how closely does the price established for compliance approximate the true social value of compliance? Requiring polluting firms to make trade-offs between investments in abatement technology and payments of emission charges will yield optimal levels of abatement only if emission charges reflect the true social costs of pollution. In the second place, the allocative efficiency of exchange mechanisms depends on the competitiveness of the input and output markets in which the costs of compliance or non-compliance may be passed along. To the extent that these markets are imperfect, exchange mechanisms may not transmit an aggregate social willingness to pay for compliance with given objectives. A fuller consideration of this point merges with our third criterion – democratic accountability and participation.

It can be persuasively argued that price-based compliance mechanisms provide a form of popular control that can be either a complement to or a substitute for democratic accountability and participation. By bringing sanctions and rewards to the level of the individual transaction, exchange mechanisms allow individuals to register their preferences much more discretely than can be done by providing or withholding generalized support for an administration through the ballot-box. Consider again the case of an emission-charge regime in which polluters are made to bear the social costs of pollution and must make decisions about how much to invest in pollution control technology. The sum of the costs of the control technology and the social costs of the remaining pollutants (the emission charges) will be passed along to consumers in the price of the product, and/or back to workers in the form of reduced wages. Efficient producers will minimize these costs, and will compete favourably in input and output markets; those who do not minimize costs will fail. Consumer decisions to buy a product whose price includes these costs, and worker decisions to seek more attractive wages elsewhere, arguably provide a more discrete measure of the public's willingness to pay for pollution control than does the political process of representation through parties and interest groups. But this supposed advantage of exchange mechanisms depends upon the accuracy with which emission charges reflect social costs, and upon the competitiveness of the markets in which these mechanisms are implicated. There are, however, a number of ways in which such competitive markets may 'fail.' Economies of scale and geographic factors, for example, may mean that certain industries or regions come to be dominated by one or only a very few firms. In such cases, workers may have to incur substantial relocating or retraining costs in order to find alternative employment: there are, in economic terms, barriers to labour mobility that interfere with the functioning of competitive labour markets. In these circumstances the theoretical advantages of markets begin to unravel, and real-world markets must be assessed against their real-world alternatives.

Negotiation-Based Mechanisms

The second category of exchange mechanisms, at a broader, system-wide, or 'macro' political and economic level, is that of 'generalized exchange' in which compliance with general social objectives is negotiated among key social and economic groups. This exchange may take place with regard to the macro-economy, as when wage demands are moderated in return for policies of full employment and 'social wages' in the form of social security benefits; or it may take place at the level of particular programs, such as occupational health and safety. The corporatist systems of Sweden, Austria, and to a lesser extent West Germany are primary examples of this model.[26] Most commentaries suggest that in these models not only the setting but the enforcement of objectives is accomplished through negotiation and accommodation.[27] Despite periodic eruptions of enthusiasm for this model in North America, there are few practical examples, though several Canadian provinces are experimenting with it in occupational health and safety.

The technical efficiency of negotiation mechanisms in achieving compliance is not clear. In the first place, these mechanisms require that substantial amounts of time and energy be expended in coming to an agreement. Moreover, the relative advantages of negotiation mechanisms and command mechanisms in minimizing police and audit costs are a matter of theoretical dispute. On the one hand, it can be argued that the fact that parties have voluntarily consented to an agreement (which presumably leaves each party better off than it would have been in the absence of an agreement) enhances the likelihood of voluntary compliance.[28] On the other hand, economists such as Williamson have argued that command mechanisms (hierarchies) are often established precisely because voluntary agreements are vulnerable to cheating.

With regard to allocative efficiency, the advantages of negotiation mechanisms are somewhat similar to those of price mechanisms: they allow for a more disaggregated expression of preferences than do command structures. They allow trade-offs between the costs and benefits of various levels of compliance to be made, ideally, by the parties who bear the costs and enjoy the benefits. As I have argued elsewhere, the negotiation model

> does not require that a central decision-maker deal 'synoptically' with all of the interrelated variables and the multiple criteria relevant to the decision; but rather makes more limited (though still substantial) demands of human intelligence. That is, it requires of each participant the capacity to perceive the effects of a variety of solutions upon his own interests, and to have sufficient appreciation of the preferences of other participants to be able to devise a bargaining strategy.
>
> The bargaining process, moreover, has the capacity to generate a wide range of potential solutions, as each participant makes proposals and revises them in the light of reactions from others. Furthermore, these proposals are generated by those directly affected by, and therefore with a 'feel' for, the problem at hand.[29]

The extent to which the outcomes of negotiating processes, like the outcomes of markets, are socially optimal depends upon the distribution of political and economic power in the relevant policy arena. Again, this consideration merges with concerns about democratic accountability and participation.

Negotiation mechanisms may appear, at first blush, to accord with the criterion of enhancing democratic accountability and participation, since they imply that representatives of affected interests participate and interact in the decision-making process. But these mechanisms are extremely vulnerable to problems arising from the differential mobilization of interests. For example, it is now a commonplace observation of political science that those with concentrated stakes in the outcome of a particular issue are more likely to organize to influence the outcome than are those for whom the stakes are more diffuse. Individual producers, for example, each have more to gain or to lose in decision-making about product safety standards than do individual consumers, though total gains or losses for consumers may be large. Typically, then, producer groups are more readily mobilized than are consumer groups – to such an extent that the concept of, for example, voluntary industry compliance with product-safety standards negotiated with consumer representatives is not likely to satisfy either the allocative efficiency criterion or the democratic participation criterion. One arena that offers somewhat more promise in this respect is industrial relations; but even here, the extent and the cohesiveness of the organization of labour and management vary greatly across jurisdictions and across sectors within jurisdictions. Given this variety, the number of North American contexts in which, say, workplace labour-management committees could be expected to deal democratically and efficiently with the control of occupational health and safety hazards is limited. But within such limited contexts, the potential of negotiation mechanisms should be explored.

Persuasion

Because persuasion (if successful) involves the internalization by the individual of standards of conduct and social objectives, continuing monitoring and enforcement costs are lowest of all in this type of compliance mechanism. But the start-up costs may be relatively high, since each individual must be instructed, trained, debated with, or otherwise persuaded.

The implications of persuasion mechanisms for allocative efficiency are somewhat similar to those of command mechanisms. There is no inherent cost-benefit equilibrating mechanism, unless one assumes that objectives and optimal levels of compliance are subject to revision in the course of reasoned arguments between the persuader and the persuaded, or unless one assumes that what is being communicated is information that allows individuals to better assess the true costs and benefits of their behaviour (a process referred to as 'consequentialization' in the case of advertisements promoting seat-belt use or discouraging drunken driving, for example). Even so, these equilibrating mechanisms apply only to those costs and benefits that can be internalized to the individual: external costs (for example, injuries to strangers in motor vehicle accidents) can be incorporated only to the extent that persuasion appeals to altruism.

With respect to democratic accountability and participation, persuasion mechanisms are arguably the most consistent of the three types. Liberal theory has long emphasized the mutually reinforcing relationship between liberal education and liberal democracy. Persuasion mechanisms, in theory, allow for the respect for individual autonomy and the competition of ideas so central to this body of thought. But persuasion mechanisms, like the other two types of compliance mechanisms, are also vulnerable to distortion and perversion. On the one hand, persuasion may 'take' too well and become indoctrination; and the capacity for dissent, on which many of the alleged advantages of this mechanism rest, may be suppressed. On the other hand, persuasion may not 'take' well enough, especially when costs of non-compliance are largely externalized, and appeals to altruism fail.

It should also be noted that, in addition to explicitly persuasive mechanisms, other command- and exchange-based mechanisms have persuasive effects as a result of their symbolic dimensions. This point is considered in more detail in the following section.

Practical Choice

Although it is useful for analytic purposes to distinguish among 'pure' compliance types, any mechanism available in practice will involve a mix of command, exchange, and persuasion features. Bureaucratic mechanisms involve exchanges of information and favours as well as command;[30] markets are populated by hierarchical actors and governed by authoritative rules. Any policy decision will involve changes to an existing mix, causing heavier reliance on command, exchange, or persuasion, and/or on the positive (reward) or the negative (sanction) dimension of each of these types.

Indeed, some policy decisions could entail an increase in social control along each of these dimensions. A move toward a Swedish-, Austrian-

or West German-style 'corporatism' in the North American context, for example, would entail an increased reliance on hierarchy (since the model implies that the participants at the bargaining table are cohesively organized and can deliver the support of their membership). It would also entail an increased reliance on negotiation. Again, since these models rely heavily on a prevailing social consensus, a major effort would have to be made to persuade social groups of the legitimacy of the structures.

These practical choices involve a variety of considerations. There is the need to consider the distinctive competencies and incompetencies of these mechanisms as set out above. In particular, if an increased reliance on one type of mechanism (for example, price-based exchange) is desired in order to take advantage of its distinctive competence (in this case, allocative efficiency), it will also be necessary to deal with its distinctive incompetencies (vulnerability to cheating or defaulting on contracts, cost externalization, or concentrations of economic power) and therefore to look closely at the political and economic characteristics of the arena in which it is being introduced. Increased reliance on emission charges to control pollution may be appropriate only in industries in which input and output markets are reasonably competitive. To take another example, reliance on insurance markets to provide incentives for the purchase of safer vehicles may be more appropriate under no-fault or first-party compensation regimes than under a tort-liability regime for third-party compensation.

In addition to these considerations of the distinctive competencies and incompetencies of the various mechanisms, a decision to increase reliance on one or other of these mechanisms requires attention to the symbolic implications of such a shift, and in particular to the fit between the symbolic implications and prevailing ideologies. The symbolic effect of an increased emphasis on command is to highlight the social significance of compliance. The signal is, 'This behaviour is socially important enough to *command.*' But placing the weight of a command structure behind the enforcement of compliance stakes, to some extent, the whole command structure on the achievement of compliance. Disobedience involves not only one type or instance of behaviour, but an entire relationship with the command structure. Therefore, in practice the issuance of commands is constrained, particularly under a prevailing ideology that emphasizes individual autonomy. Commands are likely to be symbolic fiats – though usually expressed in absolute terms, they in fact imply a range of acceptable compliance. In Murray Edelman's words, a governmental command is a 'virtuous generalization around which a game can be played.'[31] When the state says 'do X,' it signals 'do X plus or minus Y' (whether X is a speed limit or an exposure standard) where Y is to be determined through implicit or explicit negotiations between the enforcer and the target.

The symbolic effect of an increased reliance on exchange mechanisms is to signal 'this activity has a price' – or, conversely, 'nothing *priceless* is being harmed by this activity.' In a society in which there are important social myths that certain values (for example, life) are priceless, an increased reliance on exchange mechanisms involving these values (for example, emission charges) is likely to be constrained, and can be pursued only at an increasing cost to the social fabric.

The symbolic effect of the persuasion mechanism is to signal that what is desired is not just action but *agreement*, and it is this symbolic dimension that considerably constrains its effective use. Theories of attitude change emphasize the drive of individuals to maintain 'consistency' or 'balance' in their belief systems, or 'cognitive maps.'[32] For this reason, persuasive messages are likely to be most effective when they do not threaten prevailing ideologies, or when they purport to present not advocacy but information that will be interpreted within the belief system of the target group to generate the desired change. It has been argued, for example (with limited empirical support), that 'over-servicing' by physicians can be reduced by providing high-volume physicians with information comparing their practice profiles with the average for their specialties and locations. Sensitive as they are to peer norms, physicians presumably will adjust their behaviour to approximate those norms.

Compliance mechanisms are likely to be effective when they are congruent not only with prevailing ideologies but with existing organizations of interest in particular policy arenas. John Zysman, for example, has argued that the choice of industrial strategy (whether economic adjustment is to be led by firms, financial institutions, or the state) is constrained by the organization of financial and industrial capital in a nation.[33] The success of Sweden and Austria in achieving wage restraint (as compared with North America and the United Kingdom) has been attributed to the comprehensive and unified organization of labour, management, and the state.[34]

Political scientists of the public choice school (those who would explain political behaviour using a model of individual utility-maximization) argue that the choice of policy instrument depends largely on the relative concentration or diffusion of affected interests.[35] Regulatory policies, it has been argued, are more likely to be chosen when the interests to be regulated (for example, monopolies or oligopolies) are relatively concentrated and can enter into close relationships with regulators, and the alleged beneficiaries of regulation (for example, consumers) are diffuse and have less incentive to organize to deal with regulators, especially given the symbolic assurance that regulators are holding regulated parties in check.[36] This theory of regulatory 'capture' has recently undergone considerable revision. It appears to be much more useful in understanding traditional forms of 'economic' regulation – control or entry and/or rate – than newer forms of 'social' regulation focusing on the regulation of quality, largely health and safety standards.[37] None the less, the basic idea that choice of policy instrument is heavily constrained by the existing organization of interests continues to be developed within political science.

This investigation of organizational constraints extends to the consideration of the organization of potential enforcement agencies. Much of the burgeoning literature on 'implementation' addresses just such issues. Kelman[38] and Montjoy and O'Toole,[39] among others, have emphasized the significance of the ideology and structure of the enforcing agency in shaping policy outcomes. Other researchers have stressed the importance of considering the ideology and structure of private sector agencies that might play an enforcement role. Christopher Hood, for example, has pointed out the role of private agencies in promoting tax compliance.[40] Systems that rely on complicated rules and on self-assessment may paradoxically increase compliance, since they encourage the development of a private industry of tax counsellors and preparers who have an interest in ensuring that their clients comply with legal requirements while minimizing their tax exposure. As a result, in the United States with (to date) a relatively complex self-reporting scheme, collection costs (on the government budget) have been about 0.05 per cent of income tax revenue; in West Germany, which has a system of official assessment, they have been about 4 per cent. The two countries achieved relatively high and roughly equivalent levels of disclosure of personal income.[41]

If political science suggests that the organization of interests influences the choice of policy instrument, it also suggests the obverse. Notably,

Theodore Lowi has argued that policy determines politics as much as politics determines policy.[42] Lowi argues that public policies can be distinguished according to the extent to which they make the coercive presence of the state apparent to particular individuals or groups (the levying of fines, for example, contrasts in this respect with the distribution of subsidies extracted from the general tax base), and according to the extent to which they apply to individuals or to collectivities. Each of these dimensions will affect the incentives of political actors to mobilize in response to governmental initiatives, and therefore will affect the political landscape on which further initiatives must be undertaken. What Lowi calls 'distributive politics,' for example, in which benefits are distributed to individual claimants, leads to a relatively atomized form of politics; policies that clearly redistribute benefits from one major collectivity in society to another (which Lowi terms 'redistributive policies') will promote the mobilization of 'peak associations' representing those collectivities.

Others have developed and extended this insight using different categories. Schultz and Alexandroff have argued that changes in Canadian regulatory policy have changed regulatory politics: the broadening of regulatory policy beyond 'policing' to 'promoting' and then to 'planning' functions has progressively broadened and complicated the range of interests active in the arena.[43] It has also been suggested that a reliance on civil liability regimes requiring individual lawsuits to achieve public policy purposes may lead to an atomized politics, and that the introduction of liberal class action rules would facilitate the mobilization of groups for political as well as litigation purposes.[44]

The extent to which politics shapes policy and policy shapes politics remains an important matter of empirical investigation in political science. Recent developments suggest some important but so far unvalidated hypotheses about compliance. Is compliance greater when compliance mechanisms are relatively congruent with ideologies and organized interests? In the occupational health and safety field, West German and Swedish tripartite mechanisms, involving negotiation among representatives of labour, management, and the state, have apparently been successful in achieving compliance with protective occupational health standards without incurring the transaction costs and the levels of conflict that characterize the North American occupational health arena. These mechanisms are congruent with the comprehensively organized labour and management interests of Sweden and West Germany. Are they capable of being transplanted to the more adversarial and fragmented organization of interests in North America? Would attempts to introduce such mechanisms in North America lead to the evolution of more comprehensive organizations and a more consensual policy-making process? Or does the North American context demand that conflict be resolved through the traditional command-oriented mechanisms of the bureaucracy and the courts? In the absence of a cohesively and broadly organized labour movement, is the judicialized rule-making process and the penalty- and prosecution-based enforcement process followed by the U.S. Occupational Safety and Health Administration the appropriate mechanism for setting and achieving compliance with occupational health objectives? The Canadian case is particularly interesting in this regard, involving as it does some experimentation with consensual European-style mechanisms in the context of an essentially North American organization of labour and management interests. Several Canadian provinces (British Columbia, Quebec, and New Brunswick) develop and administer occupational health and safety programs through bipartite or tripartite boards; five provinces have mandated the establishment of joint health and safety committees in workplaces over a given size.[45] Assessing how compliance with occupational health policies in these provinces compares, *ceteris paribus*, with, say, West Germany on the one hand and the United States on the other would make an important contribution to the literature of political science and policy evaluation. It is but one of many areas of investigation that might be suggested by this brief review of the intersections between the discipline of political science and the study of sanctions and rewards: a few other areas are suggested in the following section.

Areas for Investigation

This section is intended not to summarize but to highlight some of the issues treated above that can inform and be informed by the study of sanctions and rewards. Some of these issues derive from the matrix of considerations presented in the first section of the paper: the distinctive competencies and incompetencies of command, exchange, and persuasion mechanisms when assessed against the criteria of technical efficiency, allocative efficiency, and democratic accountability and participation. Occupational health and safety programs and disease and accident rates might be compared, for selected industries, across jurisdictions relying respectively more heavily upon command, exchange, and persuasion mechanisms: bureaucratic inspections, fines, and prosecutions; experience-rating of employer premiums for workers' compensation; joint health and safety committees; and safety education programs. Are employers sensitive to experience-related increases or decreases in premiums? Does negotiation within a committee structure improve the 'intelligence' of decision-making about health standards (that is, the range of values and interests and the extent and quality of the information considered)? Does it lead to higher rates of compliance with the outcomes of decision-making? Does it encourage a mobilization of interests that either retards or accelerates change in prescribed standards of conduct? If, as is likely, the answers to these questions are contingent upon technological, economic, political, and institutional conditions, what are these conditions and what are their effects?

Other areas for investigation are suggested by a review of practical considerations. Much of the discussion of practical choice was marked by an emphasis on the constraints on policy choice and on the view that policy change occurs incrementally – an orientation that reflects the mainstream of political science. But we need to know more about what explains the magnitude of policy change. In what circumstances and to what extent can the constraints of ideology and organized interests be relaxed? The case of U.S. tax reform appears to offer considerable scope for investigation along these lines. The adoption of a simplified tax system is incongruent with the network of investment interests that has developed around and supported the earlier maze of tax incentives and shelters. How can this innovation be explained? Will it lead to decreased compliance as a result of decreased reliance on the private tax service industry, and hence to a decrease in 'private enforcement'? What is the effect of the reform on the overall cost of collection as a percentage of revenue? Some of the literature on another 'incongruent' policy initiative – deregulation – may be relevant here.[46]

Another promising area for investigation suggested by the review of practical considerations is the range of acceptable compliance with governmental directives. What characteristics of the directive, the enforcing agency, the target, or the nature of the relationship between target and enforcer explain the breadth of this range? Performance standards might be compared with specification standards. Examples of performance standards are injunctions to 'design automobiles so that occupants can survive head-on collisions at x kmph' or 'expose workers to lead/air levels of not more than x mg/m^3.' An analogous specification standard would be to 'install air bags (meeting specified technical design requirements) in all automobiles,' or to 'install ventilation systems (meeting specified technical design requirements) in all workplaces where workers are exposed to lead.' Which of these types implies the wider range of compliance in practice? Which is most cost-effective? What technological, economic, political, and institutional contingencies affect the answers to these questions?

This is a daunting research agenda, and it transcends the boundaries of any single discipline. Political science, like the other social sciences, raises important questions and suggests intriguing hypotheses; the answers, however, are likely to come through interdisciplinary collaboration such as that fostered by the 'Sanctions and Rewards' project.

Notes

* Professor, Department of Political Science, University of Toronto

1 Lindblom explicitly distinguishes his use of the term 'authority' from the Weberian usage that permeates the social sciences. In Lindblom's usage, to grant authority is simply 'to accept a rule of obedience': C.E. Lindblom, *Politics and Markets* (1977) 18. 'Ever since Max Weber, many social scientists have argued that the authority relationship ordinarily requires legitimacy. It can exist only when someone obeys out of a belief that he ought to do so. But people can also be simply coerced ... to follow a rule of obedience even when they believe that the commands and the commander are illegitimate': Ibid. 19. I believe that the use of the term 'command' to describe a mechanism of control based on a 'rule of obedience' is purer, and avoids the overtones of legitimacy associated with the term 'authority.'

2 This is not meant to exclude private sector hierarchies as examples of command structures, but only to illustrate the 'pure type' with reference to non-market-oriented institutions.

3 A representative sampling includes, in addition to works cited in the remainder of this section, S. Arnstein, 'A Ladder of Citizen Participation' (1969) 35 *Journal of the American Institute of Planning* 216; R.A. Dahl, *A Preface to Democratic Theory* (1956); and S.M. Miller and M. Rein, 'Participation, Poverty and Administration' (1969) 29 *Public Administration Review* 15.

4 J. Rawls, *A Theory of Justice* (1971). Of the growing body of literature spawned by Rawls, one contribution of particular relevance in this context is R. Goodin, *Political Theory and Public Policy* (1982).
5 C. Pateman, *Participation and Democratic Theory* (1970)
6 A. Wildavsky, *Speaking Truth to Power: The Art and Craft of Policy Analysis* (1979). In making this distinction, Wildavsky draws upon earlier work by C.E. Lindblom, *The Intelligence of Democracy* (1965), and *The Policy-Making Process* (1968).
7 Wildavsky, supra note 6, 17, 405
8 J. Pressman and A. Wildavsky, *Implementation* (1973)
9 Wildavsky, supra note 6, 302–8
10 R.A. Manzer, *Public Policies and Political Development in Canada* (1985) 46. See also R.V. Presthus, *Elite Accommodation in Canadian Politics* (1973).
11 J. Morone and T. Marmor, 'Representing Consumer Interests: The Case of American Health Planning' (1981) 9 *Ethics* 431
12 See, for example, O. Williamson and W.G. Ouchi, 'The Markets and Hierarchies Program of Research: Origins, Implications, Prospects' in A.H. Van de Ven and W. Joyce (eds.), *Perspectives on Organization Design and Behavior* (1981). Williamson is one of the major contributors to the growing literature on the economics of institutions. This article is an excellent summary of his transaction cost analysis of the relative merits and demerits of markets and hierarchies, and of related empirical research.
13 M. Olson, *The Rise and Decline of Nations* (1982)
14 Lindblom, supra note 1, 65–75
15 H.A. Simon, *Administrative Behavior*, 3d ed. (1976). No discussion of command structures can afford to ignore Simon's sensible, insightful, and often elegant arguments that while organizations may not exhibit 'classical' rationality, they represent (if appropriately designed) the highest degree of rationality attainable by humans under the conditions of uncertainty and complexity that characterize most decision-making situations in modern industrial nations.
16 In the Canadian context, see R.F. Adie and P. Thomas, *Canadian Public Administration: Problematical Perspectives* (1982) 20–1, 212–13, 340; and S.L. Sutherland and G.B. Doern, *Bureaucracy in Canada: Control and Reform* (1985) 2–13.
17 R.A. Dahl, *Polyarchy* (1971); Sutherland and Doern, supra note 16, 3
18 H. Jacoby, *The Bureaucratization of the World* (1973); T.J. Lowi, *The End of Liberalism* (1979)
19 J.D. Aberbach, R.D. Putnam, and B.A. Rockman, *Bureaucrats and Politicians in Western Democracies* (1981); F.C. Mosher, *Democracy and the Public Service* (1968); D. Yates, *Bureaucratic Democracy* (1982)

20 C.J. Tuohy and M.J. Trebilcock, *Policy Options in the Regulation of Asbestos-Related Health Hazards*, study no. 3 for the Royal Commission on Matters of Health and Safety Arising from the Use of Asbestos in Ontario (1982) 9:50–9:51
21 Ibid. 9:57–9:59. References are to M. Eisenberg, 'Participation, Responsiveness, and the Consultative Process: An Essay for Lon Fuller' (1978) 92 *Harvard Law Review* 410, and L. Fuller 'The Forms and Limits of Adjudication' (1978) 92 *Harvard Law Review* 353.
22 E. Chen, 'Asbestos Litigation Is a Growth Industry' (July 1984) *The Atlantic Monthly* 24
23 G. Priest, *Modern Tort Law and the Current Insurability Crisis*, a background paper for the Task Force on Insurance, Ministry of Financial Institutions, Government of Ontario (1986)
24 R. Brickman, S. Jasanoff, and T. Ilgen, *Controlling Chemicals* (1985); S. Kelman, *Regulating America, Regulating Sweden* (1980)
25 Williamson and Ouchi, supra note 12
26 The term 'corporatist' is widely but not entirely consistently used in contemporary political science. Lehmbruch's definition comes closest to capturing the interrelated dimensions of the concept: (1) the development and strengthening of centralized interest organizations – or 'peak' associations – which possess a representational monopoly; (2) the granting to these associations of privileged access to government, and the growth of – more or less institutionalized – linkages between public administration and such interest organization; (3) the 'social partnership' of organized labour and business aimed at regulating conflicts between these groups, in co-ordination with government policy (usually in the form of 'tripartism'). G. Lehmbruch, 'Concentration and the Structure of Corporatist Networks' in J.H. Goldthorpe (ed.), *Order and Conflict in Contemporary Capitalism* (1984) 61.
27 Brickman et al., supra, note 24; Kelman, ibid.
28 P. Schuck, 'Litigation, Bargaining and Regulation' (July/August 1979) *Regulation* 26
29 Tuohy and Trebilcock, supra note 20. The term 'synoptic' is Lindblom's (supra note 6) and refers to a model of decision-making in which the decision-maker has a comprehensive overview of all relevant factors.
30 A. Breton and R. Wintrobe, *The Logic of Bureaucratic Conduct* (1984)
31 J.M. Edelman, *The Symbolic Uses of Politics* (1964) 47
32 R.M. Axelrod (ed.), *Structure of Decision: The Cognitive Maps of Political Elites* (1976); D.D. Nimmo and C.M. Bonjean (eds), *Political Attitudes and Public Opinion* (1972), Part III
33 J. Zysman, *Governments, Markets and Growth* (1983)

34 See, for example, J. Goldthorpe, 'The End of Convergence: Corporatist and Dualist Tendencies in Modern Western Societies,' in Goldthorpe, supra note 26, 315–43.
35 M.J. Trebilcock, D.G. Hartle, J.R.S. Prichard, and D.N. Dewees, *The Choice of Governing Instrument* (1982)
36 J.Q. Wilson (ed.), *The Politics of Regulation* (1980)
37 R. Noll and B.M. Owen (eds.), *The Political Economy of Deregulation* (1983)
38 Kelman, supra note 24, and 'Occupational Safety and Health Administration,' in Wilson, supra note 36
39 R.S. Montjoy and L.J. O'Toole, 'Toward a Theory of Policy Implementation: An Organizational Perspective' (1979) 39 *Public Administration Review* 465. A good example of the literature on 'implementation,' this article reviews a number of case studies to test hypotheses about the influence of the 'world view,' standard operating procedures, and internal factionalism or cohesiveness of the administering agency upon the likelihood of achieving the sponsor's objectives. The influence of these variables is found to vary with the specificity of the mandate and the extent of new resources accompanying it.
40 C.C. Hood, *The Limits of Administration* (1974) 125–6
41 A.J. Heidenheimer, H. Heclo, and C.T. Adams, *Comparative Public Policy: The Politics of Social Choice in Europe and America* (1984) 183–8
42 T. Lowi, 'American Business, Public Policy, Case-Studies and Political Theory' (1964) 16 *World Politics* 677 and 'Four Systems of Policy, Politics and Choice' (1972) 32 *Public Administration Review* 298. Lowi was the initial and the major proponent of the 'policy determines politics' approach. In the 1960s, this was an important antidote to the prevalent focus on causality. Lowi's particular formulation, however, has proved problematic, and has undergone a number of reformulations by other scholars.
43 R. Schultz and A.S. Alexandroff, *Economic Regulation and the Federal System* (1985)
44 Tuohy and Trebilcock, supra note 20, at 7:43
45 T.L. Ilgen, 'Between Europe and America, Ottawa and the Provinces: Regulating Toxic Substances in Canada' (1985) 11 *Canadian Public Policy* 578
46 Noll and Owen, supra note 37; M. Derthick and P.J. Quirk, *The Politics of Deregulation* (1985)

10 Choice of Target and Other Law Enforcement Variables

CHRISTOPHER D. STONE*

What is the best way to discourage unwanted social conduct? Most of the traditional literature concentrates on the level of sanction: What punishment fits which crime? Should we supplement civil damage awards with criminal liability? Less thought is typically given to a set of prior, more fundamental questions. For example, are there any areas in which we should be replacing sanctions, whether criminal or civil, with rewards? Are there non-monetary resources that might effectively serve as incentive and disincentive currencies? To which actors are sanctions and rewards most appropriately addressed?

Perhaps the more fundamental questions have been slighted because in most traditional areas of law the answers have appeared so obvious that our imagination has not been taxed.[1] Everyone agrees that burglary merits bringing stiff penal sanctions against the burglar. But burglary and the other common law offences are in many ways unrepresentative of newer forms of conduct the society has to deal with. The paradigmatic trouble-maker is no longer the cutpurse, the hoodlum. Today it may be the fly-by-night corporation that disposes of toxic wastes after midnight, or the laboratory that engineers a destructive gene. Various social forces are focusing our attention on new, more subtle varieties of behaviour, often marked by elements that complicate our task.

Consider a few comparisons of traditional wrongs and their successors. First, we have to figure out how to abolish the unwanted conduct without restricting socially useful activity. In 'classic' crimes like burglary, there is no socially redemptive value, no other side of the ledger. The implication is that when devising ways to crack down on burglars we are unconstrained by concern that we will over-deter. By contrast, much of the misconduct that is of contemporary concern is tied to productive, socially valued activity. We need to tread with caution. Pollution is a by-product of manufacture; the more we clamp down on toxic polluters, the more we risk eliminating, along with the pollution, the associated benefits of manufacture.

Second, an expanding class of modern wrongs strains traditional remedies and forums. Consider the classic tort scenario, one with which the law is most accustomed to cope. A, a pedestrian crossing the street, is accidentally but negligently run into by B, a driver. Note that (1) A knows the *fact* that he has been injured; (2) A knows *who* has injured him; (3) anyone (presumably including jurors) can fairly well assess the *nature and extent* of the injuries; and (4) the *technical inquiry* necessary to analyse the accident is not complex – essentially, only a rudimentary knowledge of physics is required. Contrast the auto accident with the types of situations that are of increasing concern today. With regard to chemical hazards in the environment (1) we are less (or not at all) apt to know with certainty the *fact* that we are being injured; (2) even if we know that a certain chemical is harmful, it is often hard to determine *which* of several possible sources is responsible; and (3) and (4) it is far more complicated to prove the *extent* and *mechanism* of the injury. Indeed, the injury may not become apparent to the injured party until long after the wrongdoer has gone out of business.

Third, all advanced societies have been undergoing a dramatic demographic change. Activities that were once conducted by individuals are increasingly conducted through giant bureaucracies typified by, but not limited to, the mighty for-profit corporations and public agencies. The proliferation of 'corporate' activity introduces alternatives that do not arise in dealing with a burglar: when a 'corporate crime' is committed, how are the penalties to be distributed among the various participants who had a hand in, or stood to gain by, the wrongful conduct?

These and associated developments make it timely to identify and reconsider the assumptions that underlie our inherited strategies for steering social conduct, strategies that developed in response to a less complex society. In the treatment that follows, I will not undertake to propose a new set of strategies for any particular class of conduct – that is, specific means by which to deal with pollution or bribery or workplace safety. The idea is to present a general overview that might serve as the basis for further research. To that end, I have concentrated on identifying and, in a preliminary way, assessing the range of variables available to a society in its efforts to enforce modification of behaviour.

The Variables

An investigation of enforcement variables involves canvassing the *mechanisms* for law enforcement and the *targets* upon which those mechanisms will focus. In the term 'mechanism' I include a whole range of elements that give a law enforcement strategy its character. These include choice of target, discussed below (do we make parents targets of the law on account of their children's torts?). Additionally, the term denotes a more inclusive range of variables, such as the event or circumstances that trigger the authoritative response (do we wait until someone is killed?), the monitoring and enforcement apparatus (do we rely on public officials or private attorneys-general?), the forum (do we use traditional courts or agencies?), and the sanction level. More broadly, mechanisms should be understood as incorporating a host of 'background' rules, such as limited liability, indemnification, political accountability, and sovereign and charitable immunity.

Because this is too vast a field to examine in depth, I will limit myself to reviewing three principal elements. First, I will deal with some *substantive variables* of the legal mechanism; second, the selection of *target*; and third, the variables of *monitoring and enforcement*.

The Substantive Rule Variables

Control strategies can be based on several different sorts of control approaches. I find it useful to gather these under four headings: harm-based liability rules (HBLRs), penalties, standards, and rewards. Let me review these four substantive mechanism variables in turn.

Harm-Based Liability Rules

Harm-based liability rules are typified by the ordinary tort rules. They are harm-based in a double sense. First, harm is the triggering mechanism: the law stays its hand until the injury has occurred. Second, the loss that the law imposes upon the wrongdoer is calibrated to the harm. The virtues of this approach are obvious. For one thing, HBLRs minimize intrusion into private decision-making. Those subject to HBLR strategies are deterred by knowledge that if they cause harm, they will have to pay for it; how and to what extent they avoid the harm-causing activity is left to their expertise in the light of market forces. Under the shadow of the law's threat, the actors are free to calculate the most efficient cost-avoidance measure.

Penalties

Penalties can either be triggered, like HBLRs, by the occurrence of harm or tied to standards (discussed below), but in either event the loss that the wrongdoer faces – the 'bill' for misconduct – is severed from the quantum of harm that the wrongdoer has caused. For example, the violator of an antitrust standard under U.S. law may be liable not only for ordinary damages (measured by the amount of harm caused) but for punitive damages and/or criminal fine.

The obvious point to make about penalties is that they are traditionally relied upon in two types of situations. First, certain conduct is deemed so onerous, such a 'public offence,' that enforcement and condemnation are lifted from private hands and lodged in officers of the community. Second, questions of 'public statement' aside, we may be unsure whether the prospect of damages, by themselves, will reduce the flow of misconduct to a tolerable level. (Many instances of wrong will go undetected, plaintiffs with otherwise meritorious cases will fail owing to problems of proof such as joint causality, etc.)

There are two less obvious points. First, even assuming a class of misconduct for which HBLRs are inadequate, in what circumstances should penalties be preferred as a substitute over standards, which repair defects in the HBLRs by employing ex ante rather than ex post measures? Second, discussions of penalties ordinarily focus on levels of severity. There are, however, independent questions of penalty quality. By this I mean that the imposition of a penalty is the deprivation of a resource, ordinarily money and sometimes, as in imprisonment or probation, liberty. But a discussion of resource deprivation should open up the discussion of a broader range of alternative 'currencies.'[2] Some strategies rely on monetary threats, but indirectly. For example, as punishment for improper lobbying efforts, a non-profit organization may be deprived of its tax-exempt status; an errant lobbying group thus faces a reduction, of uncertain magnitude, of the donor funds on which it relies. Similarly, a hospital or university that does not comply with federal regulations may be deemed ineligible for further federal funding. Sanctions available under the antitrust law include depriving a wrongdoer of its contracts, divesting it of its patent rights, and even seizing its property. Instances of severe wrongdoing can lead to the revocation of a licence to do business or even the suspension of a corporate charter. A lawyer can be disbarred, a doctor suspended. Wrongdoers can be forced literally to advertise their mistakes – spreading the word of prosecutorial determination as well as, presumably, infusing them with a sense of shame.

One wonders, not rhetorically, why sanctions that are only indirectly or secondarily monetary have been imposed so rarely. Some of the alternatives are probably regarded as too harsh. The revocation of a corporation's charter is a rough analogue to the imposition of the death penalty.[3] Not only is 'death' a penalty of last resort, but its effects, especially in the corporate arena, fall on too many innocent persons, such as shareholders, uninvolved employees, and members of communities dependent upon the corporation's continued existence.[4] We can imagine, however, alternative fines the monetary burden of which would be within the range most courts would not find inappropriate to impose. For example, suppose that a monetary judgment of $100,000 is in order, and that the expected economic loss from, say, public dedication of a patent, or the denial of a right to advertise, would not exceed that figure. Are there cases in which the alternative sanction would more effectively deter and rehabilitate than the imposition of a (direct) money loss? Consider a company convicted of false telephone advertising or of making unlicensed 'boiler-room' stock sales. The effect of a money judgment (particularly if the culprit is a large publicly held company) may be little felt by the people who have the strongest hand in avoiding repetition of the wrong. A direct suspension of the power to make telephone solicitations (backed by the prospect of severe contempt penalties for disobedience) is calculated to 'get to' the perpetrators more effectively – to force them to develop more legitimate ways of doing business.

Standards

Penalties differ from HBLRs in that they detach the level of sanction from the level of harm actually caused (the embezzler of $1,000 can be fined $10,000); standards differ from HBLRs in that they detach the law from the harm-causing occurrence. Standards are put in place before the harm they seek to avoid occurs. Typically, the function of standards is to encourage desired performance through direct ex ante measures, rather than to influence conduct indirectly and ex post through the prospect of contingent sanction and reward *should the harm occur*.

I think there is a special reason why traditional legal scholarship has given less thought to standards than to the other mechanisms. HBLRs and harm- (or wrong-)triggered penalties are both consistent with free will and salvation: they enable the actor to choose – and to pay the penalty if the choice is wrong. The ex ante quality of standards involves a nullification or limitation of choice. Indeed, some of the most effective measures that can be brought to bear on ordinary flesh-and-blood mortals are prior direct constraints, such as the forced sterilization of sex offenders or the preventive detention (or even the lobotomizing) of those statistically likely to engage in crime. But in direct dealings with ordinary persons, such measures are resisted on moral or even theological grounds.

In contrast, when organizations, not persons, are the direct target of the law, objections of this sort (by and large, objections on grounds other than efficiency) disappear. That is, when one is dealing with the corporate or industrial sector, there are fewer compunctions about ex ante, choice-eliminating measures. To ensure workplace safety, industrial boards lay down mandatory safety rules that substitute the government's notion of the ideal harm-avoiding measure for the enterprise's. In effect, we withdraw from the enterprise the power to determine the ideal solution on its own, subject to the prospect of fines and punitive damage awards should its choices turn out badly and a worker be injured. We do not grant the licensees of nuclear plants full autonomy to decide how to protect the public, subject only to the condition that *if* there is a catastrophe, they will be held accountable. Instead, public agencies require nuclear facilities to adopt certain physical and bureaucratic preventive measures as a condition of doing business.

Generally speaking, standards fall into three classes: factor, output, and bureaucratic. *Factor* standards constrain the regulated party's input. An example is the air-quality regulations that require utilities to use coal with no more than a specified maximum sulphur content; such a mandate displaces the utility's managerial discretion with a collective choice as to a factor of production. *Output* standards preserve managerial autonomy over input, but constrain output. To continue the air-quality example, an output standard approach allows the regulated party to select and combine factors of production as it likes, subject only to the limitation that, however combined, the output from the chimneys cannot surpass x units of restricted material per day.[5] *Bureaucratic* standards impinge upon managerial discretion in organizational and bureaucratic variables. For example, companies in potentially hazardous industries have been required to adopt internal information pathways which assure that the organizations gather data of a specified sort and transmit them to a specified desk for action. Corporations have been required to establish new corporate posts and to endow existing offices with mandated powers and obligations. In other areas, the managerial level at which decisions of a certain character must be made is no longer solely a matter for managerial discretion.[6]

The arguments favouring standards. To understand the justification for standards, one has to appreciate the misgivings and alternative strategies, which rely on ex post financial rewards, either through HBLRs or through HBLRs intensified by the prospect of penalties. Either way, the predominant ex post measures seek to modify conduct through the threat of enterprise-targeting financial disincentives aimed at company profits. The theoretical justification is that the enterprise participants – especially, in the case of the giant publicly held company, the managers – are influenced by the financial well-being of the company, which affects the managers' power-base and, through compensation arrangements, their personal wealth. Faced with a threat to company profits, and without any further and more specific direction, they will be motivated to put their houses in order in the most cost-beneficial way.

Some of the assumptions on which the approach rests are imperfect or even doubtful, however. For example, at some points (presumably when profits are sufficient for the managers to stave off competitors for their power) management may be relatively insensitive to profit-threats, and may be willing to trade share value maximization for the maximization of some other value – anything from prestige to perquisites. If the enterprise is managed in such a way as to employ an abnormally high discount rate, or is a strong risk-preferrer, the expected loss that will 'correct' the course of the economically rational firm may not sway the abnormal firm into taking the appropriate action. There is the further possibility that those nominally in control of the organization will see their actual control erode, particularly in a huge and complex modern bureaucracy. Therefore, even if the prospect of the law's penalties motivates the managers to take appropriate action, there is no guarantee that they will succeed. The obstacles to managerial control range from what organizational theorists call 'subgoal pursuit' (a particular division of plant may favour its own pet projects and familiar procedures) to outright opportunism of various agents and subagents, who may pursue their own welfare-maximizing strategies in disregard for what is best for the firm as a whole. In many instances, information needed for tight managerial control simply does not flow perfectly, either up or down. (The *Challenger* explosion provides several unfortunate illustrations of what organizational theorists call 'information constipation.')

To doubt that the firm is perfectly profit-sensitive is not to say that it is entirely insensitive and that no level of threat to its economic well-being will get through the corporate skin. If prevailing levels of threat are inadequate to modify industrial performance in a certain area, it does not mean that standards are the only alternative. We have the option, among others,[7] of escalating the threat to ever-higher levels. That can be done either by intensifying monitoring and enforcement efforts (thereby raising the probability of conviction) or by increasing the penalty level for those convicted. Either way, the 'bill' the enterprise can expect to receive for its misconduct goes up. Perhaps some companies' insensitivity to profit threats is such that the expectation of a $100,000 loss from a certain course of conduct will not deter them; but only a consummate corporate dullard will fail to heed a $1 million warning.

Raising the ante for misconduct is no panacea, however. Increased monitoring and enforcement procedures cause drains on public funds. The alternative, raising the level of penalty, seems relatively attractive precisely because it appears to be cost-free. But the costlessness is only superficial: the higher we raise penalty levels, the more we risk deterring firms from engaging in worthwhile endeavours. As the magnitude of prospective judgments increases, a company may prefer to withdraw from a meritorious product line rather than take the risk that some future jury might hold it to a level of liability utterly disproportionate to the social costs and benefits of its endeavour.

Efficiency is not the only constraint on escalating the penalty level. In fact, the level of penalty, while theoretically boundless (we could threaten shop-lifters with million-dollar fines), is subject to several practical and moral constraints. First, the penalty is limited by the defendant's wealth: threats beyond that level are hollow. When the defendant is a business corporation, limited liability and bankruptcy laws shield the investors from bearing the full brunt of the hazards they impose upon the society. If a pharmaceutical product is a great success, the firm and its managers will prosper; but if the drug creates a thalidomide-like nightmare, there is no comparable level of expected losses. Witness the still-unravelling aftermath of the Johns-Manville litigation concerning asbestos-related diseases, and the A.H. Robbins litigation concerning the Dalkon birth control shield. Millions of dollars in judgments are owing, even at existing liability levels. But is there any real prospect that the investors, or even the managers, will be forced to compensate the injured, much less pay the law's penalties?

The law's roar may not only prove toothless; worse, it may be self-defeating. As the law increases its threat, the costs of enforcement rise as potential wrongdoers take more care to cover up and, if caught, to resist judgment in costly court battles.

Other constraints on the escalation of penalty level have a moral basis. Suppose that, notwithstanding the diluted impact of a corporate judgment on any individual, the institution of limited liability, etc., a fabulously high penalty level does have some value in deterring the firm. So, too, can pickpocketing be deterred, if we are prepared to make an example, by hanging, of a few pickpockets who are unlucky enough to get caught. But justice shrinks at the prospect of meting out punishment with so disproportionate a penalty and so uneven a hand. That is why, even though increased enforcement is a more expensive way to reach any level of mathematically expected threat than increasing the penalty for those convicted, it may be preferred on grounds of fairness. In fact, moral misgivings about penalty level, often debated in regard to ordinary defendants, may be more constraining in the corporate context because of the complexity of a corporate punishment. Corporate misconduct often occurs in circumstances where it is unclear that any individual was truly to blame – least of all the investors, lower-level employees, consumers, and dependent communities, on which some of the penalty's brunt will undoubtedly fall.

None of these considerations proves that we should abandon reliance on enterprise-aimed financial disincentives, or that they are necessarily inferior to the alternatives. For many classes of offence it may be perfectly feasible to increase enterprise penalties to a level so high that most firms will behave well, and perform efficiently, most of the time. But the limitations are sobering enough to give support to two principal (and closely related) alternatives: standards and individual agent liability (discussed below).

Although the weaknesses of ex post judgments, both on efficiency and fairness grounds, give an impetus to standards, standards have drawbacks of their own. HBLRs, because they are dormant until the wrong has occurred, have the obvious defect of any after-the-fact remedy. The law will have the appearance of having stepped in too late. With HBLRs, the principal fear (short of the imposition of fabulously high penalties) is that they will under-deter. Conversely, the principal objection to standards is that they will over-deter. In most (though not all) cases, the enterprise participants are better informed than the outside world about the firm's hazardous business and the alternative remedies. Whenever, in disregard of this apparent expertise, the outside world undertakes to impose its own solution, we risk saddling the firm (and through it, the society) with costs in excess of the expected social harm that constitutes the original justification for the standard. A single industry-wide standard, laid down by the government after years of hearings, may be out of date before it is enacted. The result is to stultify development of superior harm-avoiding measures – superior either as industry-wide responses, or superior on a company-by-company basis, depending upon nuances of situation that a sweeping edict fails to account for. Finally, the 'protection' afforded by standards may prove, in the end, illusory. Formal arrangements mandated by the law can be subverted by the organization's informal procedures and value structures, factors that are difficult for the outside world to counter.

The question of standards – of the appropriate place and reach of ex ante interventions – is a major issue for further consideration. My own sense is that, because the risks of overdeterrence are significant, standards ought to be employed sparingly. It seems prudent to displace managerial judgment with a standard only when there is some strong combination of the following factors:

1. There are features of the anticipated hazard that render after-the-fact strategies unacceptable, and incline us toward a more directly preventive set of strategies. Such features might include a deep societal aversion to the type of harm (nuclear radiation, for example), the apparent inadequacy of monetary compensation really needed to make victims 'whole,' and complex problems of after-the-fact litigation and proof;

2 the government's access to the relevant data regarding risk and risk-reduction techniques makes it as well informed as the industry regulated;
3 the enterprises affected are relevantly similar, or we are otherwise able to avoid the situation where the benefit of controlling 'bad' companies outweighs the costs imposed by strait-jacketing their innovative and generally law-compliant competitors;
4 there is a strong relationship between the variable the standard affects and the outcome to be avoided (in the sense in which there is a strong relationship between faulty auto brakes and auto accidents);
5 the costs that the constraint imposes, when the alternatives are considered, is not likely to exceed what society is prepared to pay for the marginal reduction in misconduct it is likely to purchase.

Rewards

Not all compliance is achieved through a threat of sanctions or, as with standards, through direct ex ante restrictions. In many areas of our lives we modify behaviour through positive reinforcement of good performance. We compliment people, promote them, award them prizes. Such positive rewards are not unsuited to organizations. For-profit corporations may capitalize on the sales advantages of a well-won reputation, or, as reliable citizens, may anticipate favourable consideration in the awarding of government contracts. But overall it appears that far less authoritative social control is entrusted to positive reinforcement than to negative sanction.

Is there room for expansion of the government's role in meting out rewards, particularly rewards of a sort that are not directly monetary? Several factors warrant retaining the present limited role of rewards. It may be thought that the language companies speak is that of profits and losses, and that any government award of 'mere' recognition would speak in a foreign, and not particularly motivating, tongue. Governments are unpractised in doling out positive recognition (as distinct from meting out sanctions), which gives rise to fears that public entry into the field would be arbitrary or, worse, subject, in the absence of recognized approaches, to improper influence. There may be some validity in both reservations, but they are easily exaggerated. We might do well to examine in what areas, if any, the employment of rewards might usefully be extended. During the Second World War the U.S. War Production Board ceremoniously handed out E (for excellence) awards in recognition of supererogatory output, quality, and safety performance. What experience has there been with positive incentives awarded to individuals, firms, or subfirm units (such as plants), and with what results?

Target Variables

The variables of target involve the question, To what individual or entity should the law address its sanctions or rewards? In the case of traditional crimes, ordinarily committed by a culprit or culprits who operate outside any organizational structure, the answer seems too obvious to have drawn the attention of traditional commentators. The law sets its sights on the responsible individual or individuals. But in large bureaucracies and, in particular, in formal organizations that have been granted independent legal status, the answer is not so obvious. The problem is to decide whether, an undesired act having occurred, the outside world ought to pursue an individual agent or impose the penalty on the principal.[8]

Assessing the range of alternatives is complex. The best way to canvass the possibilities is to recognize that for each of the substantive mechanism variables listed above, we can identify an independent set of target variables. Specifically, where A = agent, and E = enterprise (or, more broadly, any organization whether or not organized in quest of profit), we have the alternatives:

HBLR(E)   (HBLR in which the enterprise is targeted)
HBLR(A)   (HBLR in which the agent is targeted)
S(E)   (standard addressed to the enterprise)
S(A)   (standard addressed to the agent)
P(E)   (penalty addressed to the enterprise)
P(A)   (penalty addressed to the agent)
R(E)   (reward addressed to the enterprise)
R(A)   (reward addressed to the agent)

The Agent or the Enterprise

Obviously, the fundamental choice that runs through these variables is whether to pursue an E-targeting or an A-targeting strategy. In the E, or enterprise liability alternatives, the law nails its threat, as it were, on the enterprise's doorstep; how the enterprise distributes the benefit or burden among those on the inside is a matter over which the outside world has no say. In the A variations, the outside world steps inside the organization to ensure that the burden or benefit is imposed on a particular agent or agents who the outside world insists are to receive it. The difference is not one, as it may first appear, between agent liability and agent non-liability. At least, we should not view the decision to, say, impose a criminal fine on the enterprise as being inconsistent with individual responsibility. It is more nearly correct to say that when the A strategies are adopted, the outside world undertakes to identify and punish (or reward) an agent of its choice in its way. Where the E strategies are adopted, we are simply leaving it to the enterprise participants (in the case of the stock company, the managers, the shareholders, and employees) to distribute the penalty among themselves according to their own judgments, their own contracts, and their own devices.

When the choice is so viewed, there is a clear theoretical affinity between the A-targeting strategies and standards. Like standards, A-targeting strategies originate in our doubts about the efficacy of profit-affecting, enterprise-targeting mechanisms, which might be considered the predominant, and perhaps presumptively correct, response to corporate misconduct. The reasons that lead us to rebut the presumption for E-targeting strategies and employ A-targeting strategies will resemble the reasons that lead us to adopt standards: the firm may be too insensitive to the enterprise-aimed threats to respond rationally, and the law's penalties may be too broadly dispersed among the enterprise participants to make them effective constraints on the individual actors who have control over the enterprise's destiny.

Certainly, the 'corporate control' literature is replete with appeals to increase the use of agent-targeting mechanisms (or, if we view the situation historically, to return to the earlier practice of disregarding the jural status of a corporation and deeming it, as *persona ficta*, an unsuitable target of the law). Indeed, the appeal of agent-targeting strategies is often assumed to be virtually self-evident. A close examination suggests, however, that the suitability of agent liability to displace enterprise liability is not as far-reaching as many law reform critics, and common sense, suggest.

By sounding this negative note, I do not want to deny that individual liability has a place in the control of corporate misconduct; indeed, its use almost certainly ought to be expanded. In circumstances where a corporate employee has been guilty of egregious conduct, public prosecution of the individual offender is indicated. He or she ought not be allowed to take refuge in the bureaucratic thicket. But in the course of social activity that is entrusted to bureaucracies, many tragedies will occur that are difficult to trace to 'culprits.' Responsibility is diffuse, power divided, and knowledge that would forewarn of impending tragedy fragmentary and apportioned. As we enter this range of cases, the outside world may have several reasons not to target any employee for prosecution, but instead to lay its penalties on the firm's doorstep, ceding jurisdiction over any further 'prosecution' to the enterprise participants. The outside world may feel that it has done enough, symbolically, in fining the enterprise, and may now be indifferent how the enterprise ultimately distributes that burden; or, even if there is a general feeling that someone was probably more to blame than anyone else, it is usually less costly for the government to identify and convict a responsible enterprise than to press further and try to fix responsibility on a particular agent.

Of course, one worries that in some cases the judgment of the enterprise participants will be less severe than that of the outside world. A worker's colleagues may be too sympathetic, and may try to shield him from taking the blame for an act which (they know) any of them might have been guilty of. The worker's superiors may be reluctant to stir up too far-reaching an inquiry, one that may call their own roles into question. Concern about such mutual self-protection undoubtedly prompts prosecutors, in cases of very culpable wrongdoing, to carry through the task of punishment themselves. But it is also conceivable that in some circumstances the firm, itself convicted, will turn around and impose on an errant employee a judgment that is harsher than the outside world would visit on him. A firm that has suffered a million-dollar fine because of some employee's foolhardy and unauthorized conduct may be strongly motivated to identify the wrongdoer; it may be able to locate the culprit with less cost than the outside world; and in fact the enterprise, with close control over monitoring, advancement, bonuses, etc., may be able to tailor a more fitting punishment.

As we move away from the most blatant individual misconduct, the case for directly punishing the agent becomes increasingly uncertain. If individual punishment is going to be pressed into marginal areas, it has to be inflicted on the basis of strict or vicarious liability. In other words, we *can* hold a supervisory agent responsible for the misconduct of subordinates even in circumstances where the defendant did not order, or even know of, the wrongdoing. (Employers have even been held liable for the acts of agents who acted in apparent disregard of the employer's orders.)[9] Proposals to expand such liability recur, and are an understandable response to the public's frustration with the classic superior's plea, 'I didn't know what was going on' – a plea that is always greeted in the courts of common sense with a certain amount of scepticism. Yet it is one thing to entertain private misgivings; it is quite another to expand the scope of individual criminal liability. No one knows how much a superior really does know about what is going on in the bowels of the organization – certainly not everything. To make a crime out of conduct that is, in essence, beyond the actor's control will lead to a certain amount of personally defensive and socially inefficient activity. Liability on a strict and vicarious basis always seems, efficiency aside, somewhat unfair, which is why the associated penalty levels are almost always restricted to a negligible, wrist-slapping level.[10] Respect for law can suffer, too, when the state undertakes to criminalize conduct that is not really morally culpable. Moreover, even when these bills are paid, we are likely to have purchased only a slight diminution in misconduct. The further that the behaviour we aim to restrict lies beyond the actor's true control, the more inelastic its supply will be to changes in penalty level. The likely results, in practice – that is, whatever provisions we put into the law-books – are a low rate of conviction of those prosecuted, and a low level of punishment of those convicted. Witness how lightly corporate employees have traditionally been let off in the courts for offences such as bribery and antitrust violations in cases where their direct personal participation was undeniable.[11]

This discussion should not be taken to suggest that we need to select a single target, *either* the agent *or* the enterprise. In controlling the misconduct of organizations, the law can target an agent (A); the enterprise organization as an undifferentiated whole (E); or both the agent and the enterprise (A + E). Or the circumstances may be such that, although a bad act has occurred, neither the enterprise nor any agent should be penalized [−(A) and −(E)].[12] It seems most natural to support the first alternative in circumstances where there is strong evidence of individual moral culpability, perhaps with little indication that the firm authorized or stood to benefit from the agent's wrongdoing. The second strategy will be favoured in the opposite circumstances – that is, when evidence of individual culpability is slight (or not worth the expense of establishing), and the outcome was, if not mandated, inherent in the firm's way of doing business. Indeed, in such circumstances it may be appropriate to hold the organization liable in order to subject it to a structural injunction that imposes changes in its bureaucratic structure, information pathways, etc.[13] The third alternative, A + E, is in fact favoured by many prosecutors in a wide range of cases, at least when they are seeking indictments; punishment of both may be warranted.[14] And co-indictment is presumed to offer the prosecutors a negotiating advantage; they may be able to persuade the executives to plead their company guilty in exchange for the government's agreement to drop the personal charges. One can imagine that the fourth strategy would be appropriate in the case of a corporate violation that was set in motion, irreversibly, years prior to its becoming evident, so that there has been an intervening changeover in corporate employees, shareholders, creditors, and so on. A damage award might be merited in those circumstances; the desire to compensate victims (the principal aim of the civil judgment) would outweigh any queasiness about drawing the compensation from non-culpable defendants. But a penal judgment is another matter. One may balk at criminalizing either the firm as a whole or individual agents when no one seems in any way blameworthy. Or a court may wish to treat an organization favourably if the organization is prepared to demonstrate a willingness to co-operate with authorities, and a 'corporate remorse' expressed not merely in words, but in a readiness to implement measures to put its house in order.[15]

A survey of target variables must also be mindful of indemnification and other ex post 'settling-up' practices between the firm and the agent. In many cases the firm will undertake to relieve the agent of any legal losses, including legal fees, amounts paid in settlement, and even fines, that the agent incurs by reason of his employment. The effect, of course, is to make the agent less self-protective when he steps near the boundaries of legal liability; the practice also constitutes a blunting or nullification of the law's preferred strategy. The prosecutor decides, say, that an executive vice-president was to blame; a jury agrees and convicts; the fine is set at a level the court deems appropriate for the agent in those circumstances. If the agent can simply turn around and, through employee indemnification, or a sweet 'consulting' bonus, shift the burden onto the firm (so that, in effect, the shareholders become insurers against agent liability), considered public judgments are simply being undone by private agreement. The point here is that we may want the law not only to select a particular target in the first instance (A or E); if we are determined to make the sanction stick on the preferred target, we have to devise ways to restrict indemnification and its equivalents.

Other Target 'Sizings'

A survey of targets should not leave the impression that there are no alternatives to pursuing either the agent or the enterprise. There is some validity in that assumption if we consider only strategies that depend upon money sanctions: individuals and firms are profit centres in ways in which plants and industries are not. That is to say, considering the way accounts are kept, earnings distributed, etc., it is unclear how one would go about placing a fine on the organizational entity (for example, the company division or staff) that would amount to anything other than a fine of the economic unit, the entire firm itself. But as we move away from mechanisms that are not as directly profit-oriented, and consider strategies such as standards, publicity, and the manipulation of non-monetary resources, the range of feasible alternatives increases. On the one hand, we should consider the possibility of targeting *parts* of a larger political or economic entity, such as corporate divisions and plants. On the other hand, expanding outward, we might consider the imposition of losses on an industry, a result that has been effectually realized in judgment awards that, in the absence of proof to the contrary, pro-rate damages across firms in an industry.[16] That is, reverting to the symbolic notations, we might expand our list of alternatives to include thinking about:

    R(D)   for a reward to a corporate division; or

    P(P)   for a penalty that falls on the plant.

It is unclear, and I think it merits discussion, for what class of cases such variants are appropriate. One illustration was suggested a few years ago during some interviews I conducted in the course of preparing *Where the Law Ends*. The U.S. Department of Commerce regulates wood, including plywood, standards. At the time, the penalty for misgrading was the denial of the right to use the quality-grading stamp for a certain period. The penalty had the effect of suspending work at the offending plant. This was proposed to me as a much more effective control mechanism than a fine that would typically fall on a huge lumber industry conglomerate and be paid out of its New York or Los Angeles headquarters. The plant-targeting suspension of the stamp threatened the livelihood of those in the best position to avoid the infraction.

Organizational Types

Thus far I have addressed agents on the one hand and organizations on the other, as though the latter was, for law enforcement purposes, a homogeneous group. This is not the case. Any general review of compliance approaches has significant variations to deal with. The most successful strategy for disciplining for-profit corporations is not necessarily the one that works best for the governmental agency or the non-profit company. For example, money sanctions may be more effective when addressed to for-profit firms rather than to not-for-profit organizations such as charities, because of the former's profit-orientation. The donor-supported charity may be more deterred by the threat of unfavourable publicity.[17] Moreover, liability rules are only part of the strategy mechanism. Any reform that is effected will be introduced in the context of pre-existing background rules that vary among types of corporate target: rules (and application of rules) of limited liability, immunity, *respondeat superior*, and indemnification.

Enforcement Variables

A separate set of issues involves the variables of enforcement mechanism. Assuming that a set of rules are in place (of the HBLR, standard, or penalty type), that the target for non-compliance has been fixed (A, E, plant, etc.), there remain questions as to who will be charged with monitoring and enforcement. The ordinary citizen may have some casual role in the enforcement of traditional crimes (such as alerting police), but the bulk of the investigative and prosecutorial work is lodged in the hands of public authorities. Indeed, the nature of some offences and their penalties virtually assures a heavy weight of public administration: one supposes that where imprisonment, the death penalty, and forfeiture of public privileges are at issue, only the state can act. Nonetheless, *qui tam* actions, suits brought by private citizens against criminal violators (lured by damage awards or bounty), have an ancient lineage.[18] Their effect is to shift some enforcement costs away from the public coffers; to add compensation of victims to vindication of the law; and to check abuses of prosecutorial discretion. Modern statutory schemes often provide for dual public-private enforcement (as under the U.S. antitrust laws), or even for private enforcement exclusively (as under section 16(b) of the 1934 Securities Exchange Act, which restricts short-swing profits by corporate insiders). When is it appropriate to enforce public policy through reliance on private attorneys-general? What are the optimal compliance enforcement arrangements, area to area? Becker and Stigler undertook an early theoretical analysis of the alternatives in a classic 1974 article,[19] but little theoretical or empirical work has been done since then.

One monitoring and enforcement alternative that merits further systematic examination involves targeting what I call 'field' elements.[20] That is, we reduce the dangers posed by some things through strategies aimed not at the potentially harmful thing itself, but at some other factor in its environment with which the dangerous instrumentality is critically linked. For example, the obvious way to control bank default is to address a series of measures directly at the offending bank and its officers. A less evident alternative is to increase the liability of the bank's auditors. If the bank defaults, it may have no funds to proceed against; the prospect of enormous penalties may be a hollow threat. But the auditors presumably have bank accounts and a reputation to protect. They have direct access to, and the capacity to assess, the most crucial data for predicting collapse. And they may have less motivation than the bank officers to cover up evidence of defalcation. Therefore, monitoring ancillary laws aimed at the auditors may be more cost-effective than monitoring laws aimed at the banks themselves. The bank has to be audited; the auditor bears a risk if the bank fails; the auditors build into their fees the costs of assuming those risks; the result is to shift some of the cost of monitoring banks onto the industry. The enlistment of private 'outsiders' in enforcement efforts is not unique to banking. When we threaten lawyers with liability for securities fraud schemes, we are in effect dragging them into the monitoring network. In those circumstances, too, we are looking outside the organization with whose conduct we are principally concerned (the securities issuer) to locate a key non-employee (the lawyer) who occupies a critical position in controlling the incidence of harm. The outsider is made an additional addressee of the law's sanctions (and rewards?). As a general technique for social control, such a strategy deserves further systematic consideration.

Conclusion

These remarks have not been made with an eye to advocating any particular compliance technique as a solution to any particular problem.

Elsewhere I have expressed what might be considered my pet view – that of all the control techniques for organizational misconduct, the most promising innovations are bureaucratic standards.[21] But considering how diverse and complex are the types of target with which the law is forced to deal, and how varied is the nature of the conduct we are trying to affect, it has seemed best, for the purposes of this paper, to survey some of the principal variables, the building-blocks with which we may wish to work.

Notes

[*] Roy P. Crocker Professor of Law, the Law Center, University of Southern California at Los Angeles

[1] The statement in the text merits some qualification. Even with a traditional crime, such as burglary, a certain amount of attention is rightly being given to broad-ranging alternatives such as burglar-alarms, property identifications, and even the extension of punishment to persons who leave their cars unlocked. But in the main, such alternatives have been deemed peripheral to pursuing the offender after the fact.

[2] Just as a discussion of resource rewards should open up a discussion of non-monetary currencies.

[3] The analogy is only rough. Absent some special, hard-to-police restriction, the flesh-and-blood mortals who stand behind a charter-forfeiting corporation may be able to reincorporate, presumably under a different name. All that is needed are the reorganization costs, filing fees, and the forfeiture of some good (or the shedding of some bad) will.

[4] It is for such reasons that John Coffee Jr proposes as an alternative form of penalty 'currency,' the 'equity fine': a court would be empowered to exact from a delinquent company, in some circumstances, the issuance of a block of shares. See Coffee, ' "No Soul to Damn, No Body to Kick": An Unscandalized Inquiry into the Problem of Corporate Punishment' (1981) 79 *Michigan Law Review* 386.

[5] Obviously, this is a potentially less stultifying approach than that of factor standards, which impose uniformity across an entire industry without regard for differences in situation and prospects of technology.

[6] See C.D. Stone, 'The Place of Enterprise Liability in the Control of Corporate Conduct' (1980) 90 *Yale Law Journal* 1, at 36–8.

[7] Including the targeting of individual agents, discussed below.

[8] In the case of a supererogatory act, the analogous question is whom or what the outside world ought to reward.

9. See *The President Coolidge* (1939) 101 F. 2d 638 (9th Cir.), in which the defendant company was convicted for acts of its employees (throwing garbage overboard onto a harbour-patrol boatman) even though the employees had been specifically ordered not to throw refuse overboard.

10. For example, *U.S. v. Park* (1975) 421 U.S. 658, caused considerable consternation in American business circles when the U.S. Supreme Court held that the president of a large (36,000 employees) food-distributing firm could be fined for a Food and Drug Act violation on account of rodent infestation in one of its many warehouses. But the reaction may not have been warranted. Not only had the defendant personally received prior warning of the condition, but most of the discussion overlooked the fact that the fines amounted to only fifty dollars for each of five counts. Indeed, in these circumstances, when an officer is fined for a non-*mens rea* offence, he may be eligible under state law and corporate contracts to have the amount of the fine, as well as his legal expenses, indemnified. See Del. Code Ann., title 8, ss 145(a) (1974). He may not even have to pay out of his own pocket.

11. Although the traditional reluctance to mete out stiff sentences to white-collar executives may be fading, the shift is occurring in areas in which the executive's personal responsibility is undeniable and personal benefit is often an element – for example, stock fraud.

12. I review these options more fully in Stone, 'Comment on "Criminal Liability in Government" ' (1985) 27 *Nomos* 241.

13. See C.D. Stone, *Where the Law Ends: The Social Control of Corporate Behavior* (1975) chapters 17–19.

14. See *Regina v. Jetco Manufacturing* (1986), 1 CELR (n.s.) 79, holding both a corporation and its president guilty of contempt for failure, after repeated requests, to abate pollution, the president having previously testified that he 'treated the [earlier] fines as licensing fees for doing business.' But note that the conviction was set aside on appeal: *R. v. Jetco Manufacturing Ltd. and Alexander* (1987) 31 CCC (3d) 171 (Ont. CA).

15. See the opinion of Stuart CJ in *Regina v. United Keno Hill Mines Ltd.* (1980) 10 CELR 43 (Yukon Terr. Ct.) for an unusually thoughtful judicial survey of the considerations, including corporate remorse, self-imposed rehabilitation, etc., that ought to guide courts in determining sentence level for corporate offenders.

16. See *Sindell v. Abott Laboratories* (1980) 26 Cal. 3d 588.

17. Although much more thought needs be given to the constructive use of adverse publicity as a control device across all fronts, see, generally, B. Fisse and J. Braithwaite, *The Impact of Publicity on Corporate Offenders* (1983).

18. See M. Shulenberger, 'Right of Private Party to Maintain Qui Tam or Other Action for Enforcement of Provisions of Rivers and Harbors Act of 1899' (1973) 15 ALR *Fed.* 636.

19 G.S. Becker and G.J. Stigler, 'Law Enforcement, Malfeasance, and Compensation of Enforcers' (1974) 3 *Journal of Legal Studies* 1
20 The most systematic treatment is in R.H. Kraakman, 'Corporate Liability Strategies and the Costs of Legal Controls' (1984) 93 *Yale Law Journal* 857; Kraakman uses the term 'gatekeeper liability' to denote sanctions against outsiders.
21 See Stone, supra note 6, and Stone, supra note 13.